D-CUI
1F17
9XH8

W9-CKM-725

(PD is
3/95)    15⁰⁰

# STATE AND BUSINESS IN MODERN TURKEY

SUNY Series in
The Social and Economic History of the Middle East
Donald Quataert, Editor

Issa Khalaf, *Politics in Palestine: Arab Factionalism and Social Disintegration, 1939–1948*

Rifa'at 'Ali Abou-El-Haj, *Formation of the Modern State: The Ottoman Empire, Sixteenth to Eighteenth Centuries*

M. Fuad Köprülü, *The Origins of the Ottoman Empire*, translated and edited by Gary Leiser

Guilian Denoeux, *Urban Unrest in the Middle East: A Comparative Study of Informal Networks in Egypt, Iran and Lebanon*

Zachary Lockman, ed., *Workers and Working Classes in the Middle East: Struggles, Histories, Historiographies*

Palmira Brummett, *Ottoman Seapower and Levantine Diplomacy in the Age of Discovery*

Ali Abdullatif Ahmida, *The Making of Modern Libya: State Formation, Colonization, and Resistance, 1830–1932*

Ayşe Buğra, *State and Business in Modern Turkey: A Comparative Study*

# STATE AND BUSINESS IN MODERN TURKEY

## A Comparative Study

### AYŞE BUĞRA

STATE UNIVERSITY OF NEW YORK PRESS

Published by
State University of New York Press, Albany

© 1994 State University of New York

For information, address State University of New York
Press, State University Plaza, Albany, N.Y., 12246

Production by E. Moore
Marketing by Theresa A. Swierzowski

Library of Congress Cataloging-in-Publication Data

Buğra, Ayşe, 1951–
    State and business in modern Turkey : a comparative study / Ayşe
Buğra.
        p.   c. — (SUNY series in the social and economic history of
    the Middle East)
    Includes bibliogrpahical references and index.
    ISBN 0-7914-1787-5 (hard : alk. paper). — ISBN 0-7914-1788-3
(pbk. : alk. paper)
        1. Industry and state—Turkey. 2. Turkey—Commerce. 3. Turkey—
Economic conditions—1960– I. Title. II. Series
HD3616.T873B84   1994
338.9561—dc20                                                    93-18517
                                                                      CIP

10   9   8   7   6   5   4   3   2   1

# Contents

Tables and Figures                vii

Preface             ix

1. Introduction: State/Business Relations in
   Theory and Society       1

2. Private Business in Turkey: Past and Present    35

3. Political Context of Business Activity    95

4. The Turkish Holding Company As a Social Institution    171

5. Business Associations in Turkey    225

6. Concluding Remarks    263

Appendix: List of Interviewees    269

Notes    273

Bibliography    307

Index    323

# TABLES AND FIGURES

## TABLES

2.1 Sectorial Distribution of Industrial Establishments in Turkey in 1915

2.2 Relative Share of the Private Sector in Turkish Manufacturing Industry, 1950–1986

2.3 Sectorial Distribution of Enterprises in Istanbul Benefitting from the Law for the Encouragement of Industry, 1924–1925

2.4 Date of Incorporation of the Companies Represented in TÜSİAD

2.5 The Period of First Entry into Business for some Major Holding Companies

2.6 Occupational Background of Entrepreneurs According to the Period of Foundation of the Enterprise

2.7 Some Indicators of the Position of Small Industry in the Manufacturing Sector

2.8 Educational Background of TÜSİAD Members According to Their Age Groups

2.9 Comparative Figures of Average Annual Foreign Direct Investment

4.1 Turkish Foreign-Trade Companies and Their Group Affiliations

Activity diversification charts for seven holding companies include:

4.2  Sabancı Holding

4.3  Yaşar Holding

4.4  Anadolu Endüstri Holding

4.5  Borusan Holding

4.6  Tekfen Holding

4.7  Altınyıldız Holding

4.8  Akkök Holding

4.9  Tamek Holding

4.10 Group-Affiliated Banks in Turkey

4.11 The Composition of Boards of Directors of Some Group-Affiliated Enterprises

## FIGURES

2.1 Relative Share of Private and Public Sectors in the Number of Industrial Establishments

2.2 Relative Share of Private and Public Sectors in Annual Payments to Employees

2.3 Relative Share of Private and Public Sectors in Fixed Capital Investment

2.4 Relative Share of Private and Public Sectors in Value Added

# PREFACE

This study presents an evaluation of the political and social environment of big business activity in Turkey with reference to the evolution of state-business relations in the Republican period. The study is largely based on some of the findings of a research project on "The State, Policy Networks, and the New Economic Strategy in Turkey," which was carried out during the period of 1988–1990 with the financial support of the Middle Eastern Branch of the Ford Foundation. The research on Turkey was complemented with a survey of literature on state-business relations in different Western and non-Western countries. The library work for this second part of the research was completed at the London School of Economics and Political Science where I spent the fall term of the 1990–1991 academic year as a visiting fellow of the Business History Unit. I owe many thanks to both the Ford Foundation and the Business History Unit for their support.

Although it would be impossible to mention the names of all those colleagues and friends who have contributed to the study in different ways, there are a few people to whom I owe special thanks. I would like to thank, in particular, Professor Metin Heper who, in a way, initiated the whole study in 1987 by asking me to write a rewiew article on the autobiographies of three leading Turkish businessmen. I would also like to thank Professors Ziya Öniş and İlkay Sunar for many stimulating debates at the initial stages of my research, and Professors John Waterbury, Deniz Kandiyoti, Ayşe Öncü and Huricihan İnan for the interest they have shown for the subject. I would also like to mention here the name of Meral Ka-

*ix*

rasulu, without whose able and committed assistantship the completion of the research work would have been much more difficult and much less enjoyable. I should express my gratitude to the editors of the SUNY Press who undertook the task of preparing the manuscript for publication. Finally, I am grateful to Osman Kavala for his invaluable contribution to the bridging of the gap between the linguistic frameworks of the world of academe and the world of business. I remain, naturally, responsible for all the views contained in this book as well as any errors that there might be.

The major difficulty that I had to confront during my research on Turkey had to do with the state of available statistics. Given the extremely limited availability and reliability of statistical material, a healthy evaluation of historical trends with the aid of quantitative data was hardly possible. The study mostly relies, therefore, on alternative sources of information. The data derived from the analysis of company reports, reports prepared by different business organizations, and official documents was completed with an extensive survey of newspapers, the analysis of biographical and autobiographical material, and a series of personal open-ended interviews. I had about forty interviews with owner-managers, professional managers, and several individuals who were in a position to provide relevant information on the types of entrepreneurial activity to be examined. (See the list of interviewees.) These interviews were not always very easy to arrange, but, contrary to my expectations, the majority of my interviewees were very generous with their time, and they were very cooperative unless specific, enterprise-level questions were raised. I am indeed grateful to these very busy individuals for their time and for their confidence. Among many private-sector representatives who have provided me with otherwise unobtainable information on different issues, I would like to mention, in particular, the name of Memduh Hacıoğlu, the president of the board of directors of the Istanbul Chamber of Industry, who spent hours with me to depict the ownership structure of the five hundred largest Turkish companies.

While I would not contest doubts about the falsifiability—hence the scientific nature of the knowledge based on informal interviews—I also feel that the latter convey certain types of information which can hardly be obtained from any other source. I believe, for example, that there is no other method which would be more efficient than personal interviews in assessing the relative significance of personal psychology, national character, and class-bound behavior in determining professional attitudes. My interviews with private sector representatives, more than anything else, enabled me to formulate the initial hypotheses about those factors which account for the specificity of the Turkish business environment.

Since the role of the state in society is central to the analysis of Turkish business environment presented in this book, I would like to clarify, from the outset, a semantic issue concerning the use of the term *state*. In the study, I use the term *state-business relations* in order not to loose semantic harmony with most of the relevant theoretical and empirical literature. Nevertheless, the issues explored in this study pertain to the relationship between businessmen and government authorities, with their respective positions relative to the instutions of the state and civil society defined by societal characteristics. For example, characteristics of state institutions—such as the law or the bureaucracy—the autonomy of these institutions from the political authority in particular are among the significant determinants of the relationship between the government and the business community. The nature of these state institutions, too, appears as an important factor influencing the social position of the business community. I examine this influence, however, at that level where it manifests itself in the relationship between businessmen and government authorities. State institutions enter into the analysis indirectly, through their influence on the interaction between the two sets of actors on which the study focuses. Consequently, the question of the "Turkish state tradition," while in many ways central to the analysis, is specifically dealt with only to the extent that the attitudes of successive governments toward the business community are conditioned by this tradition.

# 1. INTRODUCTION: STATE/BUSINESS RELATIONS IN THEORY AND SOCIETY

The themes pursued in this book originate in a review article written in 1987.[1] The article was on the recently published autobiographies of three leading Turkish businessmen, and it constituted an attempt to highlight what was unusual in these accounts of a Turkish businessman's life and livelihood.[2] Revisited today, after several years of research and reading on comparative state-business relations, it looks like an exaggeration of the specificity of the social and political coordinates of business life in Turkey. The present study, therefore, starts out more cautiously, with an attempt to build an analytical framework in which one could study the factors that shape the nature of the business activity in a given society without overlooking the common presence of some of these factors in different societies with highly different cultural and historical characteristics.

This analytical framework in which the study is situated draws on several different theoretical approaches and currents of analysis. In spite of their sometimes substantial methodological differences, the latter share a significant common characteristic. They are largely developed as a reaction to the shortcomings of two grand theories which provide coherent models of business behavior and state-business relations, namely mainstream economic analysis and the Marxian approach. Common to both these lines of analysis is their treatment of private (or class) interest as an exogenous variable. Consequently, the social scientist adopting these perspectives is prevented from studying the content and the form of interest

in different societal contexts. Second, both approaches set a dichotomy between the state and the market, and thus restrict the scope
of analysis of different forms of interaction between the political
authority and civil society.

Mainstream economic theory is limited to the analysis of economic activity on self-regulating markets which operate on the
basis of individual pursuit of self-interest. In this context, intervention by the state merely restricts the scope of the market activity.
The possibility that the intervention itself might actually play a role
in helping the establishment of the market and/or in affecting the
nature of the market activity is virtually totally excluded. State
intervention appears in a different perspective in Marxian analyses.
There, one sees the state acting either as an instrument of the
capitalist class in pursuit of its sectional interests or, as in the
functionalist approach, less directly, to assure the survival of the
capitalist system sometimes at the cost of sacrificing the immediate
interests of capitalists. In the instrumentalist approach, capitalists
make the state do what conforms to their interests, and, in the
basically tautological framework of functionalism, whatever the
state does conforms to the long term interests of capitalists.[3] In
these two versions of the Marxian approach, business class appears
as an entity which is defined with respect to its position vis-a-vis
the means of production. It acts according to exogenously given
principles of behavior and influences the course of social and economic life.

The approach adopted in this study attempts to overcome the
limitations of these assumptions through a questioning of the notions of "interest," "class," and "state" as derived from the two
general theories in question. It is an approach, in other words, in
which interest, class, and state become endogenous variables. The
necessity of such an alternative perspective is clearly revealed by
the divergences between our standard theoretical models and the
nature of the Turkish business environment. More important than
these divergences is, however, the fact that the Turkish case largely
loses its exceptional character in the light of some empirical studies
of different aspects of business activity in other countries. Before
proceeding to the discussion of the approach adopted in the present
study, it would, indeed, be useful to show how one's perception of
the Turkish case changes when the assumptions of our well-
established general theories are questioned from a comparative per-

spective. Because these assumptions reflect the characteristics of the ideal model of a market society, questions directed at their relevance also reveal the differences between the social reality in contemporary societies and this ideal model.

## BUSINESS OUTLOOK AND BEHAVIOR IN TURKEY COMPARED TO AN IDEAL CASE AND EMPIRICAL REALITY

The nature of the model in question is reflected, for example, in J. M. Keynes's description of the essential characteristic of capitalism as "the intense appeal to the money-making and money-loving instincts of individuals as the main motive force of the economic machine."[4] This implies that the economy is divorced from the wider social, political, and cultural context, and has an autonomy contingent upon individual behavior seen as basically directed at the maximization of material self-interest. In this framework, the autonomy of the economy has its counterpart in the autonomy of the individual within the social whole. As L. Dumont puts it, in the capitalist civilization, the relations between men and things dominate the relations among people. "For all practical purposes," Dumont writes, "we are those who have, with Locke, enthroned the private property in the place of subordination, or, for that matter, have chosen to be possessing and producing individuals and have turned our backs to the social whole . . ."[5] Private property, the right of the individual to what is his own, thus appears as the key institution in the capitalist civilization which J. Schumpeter qualifies, first and foremost, by its "individualistic, rationalistic and antiheroic nature."[6] In this context, as Schumpeter argues, religious fervor, ardent nationalism and similar sentiments are eliminated with the increasing marginalization of all those values having little to do with the rational evaluation of an ends/means relationship by the individuals constituting the society. In Keynes's words, "Capitalism is absolutely irreligious, without internal union, without much public spirit, often, though not always a mere congeries of possesors and pursuers."[7]

These statements underline the disembeddedness of the economy from society. Consequently, they define a situation in which societal determinants of the interaction between state and business lose their significance. Second, when economy is disembedded from society, it becomes natural for businessmen to conform to rationally and not socially defined norms of behavior.

It is basically the internalization of this idea of rationality which is not reflected in the autobiographies of Turkish business-men. In fact, from the perspective provided by mainstream econom-ics and the Marxian theory, these businessmen's perception of their rights and responsibilities, their sense of the social power that they have, and their image of an ideal society implicitly sketched in their writings all seem to be quite peculiar. One of the most striking dimensions of Turkish businessmen's self-image seems to be a lack of confidence about the legitimacy of the activities carried out in pursuit of pecuniary gain. This is reflected in an almost desperate attempt to justify business as a walk of life with reference to its social value. In their autobiographies, Turkish businessmen rarely express their pride about successful business ventures. Instead, they try to apologize for their success and never fail to mention its positive implications for the national economy as a whole. Sim-ilarly, the inviolability of private property rights does not seem at all obvious to them. They do not, in fact, appear to be sure about their legal rights and their abilities to do what they please with their private properties. Hence, they feel the need to indicate that "wealth is not something to be ashamed of," and they justify the statement by counting the ways in which they use their wealth for the benefit of their country.

The same lack of confidence could be observed in their evalua-tion of their social power. A sense of impotence is reflected in the statements of Turkish businessmen. This sense of impotence might or might not be justified, but its expression is too persistent and too sincere to enable one to dismiss it as mere calculated rhetoric. Moreover, the feeling of insecurity expressed by Turkish business-men probably has some significant implications at a practical level. It seems to be instrumental, in particular, in hampering the develop-ment of an industrial outlook in the country. The lack of committ-ment to a particular line of industrial activity and the domination of concerns pertaining to productive activity by objectives of a financial—or even speculative—nature, which I have observed throughout the research, appear to be—at least partially—a man-ifestation of a deep-rooted feeling of social insecurity.

The overwhelming significance of the state in determining the course of business life appears as a key determinant of the character of business activity in Turkey. In the autobiographies written by Turkish businessmen, success in business seems to be related, first and foremost, to the nature of one's relationship with the state which can best be qualified as a love-hate relationship. Turkish businessmen see the state as the major source of their difficulties. They also know, however, that it is to the state that they owe not only their wealth, but also their position in society. Hence, they have no illusions about either the possibility or the desirability of capitalist development with no state intervention in Turkey. What they emphasize is the need for a greater cooperation between government authorities and the world of business, not the desirability of reduced intervention. There is, in their books, no trace of the neo-liberal orthodoxy in which the individual endeavor is opposed to the responsibility of the state in determining the livelihood of the individual. There is no reference to the autonomy of economic activities from the wider societal framework as a desirable thing, and the pursuit of individual self-interest is nowhere attributed the central role in the organization of economic life.

As they have strong doubts about the economic achievements that would be possible with the free play of the unregulated market mechanism in the absence of state intervention, Turkish businessmen are also suspicious of the possible impact of the liberal value system on the social fabric. Hence, "the right of the possessive individual to what belongs to him" does not appear to them as a significant component of a value system which could successfully serve to maintain the social concensus. They fully recognize the need for different social and ideological mechanisms to maintain stability in a societal framework in which the businessman would feel secure. In fact, the autobiographies clearly reflect a sense of precariousness of social status and seem to constitute, at least partially, an effort to deal with this problem.

On the basis of the observations previously summarized, it is not difficult to make broad generalizations concerning the limited internalization of the basic values of capitalist development by Turkish businessmen, and to emphasize the divergences between the value system and institutional basis of business life in Turkey and in the West. I could, in fact, gather ample material to support this argument from a series of personal interviews that I conducted with some leading Turkish businessmen. Public declarations of the latter also provided evidence leading to the same conclusion.

Such a conclusion would not be totally unjustified, but it would be of limited usefulness unless it contributed to the understanding of societal determinants of business activity and state-business relations. With the objective of the study thus defined, it becomes necessary to go beyond the common assumptions of mainstream economic analysis and the Marxian approach as the general rule against which the exceptional character of an empirical case is to be explored. Another level of comparison—one in which social factors shaping the business environment in other societies are taken into account—must be introduced into the analysis.

At this second level, empirical observations of business activity in different countries immediately raise certain doubts about the validity of the assumptions concerning both the social legitimacy of the motive of gain as the organizing principle of the economy and the nature of the state as an arena where the social structure of private interests are reflected. Highlighted in most of these observations is, moreover, the role of political factors in shaping both the content of private or class interest, and the form which the pursuit of interest assumes in a given society. From an empirical point of view, therefore, the two grand theories of business behavior and their social implications appear to be exceptions rather than rules. Different accounts of particular cases also suggest that empirically observed societal characteristics are of a nature which could hardly be explained only with reference to culture as the explanatory variable—unless, of course, those aspects of a particular culture which are relevant to the forms of behavior and interaction under analysis are clearly specified.

For example, although cultural factors are undoubtedly important in dealing with questions pertaining to the social legitimacy of business activity, the attempts to present the precariousness of the social status of businessmen in a given society as a cultural characteristic of that society frequently prove to be unsuccessful. Such attempts often involve a tendency to present certain features, which are shared by societies with very dissimilar cultural systems, as being unique to a particular culture. Statements such as the following abound in this literature:

"Within the traditional Japanese system the private interests of any group are not considered to be legitimate. Therefore, it is relatively difficult for any group to articulate its own interests.

At the very least, these groups have to find some way to legitimize their own interest as an aspect of the broader public interest"[8]

"(In India) the basic attitudes of the political culture are strongly antibusiness"[9]

"In Turkey the notion of the business leader is misunderstood. He is often viewed as a speculator if not a thief. Business for a long time was downgraded and looked upon as an occupation which no respectable Turk would enter."[10]

In fact, it probably would not be unrealistic to assume that there is no single non-Western society on which such an observation has not been made. It would also be reasonable to assume that, in many non-Western societies of highly different cultural characteristics, the extent of state intervention in the economy is of a nature to render as quite ambigious the distinction between the realms of private interest and public policy. It is now well documented that, even in those countries such as South Korea and Taiwan, which, until quite recently, were presented as examples of the undisputable superiority of market-oriented, outward looking development strategies[11], the role of the state in directing and shaping private sector activity has been of crucial significance. In recent interpretations of East Asian economic success, the extent of state intervention appears to be much beyond the role which the state is expected to perform in a market economy. This is reflected, in particular, in the intervention of South Korean and Taiwanese states at the level of private investment decisions and private enterprise management to "discipline big business" and to make the latter act in conformity with national objectives.[12]

The following comments of A. Amsden on Taiwanese and South Korean economic systems are quite revealing in this regard.

> We may hypothesize that the system of "bureaucratic" capitalism of late imperial China, with its total interpenetration of public and private interests, was transplanted into Taiwan, along with mainlanders. Although historical conditions were unpropitious for economic development under bureaucratic capitalism in China, they were favorable in Taiwan.[13]

In a similar vein, Amsden writes that, in South Korea, the growth of private industry was almost totally based on direct governmnet support given according to the principle of reciprocity in exchange for performance standards. Hence,

> No firm in South Korea could succeed if it openly criticized the government. No firm could flourish if it was not a staunch government supporter. Nevertheless, despite pervasive corruption surrounding the allocation of subsidies to specific companies, discipline has still been effective: generally only good performers have been rewarded and poor performers have been punished.[14]

These comments describe a situation in which the performance of the private entrepreneur is judged on the basis of a set of criteria which has little to do with profit maximization. In such a setting, private interest is subservient to nationally set objectives, and the social position of the private businessman depends on his contribution to these objectives. Just as in the Turkish case, therefore, the heavily state-dependent business classes of East Asian societies, too, can hardly be expected to refer to the uncontested legitimacy of the motive of gain as a clear justification of business activity.

What is even more interesting than this East Asian situation, however, are those empirical observations which pertain to the expanding domain of state intervention in Western societies. In the latter, too, the expansion in question seems to have resulted in a modification of the role of the relationship between private and public interest as a determinant of the economic process. Neo-corporatist forms of state-business relations which have been extensively explored present, for example, the cases of European societies in which interest articulation and representation appears as a matter of political design.[15] When private interests are influenced by political factors, it becomes increasingly difficult to talk about exogenously defined interests as the motive force of economic and political processes. While the pursuit of private interest thus ceases to appear as the main determinant of economic activity, the association-based pursuit of class interest also appears under a new light with both activities losing their intrinsically legitimate status. Business associations—which are normally created to represent the interests of their constituency—are expected, in a neo-corporatist framework, to convince the business community to act in conformity with national objectives even when this conflicts with the requirements of profit maximization. Under these circumstances, business associations appear both as state servants and advocates of business interests. With regards to this situation, some writers point to a certain uneasiness of business associations which are often equally reluctant to appear as policing for the state or lobbying for business.[16]

The findings of the literature on neo-corporatism are extremely relevant for the purposes of the present study which points to the ambiguities of the standard dichotomy between public policy and private interest. Yet, the expanding domain of state intervention does not appear to be a source of uncertainty concerning the economic role and social legitimacy of business activities geared toward private interest maximization only in societies where neo-corporatist arrangements are dominant. Even in the United States and Britain—usually presented as countries where the business class has a truely hegemonic power[17]—certain changes in the domain of state intervention seem to have led to a significant modification of businessmen's perception of their social position and power. Hence, we read, for example, about the lack of confidence of British manufacturers who have exhibited a marked reluctance to raise their voices against the Thacherite policies inimical to their interests. In his evaluation of the inability of the British industrialists to articulate and successfully pursue their interests in a way as to influence the direction of public policy in the 1980s, C. Leys refers to certain political developments which have culminated in the "social contract" implemented by the Labor governments between 1974 and 1978. According to Leys, the social contract, with its impact on the decision-making powers of businessmen through regulation and worker control, was interpreted as a real loss of power over capital by some members of the business community. He writes that "In the mid-1970s a majority of manufacturing executives had come to feel that the survival of capitalism was at stake . . . Even those who were unconvinced by the Thacherite project saw no realistic political alternative . . ."[18] Hence, the surprising silence of the British businessmen in the sector hardest hit by the Thacher program.

In the second bastion of the free enterprise economy—in the United States, too—there are doubts that the business class is completely at ease in its social and political environment. In fact, several

studies on American business history refer to the historical significance of a love-hate relationship, not too dissimilar to the one
observed in state-business relations in Turkey.[19] Other writers comment on the strong distrust that American businessmen feel toward
their state. One observer notes, for example, that "the really revolutionary changes in the role of the government and in the relation of
various groups to government produced by the Great Depression
and the war have not yet been fully accepted in this country. Where
counter revolution is still considered to be a possibility, no one is
quite willing to lay down his arms."[20] This observation was made in
the 1960s. The developments of the post-Second Word War era have
culminated in the the rising wave of industrial regulation in the
1970s. Certain writers believe that the expansion of the domain of
intervention in this decade has seriously troubled the American
capitalists who have interpreted this as a trespassing of normal
boundaries of the state's role in the economy.[21] Similar comments
were made on the Canadian situation in which government-
business relations have become quite tense as a result of the increasing state involvement in the economy in the same period.[22] In both
countries, as in Britain, the uneasy decade ended with the victory of
neo-liberalism, and with the demise—at least at an ideological
level—of the welfare state.[23]

It is not at all clear, however, that the social legitimacy of
business activity could be automatically established with the victory of neo-liberalism. In fact, at least some businessmen in North
America and in Britain seemed to think that something more was
necessary to regain the security of its social position. This was
reflected in some significant changes that have taken place in the
social attitudes of businessmen in the countries in question.

Starting with the late 1970s, there has been an unmistakable
increase in the visibility of businessmen in social life, after decades
of conscious effort to keep a low profile. This is reflected, first, in
the unprecedented media presence of businessmen who now almost
compete with movie stars in this respect. Some writers see a negative correlation between the capitalist's declining economic significance and his increasing visibility as a media figure.[24] It is
impossible, however, not to see, in the businessmen's use of the
media something more than a simple ego trip. In other words, it is
impossible to overlook the fact that businessmen have been using
the media to create a positive public image to influence both states-

men and ordinary citizens. Their increasingly conspicious social presence has served to contribute to the same objective. While corporate philanthropy and involvement in artistic projects have become increasingly important, social committee work has become a significant part of the corporate businessman's daily routine.[25]

Some writers approach this as part of a process whereby an increasingly vocal and visible fraction of the North American and British businessmen consciously attempt to define themselves as a social class, to reshape their social image, and to establish their position in society. For our purposes, the process is highly interesting because, first, the mere fact that such an attempt is undertaken indicates that the business community feels a certain precariousness with regards to its position in society. Second, the totality of the message recently put forward by the business community seems to diverge considerably from the model of an ideal market society in which the economy is separated from politics, and in which the pursuit of material interest plays the leading role in assuring the smooth functioning of the economy. That the private enterprise has a social responsibility which should dominate the objective of profit maximization is little contested. Moreover, the small group of businessmen who assume a leadership role in the process in question appears with claims not for the limitation, but for a modification of the role of the state in the economy. In other words, feeling that they did not have a sufficient say in policy matters, these business leaders have volunteered to take part in the policy process rather than asking for a more limited government along the lines of the neo-liberal ideology.[26]

These observations of business environment in different groups of countries with very dissimilar economic, social, and cultural structures tend to call for an approach which could reveal both society-specific characteristics of and universal trends in the organization of business activity and state-business relations.

## TOWARD AN ALTERNATIVE ANALYTICAL FRAMEWORK

It must be admitted, from the outset, that the analytical framework of this study of business environment in Turkey is a highly ecclectic one which lacks the coherence of liberal or Marxian models. The study forms, in fact, part of many current attempts to develop new tools of analysis on the basis of empirical research on the forms of interaction between class, state, and society. Although these attempts can hardly match the rigor of the general theories that they abandon, they have the advantage of adhering to the objective of increasing the empirical content of analysis for a more relevant approach to social reality.

However, one theoretical contribution—that of Karl Polanyi, which is central to the present study—presents a fairly comprehensive body of critical analysis based on the idea that economy is, as a rule, embedded in society.[27] Polanyi approaches the market society as a historical aberration in which, for the first time in human history, the economic activity is disassociated from the rest of the society and is organized on the principle of individual self-interest. According to Polanyi, this particular social arrangement was largely a nineteenth century phenomenon which ended with the Great Depression and the World War II.[28] These events mark, in Polanyi's analysis, the beginning of a series of developments whereby the economy would again be "instituted as a social process" in conformity with the social fabric of each society.

This historical perspective largely rests on the distinction between the market and market society. Polanyi writes that markets—as places where individuals meet to barter, truck and exchange—can be found in all societies, and at all times. In all societies and at all times, market activity is also guided by the individual motive of gain. The market society, however, is distinguished from all the other societies by the central role that self-regulating markets and, consequently, the motive of gain, play in directing the economic activity. In other societies, the totality of the activities of production, distribution and consumption—in other words the economy—is always subservient to social, cultural, and political rules. The economy is nowhere entirely left to the market, and the pursuit of material gain plays only a marginal role in assuring the livelihood of the members of the society. In most nonmarket societies, moreover, one observes a conscious effort "to contain" and control markets to protect the society from their disruptive effect.[29] In this setting where the market activity is carefully disciplined, it is only natural that trade—and the individuals engaged in trade—are closely watched and kept under control as potentially disruptive forces, with no essential difference between Western and non-Western societies in this regard.[30]

Through an analysis of the historical developments culminating in the emergence of the nineteenth-century market economy, Polanyi demonstrates that it was only through certain ideological and institutional developments that Western societies have come to accept the profit motive as legitimate. The establishment of the unquestioned legitimacy of individual property, too, appears as the end result of a long process of ideological and institutional transformation of the Western society.[31] The rise of economic analysis as a separate discipline based on a particular conception of individual rationality defined with reference to interest maximizing behavior is a reflection of this same process. Marxian theory of history—in which class interest appears as the main explanatory variable—is also a product of the same environment.

Polanyi finds the Marxian emphasis of the ownership of means of production as the most important element of class analysis to be highly misplaced. He also thinks that "class interests offer only a limited explanation of long-run movements in society." He writes that

> The fate of classes is much more often determined by the needs of society than the fate of society is determined by the needs of classes. Given a definite structure of society, the class theory works; but what if the structure undergoes change? A class that has become functionless may disintegrate and be supplanted overnight by a new class or classes. Also, the chances of classes in a struggle will depend upon their ability to win support from outside their own membership, which again will depend upon their fulfillment of tasks set by interests wider than their own. Thus, neither the birth nor the death of classes, neither their aims nor the degree to which they attain them; neither their co-operations nor their antagonisms can be understood apart from the situation of society as a whole.[32]

Several decades after Polanyi, we find C. Offe pursuing a very similar idea through the distinction which he makes between two types of rationality, one associated with "conjunctural" and the other with "structural" policies. The first type of rationality aims at optimal satisfaction of interest manifested by societal actors. In periods of institutional or economic crisis situations, however, the nature of interest and interest representation become dependent variables shaped by the political system. Offe argues that, in the domestic and international conjuncture prevailing since the 1960s, the second type of rationality and policy orientation have become prevalent in advanced capitalist nations.[33]

The idea of political determination of private interest, which is central to the discussions around the concepts of pluralism, corporatism and neo-corporatism, also appears in "state-centered" approaches where the "society shaping" role of the state is explored through analyses of the dynamics of interaction between civil society and political authority.[34] The emergence of such analyses is sometimes traced to Western developments such as the "Keynesian revolution" of the 1930s and the advent of national macroeconomic management in the 1950s, as well as to British and American responses to the challenge of increasing international economic competition starting with the mid-1970s. In all these instances, there is a rejection of a certain perception of economic development and social change as spontaneous processes. These developments reflect, instead, an environment in which voluntarist interventions of the political authority in the realm of the economic are regarded to be necessary. Relatedly, state-centered approaches emphasize the modification of the structures and activities of different states in response to the requirements set by the international context of the national economy. Shaped in this fashion, state structures and activities in turn shape rights and responsibilities—as well as the behaviors—of individuals and classes in society in conformity with the imperative of international competition and economic development. International factors acquire a central significance in "coalition models of state-society relations," in which social and political structures are jointly determined within the national strategies for "managing interdependence" at an international level.[35]

These different approaches to the state-society nexus complement Polanyi's work in several ways. They provide empirical support to Polanyi's idea of class as a socially determined category. They relate the configuration of social classes to the situation of the society in the world system, and thus highlight the relationship between the fate of classes and the fate of the society as a whole. They also support, albeit implicitly, Polanyi's view that the present situation in market societies is highly different from the nineteenth-century one characterized by the institutional separation of politics and economics. Consequently, a conceptual ground is prepared for the evaluation of late capitalism as a new paradigm in which the codetermination of the behavior of states and societal actors is to be analyzed with reference to the international context of economic and social development.

This idea forms an important component of the present analysis of Turkish business environment. There are, however, two points of central significance which must be clarified before completing the presentation of the theoretical perspective adopted in the study. One of these points has to do with the asymmetrical social and economic significance of state-business relations, as compared to the relations between the state and other social groups or classes. Polanyi writes that "it is the relation of a class to the society as a whole which maps out its part in the drama."[36] While the business class—as are other classes in society—is to be defined by the coordinates of its position within the totality of national structures shaped by international processes, "its part in the drama" is unambigiously greater than the parts of other societal actors. It seems difficult to overlook the fact that, in all societies where private enterprise has an economic role of some significance, businessmen have a special, highly privileged position relative to the state and the policy process. This is, in fact, a point central to C. Lindblom's analysis of state-business relations and the inherent tension which characterizes this relationship.[37] As Lindblom argues, because of the crucial significance of private investment decisions for overall economic performance, government leadership must often defer to business leadership. It must nevertheless do so without compromising the interests of the wider public and endangering social stability. The way this somewhat uneasy relationship is managed appears as one of the key determinants of successful economic performance.

The second point that must be clarified is that the management of state-business relations becomes both more important and more difficult in late-industrializing countries than elsewhere. In the evaluation of state-business relations in Turkey, the present study takes into account, therefore, the country's position in the world economy as a late-industrializing country. In this regard, two sets of factors relating to the idea of late coming become significant in the analysis. One set of factors pertain to the divergences between domestic and international conditions of industrialization in developed Western countries and those characterizing the industrial development of Turkey, a late-industrializing country. These historical divergences are considered, however, without overlooking the fact that ideologies and institutions of late capitalism in developed Western nations are not the same as those characterizing the early capitalist development in the same societies. This study tries, therefore, to depict the specificity of Turkish business environment on the basis of the country's position as a late-industrializing country in the international context of late capitalism.

The term *late industrialization* is used here in reference to the case of developing countries where industrialization takes place without an indigenous technology producing capacity. Hence, not only countries such as Turkey or India, but also Japan are placed in this category.[38] In these countries, industrial development takes place in an international environment in which the existence of more advanced economies condition the national objectives as well as the means to attain these objectives.

Given the technological dependence of late-industrializing countries, the main prerogative of the entrepreneur in these countries does not appear as the introduction of new manufacturing and marketing methods. The task of the entrepreneur becomes, rather, the steering of activities in a way to benefit from social and economic changes. As Cardoso argues in his study of Latin American entrepreneurs, industrial activity takes on political dimensions in these countries.[39]

Technological dependence also plays a role in limiting the possibility of a gradual development of small enterprises into modern firms because the scale economies associated with modern technology often entail the requirement of "starting big" from the outset. On the other hand, either the capabilities or the habits of businessmen rarely match the magnitude of this task which consequently requires considerable state support. In the institutional environment of a typical late-industrializing country at the initial stages of the industrializing process, the underdeveloped state of capital markets and financial organizations also makes the state the most likely actor to provide financial resources and to share the risks taken by the individual entrepreneur.[40]

As Lindblom argues, state-business relations are probably characterized by an inherent tension everywhere. Nevertheless, it is possible to hypothesize that there are certain factors which are likely to enhance the element of tension in the relationship between the largely state created big business and political authority in late-industrializing countries. Because the emergence of big enterprises is not the outcome of a gradual development whereby the institutions and ideologies of a private enterprise economy become entrenched in the social fabric, the problem of social legitimacy of business activity appears to be particularly important in the context of late industrialization. For the business class, the state often appears as the ultimate source of social legitimacy. However, it is not only the big business but also the political authority which functions under the pressure of legitimizing the economically privileged position of businessmen. In the absence of prior ideological developments through which self-interest becomes a component of the social value system, business contribution to national goals of development appears to be particularly important in justifying the social and economic status of the private enterprise. In the presence of pressing economic problems and severe discontentments, this task often becomes too difficult for the new entrepreneurs of late-industrializing countries, and their unsatisfactory performance in this area constitutes a potentially destabilizing element in state-business relations. Hence, the threat of terminating private enterprise in a firm, industry, or the entire system through a governmental decision is neither unusual nor totally empty in these countries. As it will be discussed in the following chapters, in Turkey, throughout the Republican era, businessmen have heard such threats quite often. In Nasser's Egypt, the failure of the Egyptian businessmen to comply with the objectives of the first five-year plan has actually led to massive nationalizations in the industrial sector.[41]

The nature of institutional mechanisms which could contribute to the stability of state-business relations, too, is likely to be different in late-industrializing countries than in developed Western countries. In the former, industrialization and nation-state building often takes place simultaneously, with the legal system and bureaucracy reflecting the requirements of social and economic development rather than traditionally accepted norms. The extent to which these institutions would function as stable mechanisms of intermediation in state-business relations depends, therefore, on the attitude of political authorities who may or may not expect the autonomy of bureaucracy and the neutrality of law.

These factors appear at the level of general hypotheses about the nature of state-business relations in late-industrializing countries. There are important differences, however, in the way in which they manifest themselves in different countries. Consequently, the forms of management of state-business relations do not exhibit uniform characteristics across these countries. This lack of uniformity is in turn reflected in highly dissimilar economic performances at an international level. In this regard, some recent studies of comparative economic performance in East Asia and Latin America present very interesting observations pertaining to intercountry differences in the societal framework of business activity.[42]

In these studies, the concepts of "state autonomy" and "state capacity" often have a significant place in the explanation of economic success. State autonomy refers to the ability of the state to make policy decisions independently of the interests of societal actors, and, as such, is related to the extent to which the dominant class—or classes—can dictate and determine the course of the economic strategy. State capacity, on the other hand, appears as a determinant of the effectiveness with which policy decisions are implemented by the public authority. Several factors, such as the presence or the absence of extensive state control over the financial system or the existence of an efficient and autonomous bureaucratic apparatus which could function independently of political manipulation, in turn determine state capacity in a given society. On the basis of these notions of state autonomy and capacity, successful economic development of countries such as Taiwan and South Korea is often attributed to the limited influence of private interests on the formulation of public policy and to the ability of the state to pursue a consistent economic strategy. This effectiveness of state intervention in East Asia is then contrasted with the limited autonomy and capacity of the Latin American state.

Evaluated in the light of this comparison between East Asia and Latin America, Turkey presents an interesting intermediate case which suggests that it might be necessary to further break down the concepts of state autonomy and capacity and to analyze their societal determinants in a more detailed fashion. As in South Korea and Taiwan, the conditions for state autonomy are largely present in Turkey. Yet, the nature of the policy process in Turkey is rather similar to the one which is reflected in the lack of a coherent, systematically pursued industrial strategy in Latin America. Consequently, although the state has a substantial degree of autonomy to discipline the big business in conformity with national objectives, business behavior manifests characteristics which are dissimilar to those observed in East Asia. Given the absence of a long-term committment to an industrial strategy in the country, Turkish businessmen, too, do not develop an industrial outlook and manifest a marked tendency to engage in rent-seeking activity. In a parallel fashion, in Turkey, the state control over the financial system, which is rather important—although not as pervasive as in the case of South Korea—does not significantly enhance state capacity, but appears as a component of an economic system characterized by an ineffective interventionism as in the Latin American context.

These observations suggest that, for each country, the specificity of the business environment is given by a particular configuration of factors which also appear as determinants of state autonomy and capacity. Taken individually, or combined with a different set of factors, each of these factors might yield a totally different picture concerning the relative positions of and the mutual interaction between state and business. Consequently, one could conceptualize a certain combination of elements which interdependently enhance and accentuate the significance of each other in shaping the private business environment in a given society. This is, in fact, the approach adopted in this study and, for the analysis of the Turkish case, I define the elements of the conceptual matrix defining the societal context of business activity at four levels. The issues explored at these levels form the subject matter of the four following chapters of this book.

## TURKISH BUSINESS ENVIRONMENT IN A COMPARATIVE PERSPECTIVE

Factors characterizing the historical conditions of industrialization form the subject matter of analysis at the first level. The relative strength of state and business at initial stages of industrialization constitutes a crucial element which determines both the role of the political authority in guiding early entrepreneurial efforts, and the future course of the relationship between these two actors. In comparisons of state autonomy in East Asia and Latin America, economic strength of industrial interests appears as one of the points of emphasis. In these analyses, the fact that the indigenous business community in South Korea and Taiwan possessed a negligible fraction of industrial capital during the early state-

building phase is presented as an important condition of state autonomy in these countries. The state-created character of the business
class is also highlighted with reference to industrial capital from the
colonial era that the latter has inherited through state handouts.
This situation is then contrasted with the situation in Latin American countries, such as Brazil and Mexico, where almost all of the
currently active big multiactivity enterprises were founded or were
already in existence in the 1930s and 1940s. It is thus suggested that
Latin American economic development in the twentieth century
has taken place with the autonomy of the state largely restricted by
the presence of an already strong industrial business class.[43]

However, the situation in South Korea and Taiwan does not
only contrast with the Latin American one. It is also different, for
example, from that of Japan, a country which is often presented—
along with South Korea—as one where a certain patnership between
the state and big business community is central to the national
economic development experience. Nevertheless, it is also argued
that, in Japan, the partnership in question is one between equal
parties while, in the South Korean case, the state is undoubtedly the
stronger partner.[44] The stronger position of the Japanese businessmen could be explained, at least partially, with reference to the
historical legacy of their collaboration with the state as an equal
partner.[45] The type of interdependence observed in Japan is quite
different from the one observed between the state-created South
Korean business class and its state.

As it will be discussed in the following chapter, in this area
there is a close similarity between the initial conditions of industrialization in South Korea and Taiwan on the one hand, and Turkey
on the other. In Turkey, too, an indigenous business class was
virtually nonexistent in the early years of the Republican period. As
the East Asian entrepreneurs who have built their businesses on the
basis of state-allocated Japanese colonial property, Muslim-Turkish
entrepreneurs have received the property rights of the businesses
abandoned by non-Muslim minorities who had left the country after
the foundation of the Republic.

With regards to the social position of landed interests, too,
Turkey resembles South Korea and Taiwan more than Latin American countries. While large landownership has been quite significant
in Latin America throughout the industrialization process, comprehensive land reforms in the two East Asian countries around

World War II has greatly undermined the economic and social power of landed interests.[46] In South Korea, during the process of land reform, the landowners were given state bonds which could be converted to industrial capital. It seems, however, that few land-owners have actually become industrialists.[47] Hence, the emerging business class had no claim to the wealth and social status associated with large landownership.

As will be discussed in the next chapter, in spite of the absence of an important land distribution scheme in Turkey, large land-owners do not form an important social actor which could modify the dynamics of state-business relations as in Latin America. More-over, business class in Turkey has almost no links with large land-ownership. Former land owners are largely absent among the founders of big business enterprises, who happen to be mostly small merchants and civil servants.

Another characteristic that the Turkish industrialization process shares with East Asian as opposed to the Latin American one is the limited role played by foreign direct investment.[48] In Turkey, therefore, foreign capital does not appear as a factor likely to limit state autonomy and to affect the political context of business activity. This suggests that, along with the relative socioeconomic insignificance of landed interests, Turkish businessmen, like their East Asian counterparts, do not have the opportunity to control the political situation by manipulating their relations with other economically and socially powerful interest groups. The possibility of forming alliances with foreign investors or with landowners does not appear as a factor which could shift the balance of power between state and business. State autonomy, in other words, is not undermined by socioeconomic factors such as the ones influential in the Latin American context.

In relation to the discussion of historical conditions of industrialization in Turkey, there is another factor which appears to be of some significance in determining the position of the private sector in society as well as the nature of state-business relations. The Turkish Republic was founded in 1923, but the autonomy of the new Turkish state in the area of foreign trade policy was restricted until 1929 by the conditions of the Lausanne Treaty signed with the Allied Forces. Under these circumstances, the timing of modern Turkey's first freely determined international trade strategy and the Great Depression coincided, and, in the formative years of the Republic, policy makers were exposed to all kinds of diverse information about the problems of private enterprise economies. Political and social attitudes toward the private sector were shaped in this environment in which there was little faith in the ability of private initiative to assure a stable economic development. On the other hand, national economy was built under quite different circumstances in those countries that went through the process of decolonization, either before World War I or after World War II. While the institutions and ideologies of the post-World War II era have included a good dose of interventionism, international atmosphere in this period was highly dissimilar to that which characterized the years of the Great Depression and the subsequent war, as far as the attitudes toward the future of the free enterprise system was concerned. Consequently, the international environment, in which the legitimate domain of state intervention in private business activity was defined in Turkey, was marked by an empirically well founded pessimism about the role of unregulated private business in economic success, which was not as strong in those countries where the initial stages of modern economic development were situated in a different period. This suggests that the international context of a nation's early attempts at industrialization and development constitutes a factor which might condition the future characteristics of the economic policy process.

The ways in which business outlook and behavior are shaped by the policy formation and implementation process constitutes a second area explored in the study. In this area, the similarity between Turkish and East Asian models of state-business relations give way to significant divergences. These divergences, however, do not pertain to the *extent* of state interventionism. They have to do, rather, with the *form* of state intervention. As it is highlighted in several studies, the economic successes of South Korea and Taiwan can largely be explained with reference to the committment of the state to a coherent, long-term industrial strategy, and to the ensuing uncertainty reducing role it has played in the economy.[49] Rapid economic growth in these countries appears, in fact, as an indirect result of this type of policy orientation which has exercised its impact on the economy through its influence on entrepreneurial behavior. South Korean and Taiwanese states, in other words, could successfully sustain a certain policy route which has persuaded and forced entrepreneurs to avoid rent-seeking, speculative activity, to develop an industrial outlook, and to improve the international competitiveness of their enterprises.

In contrast to this market-augmenting role played by effective state intervention in East Asia, state intervention in Turkey has appeared as a major source of uncertainty affecting business life. In fact, the limits of state capacity in Turkey is clearly manifested in this state-induced instability in its different aspects. In chapter 3 of this book, this subject is explored by distinguishing between two types of uncertainty which prevail in Turkish business environment.

One type of uncertainty pertains to the social coordinates of business activity and the boundaries of the legitimate domain of intervention, while the other stems from the frequent changes in the direction of economic policy and the ensuing instability of the values of the basic macroeconomic indicators. Both types of uncertainty have been significant, in varying degrees of relative importance, all through the Republican era. Their impact on the business life in Turkey has been further accentuated by the failure of the legal and bureaucratic mechanisms to introduce an element of stability in state-business relations.

As was previously suggested, in most late-industrializing countries where, given the legacy of Colonialism, decolonization experience, and/or modernization projects undertaken by developmentalist states, one does not expect to find, in bureaucratic and legal structures, a continuity similar to that exhibited by parallel institutions in developed Western nations. Nevertheless, the nature of bureaucratic and legal mechanisms in Turkey suggests that the role of historical traditions in shaping these institutions is not negligible. Hence, the analyses that trace the characteristics of Republican state institutions to the country's state tradition often provide useful insights for the study of the mechanisms through which the relations between political authorities and businessmen are mediated.[50]

These analyses imply that Turkish state tradition involves a rather sophisticated bureaucratic apparatus and quite well-rooted concern for the rule of law. It also involves, however, a characteristic tendency of Turkish governments to regard their political power as absolute. This tendency leads to the belief that the government in power has the right to monopolize the state power and to fully control the bureaucracy and the legal system. This does not necessarily result in a disregard for these institutions. As discussed in chapter 3, its consequence is, rather, a continuous modification and reformulation of rules according to the requirements of government policy. The legal system and the bureaucracy, thus, become subordinated to the government-set economic and social policy objectives, and, because the latter rarely reflect a coherent perspective, frequent changes in policy orientation result in equally frequent modifications in the institutional parameters of the business environment. The policy-induced uncertainty of the latter is enhanced by the limited role which bureaucracy and law can play in maintaining a stable policy network.

The role of bureaucracy in Turkey sharply contrasts with the bureaucratic structures prevailing in East Asia, where the the characteristics of Japanese bureaucracy, inherited by Taiwan and South Korea during the Japanese colonial rule, prevail. Bureaucracy in these three countries appears to be strongly unified, tightly organized, and largely autonomous from the political authority.[51] In comparisons of state capacity in East Asia and Latin America, differences in the nature of the bureaucratic apparatus in these two regions are frequently evoked. Hence, fragmented, politicized, and feeble bureaucracies of Latin American countries appear to be one of the factors which limit state capacity and hamper the possibility of effective intervention in the economy.[52]

Along with the above-mentioned factors pertaining to historical conditions of industrialization, social background of business class, the nature of policy processes and policy networks, differences in industrial structures in different late-industrializing countries, too, constitute an important element in intercountry comparisons of business environment. While, in some of these countries, small firms have a more important economic role than in others,[53] large, multiactivity enterprises, or "groups" in general, form the typical unit of big business, with the industrial environment characterized by a high degree of concentration. These multiactivity firms with highly diversified activities emerge in response to fairly similar needs in different countries.[54] The management of financial assets, the optimal use of scarce entrepreneurial resources, and risk diversification are some of the important concerns leading to the emergence of the multiactivity firm. Also, in many countries—at least at the initial stage of industrialization—the holding form, or a similar organizational structure, is chosen to maintain the control of the founding family over the expanding activities of the family business.[55]

In spite of these parallels in their historical development in different countries, big business firms still manifest society-specific characteristics with regards to their structure, strategy, and socio-economic implications. The factors that determine these characteristics are approached in different ways in the recent literature on industrial organization. As succintly put by Hamilton and Biggart, it seems possible to depict three sets of factors which receive varying degrees of emphasis in the explanations of the ways in which industrial organizations are shaped.[56] In some studies, market-emanated factors are emphasized in an approach which brings forth the economic rationale behind the adoption of a particular organizational form or business strategy. Other studies present cultural factors as the main explanatory variable. A third group of approaches—which Hamilton and Biggart call "political economy" or "authority" approaches—refer to historically developed authority relations in a given political environment to which economic activities of business organizations are in a position to adapt and conform.

An economic explanation of structure and strategy is provided, for example, by the classical work of A. Chandler, which will be discussed in detail in chapter 4.[57] More recent theoretical developments in a similar direction follow the work of O. Williamson which is centered around the idea of "transaction costs."[58] Explained along these lines, the emergence of multiactivity firms presents part of an attempt to reduce transaction costs that the purchasing of inputs on free markets entails, as opposed to their incorporation in the institutional structure of the firm. Certain studies specifically on multiactivity firms in developing countries adopt the same reasoning, whereby the organizational structure is examined as an outcome of rational calculation by profit maximizing individuals.[59] These market approaches—while justifiably highlighting the significance of profit maximizing activity of entrepreneurs in shaping the structure and strategy of business firms—tend to abstract from socially determined factors and, hence, remain of limited usefulness in comparative studies of industrial organization.

Culture-based approaches are, of course, specifically designed for such comparative studies. They focus on factors such as kinship ties, loyalty patterns, and hierarchical authority relations as culturally given variables that are reflected in enterprise structures. While the investigation of the parallels between cultural characteristics of different societies and different forms that organizational relations take in these societies provides useful insights to the study of industrial organization, as I have already suggested, culture, as an explanatory variable, can sometimes lead one to overlook the presence of similar attitudes and institutional forms in culturally different social settings. Besides—as Hamilton and Biggart put it— cultural variables in a given region "might be insufficiently distinguishable to have a clear explanatory force."[60] Perhaps more significantly, the emphasis of culture might lead to a static view of the society through the neglegt of dynamic interaction between historically given elements of a particular culture and new socioeconomic objectives and new societal actors which tend to modify and reshape these elements.

Given these reservations concerning market- and culture-based explanations, I tend to agree with Hamilton and Biggart that a political economy approach, which incorporates the elements of the first two approaches, often provides a better framework for the comparative analysis of industrial organization. A political economy approach enables one to take into account the role of the political environment in shaping organizational characteristics as it is done, for example, by G. R. Carroll,[61] without neglecting the significance of other society specific elements. Chapter 4 of this study adopts such a perspective which emphasizes the impact of political environment on enterprise development in the analysis of Turkish holding companies as social institutions which both reflect and serve to perpetuate the characteristics of business environment in the country.

From this perspective one can, for example, evaluate the elements of analysis that Whitley adopts in his comparison of Taiwanese, Japanese, and South Korean industrial organizations in the light of the Turkish case.[62] Whitney classifies the social differences that have influenced the contexts in which different business systems have developed in East Asia in four categories. These are:

1. historical extent of political pluralism and decentralization to intermediate levels of organization between the central political authority and households,

2. the extent to which market-emanated power is tolerated by the political authority,
3. the basis on which authority is claimed and obedience is justified, and
4. the degree to which family has been the fundamental unit of social identity, loyalty, and production.

For the purposes of the present study, Whitney's discussion of these categories is especially interesting because some of the characteristics of the Korean society that he depicts at these four levels—and the ensuing characteristics of the Korean multiactivity enterprise, the chaebol—present close parallels with the Turkish case. As it will be further discussed in this and in following chapters, in Turkey, as in South Korea, one finds that the extent of political centralization has traditionally been very high and the tolerance for intermediate organizations or for nonpolitical sources of power has been very limited. When the development of intermediate forms of organization between the family and the state is thus hampered, it is not surprising to see that the family becomes the primary focus of social identity and loyalty. These similarities between the political cultures of Turkey and South Korea might, in fact, have parallels in other aspects of national culture as suggested, for example, by G. Hofstede's study of cultural relativity of organizational practices and theories in which Turkey and South Korea are found to be closely similar with regards to most of the criteria used to describe national culture.[63]

The reflection of these similarities is indeed observed in parallel similarities in enterprise structure and strategy. In both countries, one observes, in particular, three common characteristics of significance. First, the extent of family control over the enterprise is high. Second, the links between the state and business enterprises are quite direct and important. Third, the activity diversification is extensive, although the extent of unrelated diversification seems to be lower in the Korean chaebol where vertical integration is probably more important than in Turkish holding companies.[64]

The comparative analysis of Turkish holding companies presented in this study further explores these parallels by, at the same time, raising some questions concerning Whitley's analysis. It highlights, for example, the fact that state-business relations and their impact on enterprise structure and strategy can be modified by the

changes that take place in the political environment via the emergence of new forces or actors. Foreign companies, for instance,
present such a new actor that often modifies the dynamics of state-
business relations. In this regard, one observes that, both in Turkey
and in South Korea, the relative insignificance of foreign direct
investment in national economy has prevented the weakening of
state-big business ties in contrast to the Latin American situation in
which foreign control over multiactivity groups has limited the
control that the public authority could exercise over big business
activity. Some writers have also suggested that, in Latin America,
the importance of foreign capital undermines the role of the family
in enterprise management which consequently reflects different
characteristics than do South Korean and Taiwanese forms of industrial organization where family control is still important.[65] Turkish
holding companies, too, largely appear to be family operations, regardless of the size and scope of their activities.

Concerning this significance of family control over enterprise
management, it also seems necessary to go beyond culturally given
explanatory variables. As it will be discussed in more detail in
chapter 4, resistance to the alleviation of family control is a fairly
common phenomenon shared by business classes of culturally very
different societies. Eventually, economic developments in all market economies have brought along new financial and managerial
requirements which have rendered the maintainance of family control quite difficult, but entrepreneurial families have not yielded to
these pressures willingly nor easily.[66] This does not suggest, however, that trends toward the professionalization of the big business
enterprise are not real. While the desire to sustain the control of the
family over business operations appears as a universal phenomenon,
the strength of this desire as well as the extent to which businessmen could and would sacrifice economic rationality for the attain-
ment of this particular objective appears to be conditioned by
society-specific factors.

In the highly unstable business environment in Turkey, the
incentive to maintain family control is likely to be higher given the
flexibility of decision making and implementing in a family enterprise.[67] Ambiguities in state-business relations, also constitute a
factor which might be instrumental in extending the lifespan of the
family enterprise in societies when legal and bureaucratic rules as
well as the social conventions determining the nature of the rela-

tionship are unclear. When a stable policy network is absent, the exchange between government authorities and businessmen acquire an informal character which lacks transparency. This renders the delegation of responsibility to professional managers highly difficult, and the direct contact of owner/managers with political authorities appears as the common means of solving the problems which stem from the ambiguities in the rules of the game.

In Turkey, the fundamental uncertainty characterizing the social and political context of entrepreneurship presents a factor discouraging possible steps toward the professionalization of management. However, in South Korea, the latter is encouraged both by deliberate state action and, indirectly, as a result of the stable environment provided by public policy. Hence, in spite of the continuing significance of family control over chaebol activity, not only the direct mechanisms of enforcement for the opening of enterprises to the public by issuing shares has been instrumental in alleviating the family controlled character of the large Korean enterprises,[68] but the resistance to the weakening of the family control, too, was probably lower in an economy where the element of uncertainty is not very important.

Also, differences in the economic performance of the chaebol and Turkish holding companies indicate that a given form of industrial organization might operate in different manners according to the characteristics of the policy process even in sociocultural environments that manifest important similarities. For example, the policy induced instability in Turkey appears to be instrumental in inhibiting the development of an industrial outlook. Consequently, Turkish holding companies largely function as financial operations in which the objective of improving productivity and international competitiveness are dominated by commercial concerns about the maximization of short-run profits. A stable, predictible policy environment in East Asia, on the other hand, seems to have led to the establishment of "positive sum" rather than "zero-sum" entrepeneurship by discouraging rent seeking, and other speculative activity.

As S. Lall argues in a recent article, industrial success in a given country is to be explained by the mutual determination of static and dynamic efficiency at the firm level on the one hand and at the level of the macroeconomy on the other.[69] This idea is, indeed, supported by the indicators of comparative performance of

the chaebol and Turkish holding companies which find their counterpart in the successful economic development of South Korea and
in the problems of Turkish industrialization. The nature of the
policy process appears here as the key explanatory variable of relative economic success to be investigated through an analysis of the
industrial enterprise as a product of a particular policy environment
which serves to perpetuate the characteristics of the management of
a given economy at a macro level. This, as I have indicated, is the
line of investigation to be followed in chapter 4.

The political economy approach to the study of industrial
culture highlights, therefore, the significance of traditional patterns
of authority relations and characteristics of political culture as manifested in and dynamically shaped by the economic policy process.
The significance of these patterns and characteristics is also observed in the ways in which the increasing importance of multiactivity groups affects the role of business associations in state-
business relations. With their activities dispersed over a large number of sectors, these big enterprises naturally have a considerable
ability to affect the direction of economic policy without necessarily requiring the intermediation of business associations. While
this possibility exists, to some degree, in all countries where economic concentration is high and the key sectors are dominated by
giant corporations, associational life hardly manifests uniform
characteristics across these countries. It reflects, rather, the historically determined forms of interaction between social classes and
state authorities within a given political culture. A given society's
response to the challenge of the forces of international
competition—which call for a stable relationship between political
authorities and big business groups—is also shaped by these same
historical and cultural factors. It is the latter that determine the
place of associations in the recently evolving forms of state-big
business relations whose social significance has been enhanced in
the new international context. The analysis of the social role of
business associations serves to clarify, therefore, the factors which
shape the general framework of business activity in a given country.
In this study, the activities of Turkish business associations through
the Republican period are approached from this perspective, as the
fourth level at which the specificity of the Turkish business environment is explored.

Traditional values entrenched in the cultural system seem to have marked, in a crucial way, the form of business interest representation in Turkey. As was previously discussed, in many societies, business activity geared toward profit maximization does not have a respectable social status. However, one could hypothesize, that, in "hierarchy-conscious" societies in which the dominant culture endorses the existence of social inequality, business interest could be more readily justified and more easily articulated.[70] This is not the case in Turkey, where the private enterprise economy has emerged against the background of a traditional value system characterized by the centrality of equality. This emphasis of equality as a value of crucial significance is traced, by many scholars, to the legacy of the Ottoman Empire in which the institutional structures were deliberately designed to prevent the emergence of a social hierarchy independent of the status conferred by the political authority. Inequalities stemming from nonpolitical sources—from the market process in particular—were regarded with suspicion and were carefully kept under control.[71] The emphasis of the idea that Turkey is a "classless society," which formed an important component of the early Republican ideology, was, therefore, in close conformity with the Ottoman tradition.

While the institutional and ideological devices designed to maintain a single axis dividing the state and the society to the exclusion of divisions between different social strata could not produce economic equality in Turkey, they have led to the emergence of strong inhibitions to the recognition of social hierarchy on the one hand, and to the pursuit of sectional interest on the other. In this context, it is quite natural to observe that the business community has been extremely cautious not to appear as a class in pursuit of its sectional interests. The same cautious attitude could be observed in the wording of any criticism that community representatives directed against government policies throughout the Republican era. Association-based pursuit of group interest and overt criticism of policies inimical to business activity are replaced, in this environment, by the attempt to establish informal ties with political authorities for particularist favors.

Current trends in the role of business associations in Turkish society reflect certain changes in the attitudes in question. Words such as *class, interest,* or *lobbying* are still avoided carefully, and the demands are always formulated with reference to national objectives. The business community, however, has been increasingly critical of the economic policies in application, and the tone of the criticism has been accelerating since the beginning of the 1980s. While relations with the government have continued to be marked by a strong particularism that is characteristic of Turkish business history, certain voluntary associations have been extremely vocal in expressing the will of big business to take part in the policy process.

Although government authorities still have, at the best, a lukewarm attitude toward such initiatives, the idea that the business community has a role to play in the policy process is being increasingly established in political circles. Some voluntary business associations are, in fact, given a quasi-governmental role especially in the realm of foreign economic relations. That the big business community currently has an important position in the social and political scene could hardly be denied.

These recent trends in state-business relations in Turkey have close parallels with the developments observed in other societies in which, as has already been mentioned, the collaboration between the business community and policy makers is increasingly recognized as a necessary condition of successful economic performance. As such, they take place in a very competitive international economy in which countries closely watch and learn from each other's experiences. In this environment, close collaboration between political authorities and big business leaders is often recognized as an important determinant of economic success in East Asia and in European countries such as Germany where neo-corporatist forms of state-business relations prevail. Hence, it is not surprising to see that this type of state-business cooperation is consolidated when it already exists and emulated when it is absent.[72]

As previously discussed with reference to some analyses of the new trends in business outlook in Britain and in North America, it is often a small group of "enlightened" businessmen forming a small but important fraction of the big business community who emerge as the vanguard of their class, attempting to redefine class interest in such a way as to incorporate social stability and economic development. These businessmen also appear to be conscious of the necessity of adopting an attitude of good corporate citizenship to consolidate the position of private enterprise in a world where there is little possibility of reversal in the expansion of interventionism. In chapter 5, I discuss the social characteristics of this vanguard of the business community as it appears in different countries, with business associations playing different types of roles in the class mission in question.

In Turkey, the few businessmen who have recently revealed a certain class consciousness which embodies a sense of social responsibility come from the ranks of those big businessmen that form the sample of this study. Naturally, not all of the latter share the social awareness of the small group in question. Yet, with the social background against which they have made their fortunes, and with the institutional setting and political environment in which they function, the characteristics of the big business community that the study covers are expected to shed some light both on the forms in which current international trends manifest themselves in Turkey and on their probable outcome at the level of the national economy and society.

## 2. PRIVATE BUSINESS IN TURKEY:
## PAST AND PRESENT

This chapter is about the making of the Turkish business class. The reader will notice, however, that the discussion of economic policy orientation—which forms the subject matter of the next chapter—also enters into the analysis of the historical development of Turkish business in a crucial manner. This reflects the nature of state-business relations in the Republican period, and highlights the state-created character of the Turkish business class. The idea that the Turkish business class appears as part of a national development project is, in fact, central to the discussion presented in this chapter.

While this idea is pursued by concentrating on the evolution of the business class after the formation of the Republic in 1923, the chapter begins with a discussion of certain developments during the Young Turk experiment when the Committee for Union and Progress (CUP) was in power in 1908–1918. In some ways, these developments anticipate the future trends in state-business relations. This discussion will be followed by a general historical overview of big business enterprises and their founders. I will then present, on the basis of autobiographical material and the information gathered in the course of interviews, some typical cases of business career orientation in Turkey.

### TURKISH BUSINESSMEN AND THEIR STATE

Many studies on Turkish economic history adhere to a widely shared idea that social attitudes toward business activity that are embedded in the cultural fabric of the society have been critical in shaping the business behavior and economic development in the country. These studies emphasize the traditional lack of respect toward and absence of recognition of the worth of business activity in their analysis of Turkish economic history. This argument is closely related to the view that the Muslim population in the Otto- man Empire was not involved—or was only marginally involved— in commercial activities which were largely controlled by non- Muslim minorities. As pointed out by one historian, the idea is so deeply rooted in Ottoman studies that one can hardly find efforts to substantiate it.[1]

In the previous chapter, certain questions were raised about the limitations of explaining business behavior with reference to cultural factors. Furthermore, in this particular case of the Ottoman Empire, the reason why Muslims were to be excluded from the realm of commerce is quite difficult to understand. One can hardly explain it with reference to Islam which, unlike Christianity, does not pass any moral judgement against money-making activity. The fact that Mohammed himself was involved in commerce seems to be sufficient to render a religion-based explanation difficult to sus- tain. While it would be possible to conjecture that Ottoman rulers may have been unfavorable to commercial dealings between Mus- lims and non-Muslims, that, too, does not seem to be the case. A recent study, in fact, argues that "there is no evidence that any reaction on the part of the Ottoman government or the religious authorities was aimed at stopping Ottoman merchants from trading with foreigners within and outside the empire . . . "[2] The same study also documents the extensive involvement of Muslim mer- chants in extraterritorial trade during the fifteenth through seven- teenth centuries.

The culturally explained exclusion of Muslims from commer- cial activities, therefore, remains to be substantiated. The idea ap- pears, however, as a significant element of the nationalistic discourse during both the 1908–1918 Young Turk experiment and the early years of Turkish Republic. That the Muslim Turks did not figure significantly in the business community in the early twen- tieth century is indeed confirmed by existing statistics. This under- representation of Muslim Turks in commercial life of the late Ottoman Empire could be explained, at least in part, with reference to the particular pattern of integration of the Empire into the European economy after the industrial revolution. On the one hand, the traditional industry in the country was unable to compete with modern European industry, and it was in decline since the eighteenth century. While this development in itself was of a nature to affect Muslims and non-Muslims in the same way, the unequal insertion of the Empire into the European economy led to other developments which were unfavorable to Muslims. Changes in the capitulary regime, in particular, were important in this regard. With these changes, foreign ambassadors in the Empire acquired sovereign rights of legal and administrative control over commercial activities within their communities. The protection offered by European ambassadors to their passport holders eventually led to the creation of merchant groups of different, real, or adopted national identities. These groups formed the Levantine population that played an important role in the economic relations between Europe and the late Ottoman Empire. Throughout these developments, non-Muslim Ottoman subjects also acquired a privileged position as chosen intermediaries between European merchants and Turkish authorities. In the nineteenth century, representative agencies and merchant houses that were controlled by European passport holders and employed non-Muslim Turks dominated the commercial life of the Empire.[3] Muslim population was largely excluded from this area and, eventually, from the business life of the country all together.[4]

Another explanation of the same phenomenon seems to have been quite popular in early Republican period. In this period, certain writers tried to expain the underrepresentation of Muslim Turks in the business community as a product of Tanzimat (Reform Period, 1839–1876). According to them, it was during the Tanzimat era that the Muslim population of the Empire began to leave the realm of business. This development was explained with reference to the establishment of a modern bureaucracy providing attractive jobs to the Muslim population. Given the appeal of a brilliant career in public bureaucracy, commerce and industry have acquired their current status of second class occupations. What was observed in early Republican period was, therefore, not a deep-rooted cultural phenomenon, but the end result of a particular phase of social history.[5]

Regardless of the type of explanation offered for the ethnic and religious makeup of the business community, the significance of the

38    State and Business in Modern Turkey

TABLE 2.1
Sectoral Distribution of Industrial Establishments in Turkey in 1915

| Sector | Number of Enterprises | Public Company | Join Stock Company | Private Company |
|---|---|---|---|---|
| Food Industry | 75 | 1 | 8 | 66 |
| Cement, Clay, Pottery | 17 | 1 | 5 | 11 |
| Leather Industry | 13 | 1 | 1 | 11 |
| Timber Industry | 24 | — | — | 24 |
| Textile Industry | 73 | 18 | 10 | 45 |
| Paper and Printing | 51 | 1 | — | 50 |
| Chemical Industry | 11 | — | 4 | 7 |
| Total | 264 | 22 | 28 | 214 |

Source: Gündüz Ökçün, ed., Osmanlı Sanayii: 1913–1915 Yılları Sanayii İstatistiki, 299 (Ankara: Ankara Universitesi Siyasal Bilgiler Fakültesi Yayını 1971) 13

private sector in the economic development of the country during the twentieth century was always emphasized, and the low participation rate of the Muslim population in business activity was lamented as a serious problem by both politicians and intellectuals. These considerations were accompanied by the attempts of both the CUP and the Republican governments to "create" a group of indigenous businessmen.

Two censuses of industry conducted in 1913 and 1915 were, in fact, a part of the attempts undertaken during the period when the Young Turks were in power. The census results—which were far from being complete—showed that in 1915, there were, within the frontiers of the Empire, 264 industrial enterprises employing more than ten workers (see table 2.1). More than half of these enterprises were located in Istanbul and its vicinity. Half of the remaining ones were in Izmir followed by Bursa as another important industrial center.[6] As shown in table 2.1, the form of ownership for 214 enterprises was private ownership by a single proprietor, and only 28 enterprises were corporations. There were 22 state-owned enterprises among the 264 mentioned in the 1915 Census results. The state enterprises were mostly in the textile industry, with public ownership being negligible in other sectors.

The census data included the name of the owner of each enterprise. It was possible, therefore, to estimate the ethnic and religious distribution of ownership. According to such an estimation, of the firms which belonged to private individuals, only forty-two, or 19.6 percent, were owned by Muslims. 172 enterprises, 80.4 percent of the total number of individually owned ones, belonged to non-Muslim minorities. It was indicated that of the twenty-nine individually owned flour mills, twenty-four belonged to non-Muslims. Of the nine pasta factories, eight were non-Muslim owned, and of the eighteen sugar refineries, sixteen were owned by non-Muslims. None of the existing canned food factories were owned by Muslims.[7]

In spite of the opportunity these results have given many writers to elaborate at length on the necessity of creating an indigenous business community, they were not at all surprising. In fact, the objective of developing an industrial base controlled by national elements had been on the agenda since the formation of the CUP government in 1908. Debates around this issue naturally involved policy measures that had to be taken for the promotion of industrial development. At the time, several such policies had been in application since the end of the nineteenth century and were designed to protect national industry from foreign competition. These policies were, however, largely ineffective because of bilateral trade agreements which, as a part of the capitulary regime, prevented the implementation of protectionist policies. Partly in consideration of the restrictions imposed by the existing trade agreements, some of the groups involved in the industrial policy debates opted for a system of government-granted privileges and monopolies. The Istanbul Chamber of Industry and Commerce, while expressing its opposition to restrictive practices in general, was also among the advocates of this approach.[8] Nevertheless, with the opposition of the liberal members of the CUP, granting of privileges and monopolies was excluded from the industrial promotion policy to be adopted.

The Law for the Encouragement of Industry—which was prepared in 1913 as a temporary measure—involved some tax exemptions and exemptions from customs duties in the importation of inputs to be used in local industrial production. It also involved provisions for the free-of-charge allocation of state lands for the installation of industrial plants. Although it was designed to provide temporary privileges which were to end after fifteen years—partly because of the unusual circumstances of the World War I years—the 1913 Law remained in application until it was replaced by another law for the promotion of industrial development in 1927, four years after the foundation of the Republic.

While the 1913 Law was important in reflecting the committment of the government to the development of national industry, it was not the most important step taken by the CUP in its attempts to create an indigineous business class. More important than this particular policy tool were the attempts to transform the commercial code and the property regime with a view to make them more consistent with a private enterprise economy, as well as the direct involvement of some CUP members in the establishment of private enterprises.[9] One sees a clear manifestation of the second element of CUP strategy for development of the national economy in the industrial and banking joint stock companies founded during this period.

The joint stock company was the solution found by the Unionists to solve the problem of capital scarcity in the country. While the absence of a commercial outlook among the Muslim Turks was underlined as the key problem of industrialization during the early years of the Unionist rule, the shortage of capital soon surfaced as a major problem dominating other, mentality-related obstacles to the national industrialization strategy.[10] It was especially during the war years that the leaders of the CUP attempted to raise industrial investment funds through the creation of joint stock companies both in Istanbul and in Anatolian towns. Although the statistical information on these ventures is largely incomplete, we have, for example, one reference to seventy-two such companies in existence in 1918.[11] A study on the banks founded as joint stock companies during the period of 1909–1930 mentions twenty-four banks established under the CUP government between the years 1908–1918.[12] According to this study, six of these banks were founded by foreigners, one by Armenian minorities, and the rest by Muslim Turks. Eight of the latter were situated in Istanbul, with the remaining ones located in several Western and Central Anatolian towns.

The information given on the composition of the boards of directors of these joint stock companies is extremely interesting in revealing the nature of the state's role in the industrialization strategy adopted in this period. What we see here is not merely a heavily interventionist state guiding and directing the private entrepreneurial efforts. Neither do we have a case with important state investments in infrastructure or in other areas to which private funds are not attracted. Rather, what we observe is a curious inter-mingling of the public and the private, in which it is often difficult to say whether a certain member of the board is there as an ordinary citizen or as a representative of the ruling government. A factory in the town of Adapazarı that produces iron and wooden implements appears to be, for example, a typical venture of the CUP era. The factory was founded as a partnership between private business and the state—more specifically, between the members of the local CUP branch and the War Ministry. These members of the CUP were also the local notables of the town, but it is quite clear that their role in the venture was more directly related to their political position which was instrumental in assuring the support of the War Minis-try. The latter element played, in fact, a rather significant role in fostering the development of defense-related industry during World War I through partnerships of this type.[13]

The composition of the founding members of the banks estab-lished between 1908–1918 also reveal the same direct involvement of the ruling party members in the business life of the country. One finds many landowners and merchants to be prominent among the founders of these banks. It would be misleading, however, to use this information, as it is, in an analysis of the social origins of the Turkish business class. Interpreted in the light of parallel informa-tion on the founders of other companies established in the same period, the businessmen of this era seem to be characterized more by their political affiliations than their social origins. The social fabric of the indigenous business class that the Unionists were trying to create was formed by the landlords, merchants, and small tradesmen organized around "tradesmen's associations" with the initiative of the government. Former statesmen who were not pre-vented from using the fortunes they accumulated when they were in office in the new atmosphere of flourishing business activity also constituted an element of the same class. Yet, the ownership of capital, social status, or expertise in a given line of trade were not as important as Unionist connections. The members of the ruling party—who sometimes included members of the parliament or lo-cal governors—were in the forefront among the pioneers of Turkish business. In this regard, the composition of the founding members of the Turkish Vineyardists' Bank established in Manisa in 1917 is quite typical. Among the founders of the bank one finds individuals from different professional occupations to which the local notables belong. The common denominator, however, is the CUP affiliation that most of them share. Among the fifty-eight founders, thirty-five were CUP members, often holding important positions in the local party organization.[14]

Direct involvement of the Union and Progress Party members in commercial activities extended even to wartime profiteering in the cities. During the war years, the control of distribution channels for basic necessities in big cities—particularly in Istanbul—appeared to be one of the most important problems facing the government. While the municipalities were initially in charge of city provisioning, eventually the best-organized entity of the country, the CUP, took charge of the task. The Special Commission for Commerce (Heyet-i Mahsusa-i Ticariyye), controlled by the party organization, thus began to control the distribution of basic necessities to Istanbul and other big cities. The party members seem to have fulfilled this task in a way that assure a significant accumulation of capital funds for the establisment of joint stock companies founded with their initiative.[15]

In fact, during World War I, black market activity appeared to be a source of capital accumulation for all individuals who were in a position to take advantage of the unusual circumstances. Initially, the non-Muslim minorities who were important in the business life of the country were the ones best-situated in this regard. Yet, given government polies aimed at the creation of an indigenous business class, the measures against profiteering were mostly used against this group, affecting the aspiring Muslim entrepreneurs less deeply.[16] The activities of a special commission formed to prevent speculative activity in Istanbul (Men-i İhtikar Heyeti) might not have been very effective in controlling wartime inflation, but they probably contributed to a significant accumulation of capital in the hands of Muslim Turks. At least a portion of these capital funds must have been used in the formation of new businesses in the Republican period.

The CUP has been called "the vanguard of the nascent Turkish bourgeoisie."[17] The Unionists were, in fact, in the forefront of the business life of the Muslim population in its formative years. The role that they assumed in this area was well beyond that of statesmen encouraging the development of national commerce and industry. They not only supported aspiring businessmen, but they became businessmen themselves. The period when they were in office was characterized, therefore, by a certain blurring of the distinction between the economic policymaker and the private businessmen, and between the realm of public policy and private interest. The distinction between the public sector firm and private enterprise, was also blurred by the popular Unionist model of partnerships between the state and private capital.

After the foundation of the Republic, the state continued to occupy a central place in the business life of the country. In the early years of the Republic, activities pertaining to public office and business enterprise could still be jointly undertaken. Many statesmen had an interest in business life, and it is possible that some of them genuinely believed that business investment constituted, for them, an additional way of serving the country. After all, Mustafa Kemal Atatürk and his close associates in the governmental circle were among the founders of the İş Bankası with other politicians and private businessmen.[18] Political connections were undoubtedly an important asset used in accumulation of private capital. Yet, in time, jointly undertaken activities in politics and business eventually gave way to the choice of a distinct career path in one of these areas. Rising sensitivity toward the abuse of political power and political connections in commercial deals was probably instrumental in imposing such a choice on public office holders.[19] While the public sector has been an important source of entrepreneurial talent to the private sector, once the choice is made, the transfer appears to be complete and final. Even in the case of professional managers in the private sector, the possibility of returning to their former public sector positions seems to be largely excluded. Hence, in spite of the significance of the role the state has played in economy all through the Republican era—and in spite of the continuing tradition of joint shareholding of enterprises by private and public companies—the boundaries of the private sector was eventually consolidated.

The acknowledgement of the state-dependent character of capitalist development in Turkey should not lead to an underestimation of the social and economic role of private business in the country. As table 2.2 and figures 2.1, 2.2, 2.3, and 2.4 show, the private sector has had an increasingly significant role in Turkish economy despite the rather significant fluctuations in its share in total payments to employees, total fixed investment, and the value

TABLE 2.2

Relative Share of the Private Sector in Turkish Manufacturing Industry, 1950–1986

| Years | Number of Establishments | | Annual Payments Made to Employees | | Gross Additions to the Fixed Assets during the Year | | Value Added | |
|---|---|---|---|---|---|---|---|---|
| | Public | Private | Public | Private | Public | Private | Public | Private |
| 1950 | 3.93% | 96.07% | 59.37% | 40.63% | 53.98% | 46.02% | 58.33% | 41.67% |
| 1951 | 4.04% | 95.96% | 58.68% | 41.32% | 55.90% | 44.10% | 59.24% | 40.76% |
| 1952 | 3.80% | 96.20% | 55.74% | 44.26% | 46.89% | 53.11% | 61.34% | 38.66% |
| 1953 | 4.25% | 95.75% | 53.98% | 46.02% | 44.79% | 55.21% | 55.77% | 44.23% |
| 1954 | 3.79% | 96.21% | 51.38% | 48.62% | 61.55% | 38.45% | 50.55% | 49.45% |
| 1955 | 3.66% | 96.34% | 50.42% | 49.58% | 59.51% | 40.49% | 50.14% | 49.86% |
| 1956 | 3.66% | 96.34% | 50.77% | 49.23% | 61.13% | 38.87% | 47.03% | 52.97% |
| 1957 | 3.95% | 96.05% | 47.39% | 52.61% | 54.36% | 45.64% | 44.47% | 55.53% |
| 1958 | 3.81% | 96.19% | 44.28% | 55.72% | 57.09% | 42.91% | 45.09% | 54.91% |
| 1959 | 3.95% | 96.05% | 47.30% | 52.70% | 36.55% | 63.45% | 54.34% | 45.66% |
| 1960 | 3.98% | 96.02% | 49.08% | 50.92% | 48.36% | 51.64% | 59.11% | 40.89% |
| 1961 | 3.29% | 96.71% | 45.78% | 54.22% | 47.80% | 52.20% | 51.41% | 48.59% |
| 1962 | 5.71% | 94.29% | 48.24% | 51.76% | 78.21% | 21.79% | 52.64% | 47.36% |
| 1963 | 7.87% | 92.13% | 51.09% | 48.91% | 51.74% | 48.26% | 52.69% | 47.31% |
| 1964 | 8.03% | 91.97% | 49.09% | 50.91% | 59.24% | 40.76% | 51.73% | 48.27% |
| 1965 | 9.26% | 90.74% | 50.46% | 49.54% | 44.60% | 55.40% | 57.13% | 42.87% |
| 1966 | 9.35% | 90.65% | 50.76% | 49.24% | 36.56% | 63.44% | 54.67% | 45.33% |
| 1967 | 8.68% | 91.32% | 49.19% | 50.81% | 36.84% | 63.16% | 62.89% | 37.11% |
| 1968 | 8.65% | 91.35% | 48.32% | 51.68% | 35.05% | 64.95% | 61.99% | 38.01% |

|  | | | | | | | | |
|------|--------|--------|--------|--------|--------|--------|--------|--------|
| 1969 | | | | | | | | |
| 1970 | | | | | | | | |
| 1971 | 6.73% | 93.27% | 41.40% | 58.60% | 37.79% | 62.21% | 56.01% | 43.99% |
| 1972 | 6.72% | 93.28% | 40.46% | 59.54% | 38.47% | 61.53% | 51.81% | 48.19% |
| 1973 | 6.37% | 93.63% | 38.36% | 61.64% | 36.39% | 63.61% | 46.52% | 53.48% |
| 1974 | 6.60% | 93.40% | 38.85% | 61.15% | 34.84% | 65.16% | 50.24% | 49.76% |
| 1975 | 6.41% | 93.59% | 41.74% | 58.26% | 32.96% | 67.04% | 48.05% | 51.95% |
| 1976 | 5.65% | 94.35% | 44.05% | 55.95% | 31.69% | 68.31% | 35.54% | 64.46% |
| 1977 | 5.81% | 94.19% | 43.15% | 56.85% | 30.69% | 69.31% | 39.89% | 60.11% |
| 1978 | 5.34% | 94.66% | 42.39% | 57.61% | 38.10% | 61.90% | 33.40% | 66.60% |
| 1979 | 5.31% | 94.69% | 44.35% | 55.65% | 18.38% | 81.62% | 33.14% | 66.86% |
| 1980 | 4.68% | 95.32% | 46.49% | 53.51% | | | 40.41% | 59.59% |
| 1981 | 4.63% | 95.37% | 44.47% | 55.53% | 24.57% | 75.43% | 49.26% | 50.74% |
| 1982 | 4.48% | 95.52% | 40.46% | 59.54% | 29.01% | 70.99% | 46.84% | 53.16% |
| 1983 | 8.93% | 91.07% | 40.77% | 59.23% | 29.09% | 70.91% | 43.52% | 56.48% |
| 1984 | 8.37% | 91.63% | 37.53% | 62.47% | | | 38.47% | 61.53% |
| 1985 | 8.05% | 91.95% | 34.73% | 65.27% | | | 39.44% | 60.56% |
| 1986 | 7.86% | 92.14% | 33.01% | 66.99% | 32.24% | 67.76% | 40.72% | 59.28% |

*Source:* State Statistical Institute Census of Manufacturing and Business (1950–1986). Separate information on private and public sector not available for 1969 and 1970. No relevant data on "Gross additions to fixed assets" for 1980, 1984, and 1985.

FIGURE 2.1

Relative Share of Public and Private Sectors in the Number of Manufacturing Establishments

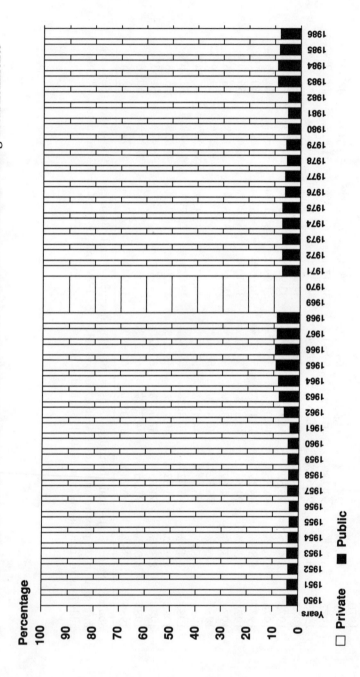

□ Private   ■ Public

*Source:* Based on the information given in table 2.2

FIGURE 2.2
Relative Share of Private and Public Sectors in Annual Payments to Employees

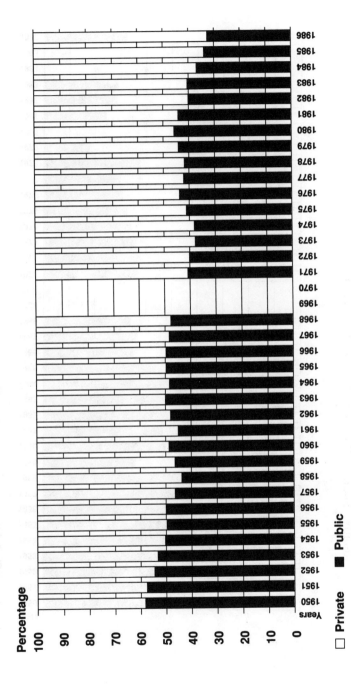

☐ Private  ■ Public

*Source:* Based on the information given in table 2.2

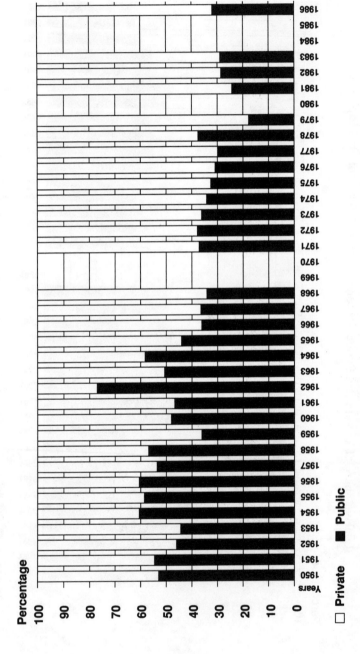

FIGURE 2.3
Relative Share of Private and Public Sectors in Fixed Capital Investment

Source: Based on the information given in table 2.2

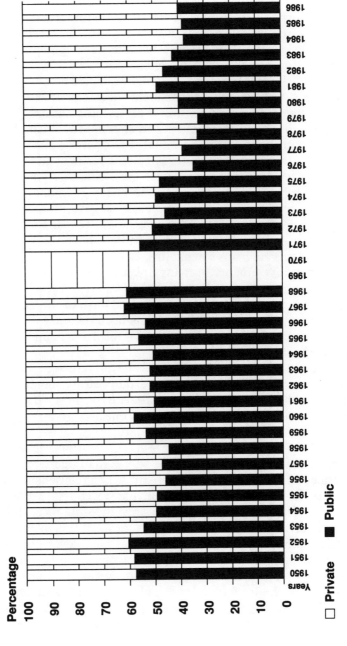

FIGURE 2.4

Relative Share of Private and Public Sectors in Value Added

□ Private   ■ Public

Source: Based on the information given in table 2.2

added. While the figures in these areas suggest that the economic share of the public sector has also been quite important, they should be interpreted by taking into account some characteristics of the Turkish experiment in mixed economic development which will become clearer in the next two chapters.

Until the 1980s, mixed economy remained an ambigious term which, at times, created a considerable degree of uneasiness among private businessmen concerning their social positions. While this ambiguity has been instrumental in shaping the business attitude prevailing in the country, the actual growth of the public sector has not taken place in a way that threatens the realm of private industry. The latter has always had sufficient investment outlets as demonstrated by its lack of interest in the purchasing of public enterprises during the privatization attempts of several governments, especially in the 1950s and 1980s. Second, joint ventures with public enterprises—especially with public banks—have facilitated the expansion of private firms by enabling them to realize large-scale, high technology investments in many areas of the economy. Third, the growth of private enterprise in Turkey has taken place along with the development of the highly structured form of the Turkish holding company. Private wealth has thus been organized in the structure of large multiactivity firms, which form a dynamic force in the development of Turkish economy.

Nevertheless, development of the private sector in the Republican period bears the mark of certain features of state-business relations which manifest close parallels with those observed in the Unionist era. In the Republican period, one also finds the emergence of a business class characterized, before anything else, by its position vis-à-vis the political power. Yet, the relationship of this class with the state appears to be more subtle than one which could be described in terms of sheer nepotism. It is a relationship in which the businessman, to be successful, has to convince political authorities of his desire and ability to serve the state through entrepreneurial activity. Relatedly, the social status of the business class is largely defined by the nature of the national development project undertaken by the political authority. Consequently, the latter becomes the main source of any legitimacy that the new class possesses. Even the legal foundations of entrepreneurship are not very solid because many newly emerging entrepreneurs built their careers on the implicit attempt at the displacement and even dispossession of non-Muslim businessmen. Attempts at the creation of an indigenous business community through replacement of minorities continued in the Republican period, and at times, led to flagrant violations of moral and legal norms. One example is the case of the infamous Wealth Levy of the 1940s which will be discussed in chapter 3. In the Republican period, therefore, the state also contributed to the creation of private wealth through selectively used mechanisms of reward and punishment. Turkish businessmen carrying these birth marks could have little claim to moral and legal arguments to face any challenge from different societal actors or from the state authority itself. There has been little autonomous moral basis or legal framework to be used for the justification of business activity.

Furthermore, financial dependence of the private sector on state subsidies has been too significant to enable businessmen to acquire an autonomous social position. The findings of a study conducted in the 1980s give us a good idea about the extent of the financial dependence in question. The study estimates that, in developed regions of the country, different types of incentives form 67.6 percent of total investment costs at the stage of investment and 58.2 percent at the stage of operation. For underdeveloped regions which are given priority in the access to incentives, these figures are, respectively, 96.6 percent and 95.2 percent.[20]

Therefore, a significant lack of financial autonomy limited the social strength of the business class throughout the Republican period. Social origins of the business community, were also not of a nature to provide a social context of legitimacy with reference to traditional social status, accumulated wealth, or trade expertise of the individuals forming the new entrepreneurial class. The following section on the social background of big businessmen in Turkey highlights this original weakness of the business community. This discussion might provide a partial explanation to certain elements of the business outlook and behavior now prevailing in the country.

## SOCIAL ORIGINS OF TURKISH BUSINESSMEN

One could surmise that the policy of indigenization adopted in the CUP era was of a nature to contribute more to the accumulation of capital in the hands of Muslim businessmen than to the establishment of a solid, long-lasting industrial base. This policy was aimed at fostering a trade mentality among the Muslim population and helping the latter to raise the necessary investment funds. While economic rationality would have imposed a policy of using the existing entrepreneurial talent and capital resources to the maximum, the Unionist policy was, by its very nature, dominated by a political attempt to create these resources exactly where they were absent, with the right political affiliation being the ultimate criterion of choice for the encouragement of a particular business venture.

The political nature of the Unionist business development strategy was also inimical to the survival of the business initiatives undertaken in this period. After the fall of the CUP with the military defeat for which they were accused of being responsible, the new government took a hostile position against the ventures most heavily associated with the party. The closing of the National Factory Builders' Association (Milli Fabrikacılar Cemiyeti) founded by Unionists to encourage private enterprise in industrial production is an example of the new government's hostility against the economic initiatives of its predecessor.[21]

Nevertheless, these initiatives were probably instrumental in the establishment of a number of industrial enterprises which were in operation in the beginning of the Republican period. It would not be justifiable, in fact, to suggest that Muslim businessmen were practically nonexistant in the beginning of the Republican period. Table 2.3. shows, for example, that, in this period, there existed in the Istanbul region a nonnegligible number of industrial enterprises of a fair size and owned by Muslim businessmen.[22] Although the dates of foundation of these enterprises are not known, support of the CUP government might have played a role in the establishment of some of these factories. However, what seems to be more interesting to highlight, for the purposes of this study, is that one is unable to trace to these early units of production the origins of any of the big business enterprises that exist in Istanbul today. The few empirical studies available on Turkish business history suggest, in fact, that most of the big business enterprises were founded after World War II.

In a study of private industrial enterprises employing fifty or more workers conducted in 1960, for example, we find information on 126 firms.[23] The study indicates that 2.4 percent or three of these enterprises were founded before 1923. The period of establishment

## TABLE 2.3
### Sectoral Distribution of Enterprises in Istanbul Benefitting from the Law for the Encouragement of Industry, 1924–1925

| Nationality and Ethnic Origin of the Owner | Food Processing | | | Leather and Leather Products | | | Textiles | | | Construction Materials | | | Carpentry | | | Mining and Metal Products | | | Chemicals | | | Paper Products and Miscellaneous | | | Total |
|---|---|---|---|---|---|---|---|---|---|---|---|---|---|---|---|---|---|---|---|---|---|---|---|---|---|
| | a | b | c | a | b | c | a | b | c | a | b | c | a | b | c | a | b | c | a | b | c | a | b | c | |
| Muslim | 8 | 2 | 3 | 1 | 5 | 2 | 2 | 6 | 3 | | 3 | 2 | 2 | 1 | 2 | 5 | 3 | 1 | | 4 | | | 3 | | 55 |
| Non-Muslim | 10 | 9 | 3 | 1 | 4 | 1 | 1 | 1 | | | 4 | 2 | | 5 | | 3 | 3 | 3 | | 1 | | | 4 | 3 | 58 |
| Total TC* | 18 | 11 | 3 | 2 | 9 | 3 | 3 | 7 | 3 | | 7 | 4 | 2 | 6 | 2 | 8 | 6 | 4 | | 5 | | | 7 | 3 | 113 |
| Non-TC* | 1 | 2 | | | 1 | | | | | | | | | | | 1 | | | | | | | | 1 | 6 |
| Total | 19 | 13 | 3 | 2 | 10 | 3 | 3 | 7 | 3 | | 7 | 4 | 2 | 6 | 2 | 9 | 6 | 4 | | 5 | | | 7 | 4 | 119 |

*: Turkish Citizens
a: Employing 10 or less workers
b: Employing more than 10 workers
c: Information on the number of employees not available

Source: Estimated on the basis of T.C. Devlet Salnamesi: 1925–26, İstanbul, 1927, presented in I. Tekeli ve Selim İlkin, 1923 yılında İstanbul'un İktisadi Durumu ve İstanbul Ticaret ve Sanayi Odası İktisat Komisyonu raporu, Tarih Boyunca İstanbul Semineri Bildirileri, İstanbul Üniversitesi Edebiyat Fakültesi, 1989.

was 1923–1939 for 16.2 percent or twenty-one businesses, 1940–1945 for 18.4 percent or twenty-three firms, and 1946–1960 for 59.7 percent or seventy-five companies. The information on the date of establishment of four of the 126 enterprises covered is not available.

Another study on 103 big business enterprises operating in Turkey in 1965 indicates that the majority of these firms were established after 1940.[24] More specifically, it is indicated that the period of establishment was before 1923 for 14.6 percent or fifteen of the enterprises in the sample, 1923–1930 for 16.5 percent or seventeen businesses, 1931–1938 for 12.6 percent or thirteen firms, 1939–1950 for 19.4 percent, and 1951–1960 for 32 percent or thirty-three companies. Also 4.9 percent or 5 of the 103 enterprises in the sample were founded after 1960.

The results of a third study carried out in 1970 give a similar picture. Of the 224 big enterprises covered, 10.46 percent were founded before 1900. The study includes no business firm established in the period 1901–1910, however 2.26 percent of the businesses were established between 1911–1920, 3.22 percent between 1921–1930, 5.40 percent between 1931–1940, 13.42 percent between 1941–1950, 40.54 percent between 1951–1960, and 24.70 percent between 1961–1969.[25]

The fact that the last two studies show a larger number of enterprises established before 1923 than did the first study probably reflects the differences in the sectoral distribution of the enterprises of different vintage. The first study includes only those enterprises in the manufacturing sector, while the second one also covers mining, commerce, finance and banking. In the third study, enterprises in the agricultural sector, are also covered and, as the latter shows, the overwhelming majority of the existing enterprises established before the Republican period are in agriculture. In the manufacturing sector, the food processing industry is almost the only area in which firms were founded before the Republican era.[26]

In fact, the membership structure of the Istanbul Chamber of Industry and Trade in the 1920s, also reflects a limited number of industrial enterprises compared to a larger number of commercial businesses. For example, in the memoirs of one of the early industrialists, it is noted that, in this period, among the thirty members of the assembly of the Chamber, there were only five industrialists. The rest of the members were merchants.[27] The author of these memoirs bitterly complains about the underrepresentation of the

TABLE 2.4
Date of Incorporation of the Companies Represented in TUSIAD[1]

| Period of Incorporation | Number of Companies |
| --- | --- |
| Prior to 1910 | 1[2] |
| 1910–1919 | 2 |
| 1920–1929 | 6 |
| 1930–1939 | 4 |
| 1940–1949 | 9 |
| 1950–1959 | 49 |
| 1960–1969 | 87 |
| 1970–1979 | 150 |
| 1980–1989 | 94 |
| Date not available | 3 |
| Total Number of Companies | 405 |

[1]When the date of foundation of the enterprise is given along with the date of incorporation, the former is chosen to show the vintage of the business unit in question.
[2]The Canadian Company Northern Telecom, Ltd. (1882).
Source: TÜSİAD Members' Company Profiles, Istanbul: TÜSİAD, 1989

industrialists in the business community, as well as about the neglect of the sector by economic policymakers.

In Turkey, the typical big business enterprise is a quite young operation. While this is most clearly observed in the manufacturing sector, big enterprises in general conform to the same pattern. The insignificance of older firms among the companies represented by the membership of Turkish Industrialists' and Businessmen's Association (TÜSİAD), for example, highlights the same characteristic of the business scene. As table 2.4. shows, of the 405 companies included in the hand book of TÜSİAD Members' Company Profiles, the companies incorporated in the 1970s form the majority or 150 enterprises. Those formed in the 1980s were next in numbers with ninety-four of the companies involved being incorporated in that decade. We find eighty-seven companies incorporated in the 1960s and forty-nine in the 1950s. There are only twenty-two companies incorporated before 1950 among the 405 represented in TÜSİAD. Because TÜSİAD is an organization which groups together the most prominent business leaders in the country, the companies represented are likely to be among the most important and dynamic ones. Therefore, the given age structure might also be interpreted as an indication of the vitality of younger firms in the current business environment.

In addition to the histories of individual enterprises, the business histories of the families that control the most important groups—the holding companies—in which enterprises are situated cannot typically be traced further back than the early days of the Republic. Table 2.5 presents the dates of the first business operations of the founders of some of the most important holding companies. The holding companies included in the list are among those which appear as the shareholders of one or more of the five-hundred largest enterprises in Turkey.[28] In fact, the affiliates of the eight holdings—Koç, Sabancı, Yaşar, Anadolu Endüstri Holding, Eczacıbaşı, Çukurova, Akkök, and Kutlutaş—presented in the table constitute 103 of these largest 500 establishments of which 95 are public firms and 9 belong to cooperatives. More than 150 of the 395 largest private enterprises are affiliates of the 30 holding companies included in the table. As the table shows, the business careers of the owners of these holding companies begin, at the earliest, in the 1920s, and, in most cases, the date of entry into business is situated in the 1950s. The fact that most of the business careers begin in the 1950s is consistent with the results of the three empirical studies previously discussed. This can be explained with reference to the probusiness policy orientation of the Democratic Party governments in power in this period. It would be misleading, nevertheless, to overemphasize this point. In fact, as shown by Table 2.6., the 1930s and 1940s—two decades associated with Etatist policies—appear to be periods when a considerable number of business enterprises were established. Moreover, the same table indicates that these "Etatist" decades also appear as the ones in which the number of individuals leaving public-sector jobs for business careers is at its highest—a phenomenon which would be difficult to explain in the light of the popular belief about the culturally downgraded status of private business activity and the privileged position of state employment.

In fact, employment in the public sector appears to be the former occupation of the majority of big businessmen in Turkey, as can be seen in table 2.6. which presents the occupational background, as well as the date of entry into business, of big entrepreneurs active in the 1970s. The table indicates that former merchants also form an important group among these businessmen. After gov-

TABLE 2.5
The Period of First Entry into Business for Some Major Holding Companies

| Decades | Holding Companies |
|---------|-------------------|
| 1920s | KOÇ <br> ÇUKUROVA <br> SÖNMEZ <br> ÖZAKAT <br> SANTRAL MENSUCAT |
| 1930s | SABANCI <br> SAPMAZ <br> VAKKO |
| 1940s | YAŞAR <br> ECZACIBAŞI <br> ERCAN <br> TRANSTÜRK |
| 1950s | AKKÖK <br> KUTLUTAŞ <br> BORUSAN <br> BODUR <br> TEKFEN <br> ENKA <br> E.C.A. <br> PROFİLO <br> STFA <br> ALARKO <br> AKIN <br> DEVA <br> TAMEK <br> ALTINYILDIZ |
| 1960s | ANADOLU ENDÜSTRİ <br> ÖZSARUHAN <br> İZDAŞ |
| 1970s | EKİNCİLER |

*Source:* Company reports and interviews.

## TABLE 2.6
### Occupational Background of Entrepreneurs According to the Period of Foundation of the Enterprise

| Period of Establish-ment | Previous Occupation (Percent) | | | | | | | | | Number of Enterprises |
|---|---|---|---|---|---|---|---|---|---|---|
| | Mer-chant | Industrialist | Farmer | Professional | Civil Servant | Shop Keeper | Artisan | No. of Occu-pation | Total | |
| Prior to 1900 | 19.17 | — | — | — | 10.83 | — | — | 70 | 100 | 120 |
| 1901–1910 | — | — | — | — | — | — | — | — | — | 26 |
| 1911–1920 | 3.85 | — | — | — | 3.85 | — | — | 92.3 | 100 | 37 |
| 1921–1930 | 27.03 | — | — | 2.7 | 10.81 | 27.03 | — | 32.43 | 100 | 62 |
| 1931–1940 | 3.23 | 1.61 | — | — | 74.19 | — | 1.61 | 19.36 | 100 | 154 |
| 1941–1950 | 35.71 | — | — | 4.55 | 31.17 | 6.49 | — | 22.08 | 100 | 465 |
| 1951–1960 | 18.92 | 4.3 | 5.16 | 6.45 | 18.93 | — | 1.51 | 44.73 | 100 | 283 |
| 1961–1969 | 22.97 | 0.35 | 4.24 | 13.08 | 26.15 | 4.59 | | 28.62 | 100 | |
| Total | 239 | 21 | 36 | 75 | 280 | 33 | 8 | 455 | | 1147 |
| Percent | 20.83 | 1.83 | 3.14 | 6.54 | 24.41 | 2.88 | 0.7 | 39.67 | 100 | 7 |

Source: E. Soral, Özel Kesimde Türk Müteşebbisleri (Ankara: İktisadi ve Ticari İlimler Akademisi Yayınları, 1974) 36

ernment employees and merchants, professionals, also constitute an occupational category which leads to a business career for many individuals. Landownership, on the other hand, appears to be a relatively unimportant category as far as the social background of Turkish businessmen is concerned. Finally, conspicious with their insignificance among Turkish big businessmen are former crafts-men. A career path which leads from artisanal production to modern industry does not, therefore, seem to be a characteristic of Turkish business history.

These observations are also confirmed by other empirical stud-ies. For example, on the basis of a study conducted in the early 1970s, D. La Vere Bates writes that "almost one-half of the [busi-ness] elite are from similar occupational origins, commerce related. The significant point is that 77 percent of the elite are from the two occupational origins of commerce related (small- and medium-sized business owner and business executive) and government associated . . . The occupational origins of the fathers of the elite are almost exactly the same as the occupational origins of the elite."[29] The findings of another study conducted in the 1960s present a similar picture especially with regard to the insignificance of landowner-ship and craftsmenship in characterizing the social background of the business community. Among the 103 businessmen covered in this study, 35 have fathers holding different types of public sector jobs, and the fathers of 25 businessmen in the sample are small merchants. There are only 7 businessmen whose fathers were farm-ers, with the type of land holdings unknown. Craftsmanship is not even included as an occupational category in this classification of entrepreneurs according to the profession of their fathers.[30]

Among the prominent holding companies that are active to-day, there is only one, Çukurova Holding, whose founders are known to be wealthy landowners. Nevertheless, the fact that the two founding families, Karamehmet and Eliyeşil, were very close to the founders of the Republic because of their active participation in the War of Liberation somewhat modifies the picture and suggests that the determining factor in this case is something different from the advantage derived from material wealth and social status associ-ated with the ownership of landed property.

In fact, it would even be possible to argue that the success of Çukurova Holding as a commercial and industrial operation was in spite of, rather than because of, the social background of its founders as they belonged to a social category from which the Republican state has not chosen to recruit the elements of the new business class it had set out to create. It is indeed worth asking why, while encouraging the emergence of a class of indigenous entrepreneurs, the founders of the Republic did not direct their efforts to raising industrial capital at the most obvious source of accumulation—that is, from landed property. Some writers have attempted to explain the fact that landed property does not appear to be source of capital accumulation with reference to the general pattern of land tenure in the country. According to them, in Turkey, small family holdings have traditionally been the typical production unit in land. Consequently, agrarian fortune could not form the basis of capitalist accumulation.[31] While this observation about the significance of independent family holdings is valid for some parts of the country, we know that, in the early twentieth century, large landownership existed and was significant, at least in Southern and Eastern Turkey.[32] Therefore, we need an additional explanation to the absence of special incentives to encourage the existing landlords to convert their wealth into industrial and commercial capital. Another explanation could be found, for example, in the distrust of the builders of the new state for the alternative, nonpolitical sources of power which might have been inimical to the radical project of social transformation. The nature of the discussions around the land reform bill of 1945, for example, supports this view. In some of these discussions, it is explicitly suggested that land reform is necessary because large landed property constitutes a threat to the state authority and conflicts with the mentality of the new Republican state.[33]

As already mentioned, craftsmen, like landowners, are largely absent in the family background of Turkish big businessmen. The fact that very few of leading Turkish businessmen were originally artisans or the sons of artisans might reflect, first, the significance of minorities in artisanal occupations in the Ottoman era. Policies aimed at creating an indigenous business class would naturally exclude encouragement of Greek and Armenian craftsmen to use their skills in the establishment of modern industry. Moreover, the emigration of minorities is likely to have led to an important shortage of artisanal skills in the country.[34] While the exclusion of Muslims from commercial activities in the Ottoman Empire is often emphasized, one finds fewer references to this absence of artisanal skills among the Muslim population. Yet, the shortage of indigenous craftsmen might be an important factor determining the original sources of entrepreneurship in the country.

Apart from the supply factors affecting the sources of entrepreneurship, government policies are also likely to have played some role in this area. Deliberate neglect of small industries and the lack of initiatives designed for the modernization of small enterprises by successive governments constitute another important factor limiting the opportunities of transition from small artisanal production to modern industrial activity. In this regard, the attitude of Turkish governments is probably not dissimilar to that of policymakers in many other late-industrializing countries. In these countries, government authorities often share an "esthetic concern" whereby small enterprises which do not resemble the modern, large-scale production units of developed Western countries are regarded with distaste.[35] The political discussions in the early Republican period—especially in the 1930s—indicate that the same distaste was quite widely shared in Turkey. Moreover, an equally strong belief in the wastefulness of competition which prevailed in the same period probably played some role in shaping policies unfavorable to small enterprises.[36]

As table 2.7. shows, although they are important in number, small enterprises have been increasingly insignificant in terms of their place in Turkish economy. A recent survey of small and medium businesses conducted by the Istanbul Chamber of Commerce indicates that 89.4 percent of the enterprises covered in the survey do not benefit from any incentives. Most of the enterprise managers who answered the researchers' question concerning the reason behind this indicated that they had either no valid knowledge of available incentives or were discouraged by the amount of bureaucratic red tape.[37]

In Turkey, individuals who have contributed to the development of modern industry rarely came from sectors of domestic industry linked to the branch in which they built factories. One sector in which there is some evidence of the existence of insiders—that is, individuals who have traditional links with the industry as artisans, merchant manufacturers, or middlemen putters-out who have played some role in the emergence of modern production processes—is the textile industry.[38] For example, two major holding companies presented in table 2.5., Akın and Altınyıldız, are com-

TABLE 2.7
Some Indicators of the Position of
Small Industry in the Manfacturing Sector* (%)

|  | 1950 | 1980 | 1985 |
|---|---|---|---|
| Total Number of Enterprises | 97 | 95 | 95 |
| Number of Employees | 51 | 38 | 36 |
| Total Number of Wage Earners** | 29 | 22 | 22 |
| Value of Production | 21 | 14 | 11 |
| Value Added | 22 | 12 | 13 |

*Small enterprises include those employing 25 or fewer workers.
**Figures for total number of wage earners are less than those for number of employees because some of the individuals employed in these enterprises are not officially registered.
Source: Istanbul Ticaret Odası, Türkiye'de Küçük ve Orta Ölçekli İşletmeler; Yapısal ve Finansal Sorunlar, Çözümler, Istanbul, 1991. 31

panies whose main activities are concentrated in the textile industry. The period of entry into business for both companies is the 1950s, yet the owner/managers of these companies refer to several generations of merchant manufacturers through whose activities their families have established strong traditional links with the industry.[39] These, however, largely remain isolated cases in a business environment in which the trade tradition does not appear to be an important factor affecting business success. It is even doubtful that businessmen who have traditional, family links with a given industrial branch would necessarily have a different outlook than, say, former civil servants whose business careers are largely based on their connections and internal knowledge of the policy process. As will be discussed in more detail in chapter 4, in an environment where business success mostly depends on the ability to take advantage of the changes in government policy orientation, activity diversification appears as an unavoidable component of business strategy. Under these circumstances, the existence of a family tradition in a particular line of production might not prove sufficient to maintain the committment to that line of production.

As was mentioned in the previous chapter, the lack of committment to a particular branch of industry appears, in fact, to be one of the characteristics of business behavior in Turkey. A related feature of the business mentality in the country is that it is dominated by a commercial rather than an industrial outlook. Several studies conducted at different periods of Republican history have highlighted this particular aspect of the Turkish business mentality which can be explained, at least partially, with reference to the origins of the business class. R. W. Kerwin argues, for example, that the trading nature of Turkish industry inhibits effective industrialization. According to him, Turkish businessmen lack a long-term committment to industrial activity. They demand abnormal returns and rapid amortization, and the tendency to sink a large portion of funds in inventory seems to indicate that objectives of a speculative nature often dominate the goal of enhanced efficiency and profitability of industrial production.[40] Another study documents that an overwhelming majority of industrial enterprises in Turkey are also involved in commercial operations and real estate speculation. As the author comments, "In Turkey, industry, by virtue of its origins, its character, and the manner in which it is operated, manifests close ties with commerce and does not appear as an independent field of activity."[41] Moreover, he writes that a large number of the industrialists interviewed by his research team indicated that they felt more comfortable in commerce than in industry, and they expressed a desire to return to their original trading activities.[42] A similar account of the industrialists' desire to shift back to original commercial undertakings, expressed with obvious signs of regret for having ventured into industry, is found in a later study on Turkish big business.[43] This last study also draws attention to the lack of committment of Turkish industrialists to the sectors in which they operate.

In fact, given the social backgrounds of Turkish businessmen, commercial skills appear to be their major asset, apart from two other important factors affecting business success. One of these factors appear as initial support from the family. While the wealth of the family does not seem to be an important source of capital accumulation as suggested by the preceeding discussion, a relatively small amount of funds raised by the family often constitutes some part of the initial capital outlay, which is rather limited especially in the case of business careers beginning in the early years of the Republic. The importance of this initial family funding—as well as the significance of partnerships between family members who raise, among themselves, the initial investment funds—is highlighted by several writers.[44] These writers discuss this phenomenon in relation to the importance which Turkish businessmen attach to the solidarity of family members and their desire to maintain the family's control over the activities of the enterprise. Also highlighted in this context is the close link between the position held in the enterprise and family ties with the founder. As will be discussed in chapter 4, Turkish business enterprises, no matter how big and diversified they are, largely remain as family firms.

I have been repeating that another major asset of crucial significance in business life is the connections with policymakers. Family background would naturally play some role here, but these connections are also established through other channels, such as formal education which contributes to the ease with which a businessman would move in government circles. Hence—and probably related to the importance of the connections with government authorities— Turkish businessmen appear as a very well-educated group that highly appreciates the value of formal education. As one student of Turkish business history writes, "The illiterate business leader who can hardly sign his name, but deals in millions of dollars, generally makes sensational news, but such a person is not the prototype of the business leader in Turkey."[45] This writer found, among the businessmen that he interviewed in the 1960s, not one individual who was without some kind of formal education. In his sample of 103 businessmen, there were 90 who had completed high school and 56 of those had gone through college. 17 of them had masters' degrees and 1 held a doctorate degree. In a similar vein, in another study conducted in the 1970s, it is noted that "If it is recalled that Turkey is considered an "emerging" nation, its business elite appears very highly educated, with 79 percent having obtained college degrees. A closer examination is more revealing: 60 percent of the business elite have completed an undergraduate degree, 14 percent hold master's degrees, and 5 percent possessed Doctorate degrees. To state it in another way, fewer than 25 percent of the business elite have not graduated from college."[46]

Leading businessmen in the country—at least those who have a significant public presence through their activities in business associations—indeed appear to have an educational background which is far superior not only to that of the average population, but also to that of most politicians and bureaucrats, especially when the knowledge of foreign languages and degrees obtained in prestigious foreign universities are taken into account. As is shown in table 2.8., among 217 members of TÜSIAD for whom we have education-related information, 194 have a graduate or post-graduate degree. 21 have a high school education with only two in three generations of businessmen having less than high school education. One hundred twenty-seven of them have perfect knowledge of at least one foreign language, having either attended a high school or university in which the language of instruction is different from Turkish or held a position abroad for a certain period of time.

The table indicates that it is not only the younger members of the big business community that are so well-educated. The percentage of university graduates among older businessmen born between 1900 and 1940 appears to be even slightly higher than the average. Knowledge of foreign languages also appears to be common among these older entrepreneurs. In fact, one would probably find that the businessmen active before the Republican period had similar educational backgrounds. A study on the history of the Istanbul Chamber of Commerce, for example, includes short biographies of about twenty businessmen who were active in the Chamber in the first quarter of the century and in the early Republican period. We see that most of these individuals had a degree from a higher education institution and had a good knowledge of either French or German.[47]

Another interesting point that table 2.8. highlights is the significance of the number of engineers in the Turkish business community. More than one-half of the businessmen born between 1910 and 1950 hold an engineering diploma. Among the younger businessmen, the position of engineers is less prominent, largely indicating a shift toward economics and business administration as fields of education now considered to be more relevant for a business career. In fact, this trend was already noted in a study of Turkish business community in the early 1970s.[48]

Formal education becomes an important asset in an environment where good connections with government authorities is crucial to business success. In fact, the level of education of big businessmen appears to be quite high in most late-industrializing countries where the state is an important actor in business life.[49] The significance of knowledge of a foreign language, on the other hand, points to the presence of another factor influencing the course of a business career, namely that of a foreign enterprise which might appear either as an investor or an exporter to the local market.

## TABLE 2.8
### Educational Background of TÜSİAD Members According to Their Age Groups

| Date of Birth | University Graduated | High School/ Technical College | No High School Diploma | Knowledge of At Least One Foreign Language | Engineering Diploma |
|---|---|---|---|---|---|
| 1900–1909 | 3 | 2 | 1 | 3 | — |
| 1910–1919 | 16 | 3 | 16 | 2 | — |
| 1920–1929 | 49 | 8 | — | 24 | 29 |
| 1930–1939 | 49 | 2 | 49 | 24 | 1 |
| 1940–1949 | 56 | 1 | — | 46 | 21 |
| 1950–1959 | 18 | 1 | — | 16 | 4 |
| 1960–1969 | 3 | — | — | 3 | — |

Source: *Kim Kimdir? (Who Is Who?)* 1988–1989, Istanbul: TÜSİAD, 1989

TABLE 2.9
Comparative Figures of Average Annual Foreign Direct Investment*

|         | Brazil  | Korea | Mexico  | Turkey |
|---------|---------|-------|---------|--------|
| 1983–87 | 974.25  | 191.8 | 1,015.2 | 88.4   |
| 1978–82 | 1,735.6 | 6.4   | 1,403.4 | 76     |
| 1973–77 | 1,027.4 | 72    | 493.8   | 89     |
| 1968–72 | 215     | 39.8  | 286     | 40.2   |
| 1963–67 | 122     | 5.74  | 162     | 22.2   |

*1967–1988: in SDRs
 1967–1983: in US Dollars
 (millions of Dollars)
Source: IMF Balance of Payments Yearbooks, 1967, 1974, 1983, 1988

Although, as indicated by table 2.9, foreign direct investment has not traditionally played an important role in Turkish economy and, consequently, has not appeared as a factor which could significantly alter the nature of state-business relations as it has, for example, in the Latin American setting where foreign connections have played a non-negligible role in many business careers. Working as the representative agency of a foreign exporter to Turkey is—as it will be seen in the following section—an important step in the business careers of some prominent Turkish businessmen. Joint ventures with foreign firms also appear to be important for some Turkish businessmen in their entry into the industrial sector. At a more general level, one could suggest that, in a late-industralizing country which professes a committment to the objective of Westernization, in a country where technology is imported and, along with it, new needs are created, some knowledge of foreign production processes and markets naturally appears as a business asset of significance. Hence, in Turkey, entrepreneurs who possessed such a knowledge have entered the business scene with an initial advantage. Those who did not have it often attempted to introduce this type of know-how in their operations through partnerships with non-Muslim minorities better acquinted with the West.

In the tripartite relationship among Turkish businessmen, foreign interests, and the Turkish state, the state, once again, appears to be the key actor setting the dynamics of the relationship. The protectionist attitude toward foreign trade and investment, and the terribly intricate rules and regulations governing these activities have traditionally put Turkish businessmen in a position of power vis-à-vis their foreign associates who could, in no way, function alone in this complicated policy environment.[50] In other words, foreign trade and investment policy has created, by its nature, a lucrative business area in which entrepreneurial success largely depends on good connections in governmental circles. On the other hand, in this particular relationship Turkish businessmen have been especially vulnerable to the decisions of state authorities and their weaknesses vis-à-vis the latter has probably been clearer than in any other area. One could thus suggest that the particular role played by foreign interests in the Turkish economy, rather than contributing to an increased autonomy of the business community from the state, has tended to enhance the state-dependent character of the former. This particular characteristic of the business community is highlighted by the following discussion of some case histories.

## MAKING OF A BUSINESS TYCOON IN TURKEY

The eight autobiographies that will be surveyed in this section were written by individuals who started their business careers with different assets and motivations. Moreover, the personality traits, as well as the social backgrounds, of these individuals appear to be quite different. Nevertheless, there are certain crucially important common points which characterize thir career orientations and, consequently, shed light on the nature of the business environment in Turkey.

One of these common points has to do with the insignificance of the initial capital resources possessed in beginning the business career. The source of initial capital funds, also does not manifest a diversity of any significance. Family support or/and commercial activity largely exhaust the possible sources of investment funds, unless the business career begins with virtually no capital but on the basis of a certain knowledge of the field. In conformity with the points made in the previous discussion, the source of this knowledge is not, in any of the eight cases presented, an occupational background in artisanal production.

Excluding two autobiographies—written by A.Bilen and F.Akkaya—they also point at the fairly arbitrary choice of the field or fields of specialization as a characteristic of the career-path orientation of Turkish businessmen. In all of the six cases of business career to be discussed, entry into a particular line of business is determined by opportunities that arise at a particular moment in time. These opportunities also appear to be instrumental in the emergence of a common pattern of extensive activity diversification in many unrelated fields. On the contrary, in Bilen's and Akkaya's cases, not only are the fields of specialization chosen on the basis of these entrepreneurs' academic formations, but the extensive diversification observed in other cases is also absent. Bilen himself mentions this as an exceptional characteristic of his business life and explains it with reference to his affiliation with an important, highly specialized foreign enterprise. As for Akkaya, in this—and in many other respects—he appears as an accomplished engineer more than a successful businessman. Although Akkaya is not a typical specimen of the Turkish business community, his career path also manifests some characteristics of the business environment in the country. For example, along with the seven other autobiographies, Akkaya's book also highlights the importance of the state as a crucial element of business life. In all these cases, even if the state does not appear as a source of credit at the initial stage, the turning point in business life can often be traced to a project in which the state plays the key role as the contractor, principal buyer, or the provider of the capital necessary to take the step that would change the course of the businessman's career orientation.

In the relationship between the state and businessmen, foreign connections of the latter also appear to be an important factor. When the Turkish entrepreneur does not appear as the representative of a foreign company exporting to the Turkish market or the local partner of a foreign investor, foreign connections still remain important in the area of technology transfer and the importation of capital equipment. As previously suggested, in a closed economy in which foreign economic relations are subject to extensive state control, each connection with foreigners also involves an encounter with the state authority.

It seems surprising that these recurrent encounters with government authorities do not, in themselves, form a subject matter of complaint in the autobiographies. The state is, for these businessmen, undoubtedly the major source of their difficulties, and it is their central concern. Yet, the autobiograhies—as well as my personal interviews with other businessmen—indicate that they accept the overwhelming presence of the state in the economy as a normal phenomenon. Frequently, they even refer, with envy, to the case of some economically successful countries where the state takes a more active role than it does in Turkey in business activity. In most cases, it is not the bureaucracy that is the focus of their complaints, as will be discussed in more detail in the following chapter. The problem is depicted quite clearly in many cases, as the uncertainty inducing character of state intervention in Turkey. Hence, frequent changes in economic policy, constant reshuffling in bureaucratic positions, and even the absence of planning appear as the issues underlined in Turkish businessmen's criticisms of the state's role in the economy.

Two of the eight autobiographies that will be discussed here are by rather important Ottoman pashas. One of them—Süreyya İlmen, whose father was also one of the prominent pashas of Sultan Abdülhamid—entered the field of business in the CUP era right before World War I. He also combined his business life with a political career in the early Republican period. He was involved in the foundation of the very short-lived Free Party experiment in 1930 when he was a deputy from Istanbul. This was the end of his political life as a member of the parliament, but he continued to be involved in many social activities, especially relating to the improvement of municipal services. His business life, too, continued with some new ventures closely related to his interest in urban development.

In his autobiography, Süreyya İlmen appears as an individual who would not do anything except to please himself and to serve his country in ways which seem to be appropriate to him.[51] He has many interests, among which military and civil aviation has an important place.[52] In many ways, he is a typical *paşazade* (son of pasha) who would not dream of living below the standards appropriate to his social status. At the same time, however, he could hardly associate the satisfaction of his needs with the private pursuit of pecuniary interest. He is an individual who defines his responsibilities in terms of living according to the requirements of his social position, much as a servant of the state is expected to live. In this particular way of defining personal responsibility, the activities in the realm of business can not be easily dissociated from the rest of the social life. A pasha is a servant of the state, expected to work for the public good. As a product of a social environment in which the creation of an indigenous business community was emphasized as a national goal, it was natural for Süreyya Pasha to approach business

activity as an appropriate occupation that he could chose in conformity with his public responsibilities.

The first enterprise of Süreyya İlmen was the purchase of a
farm in the outskirts of Istanbul in 1902. He tells us that, after
buying the farm, both his father and mother, separately presented
him with a small capital for the construction of a farm house and
the purchase of some farm animals.[53] İlmen ventured into vegetable
and vine growing and dairy production, and imported some machinery and equipment to modernize production in these areas. However, he does not appear to have been very succesful in any of these
ventures. It is possible that it was partly this lack of success which
led him to develop an interest in industrial production. It should not
be forgotten, however, that those were times when the importance
of industrialization was a major political theme pursued by the CUP
in power. His interest in industry, therefore, closely reflects the
atmosphere of his times.

The choice of the sector in which he decided to invest—textile
industry—seems to be rather random. In his autobiography, he refers to a family friend, another pasha, who had done quite well by
establishing a factory producing woolen yarn near Istanbul. This
was instrumental in İlmen's decision to venture into the same field.
In the realization of the project, a foreign acquaintance through
İlmen's previous activities in the field of aviation played an important role. This was a German engineer who was, at the time, planning to establish a woolen yarn production plant in partnership with
a Turkish citizen of Armenian origin. İlmen was invited to join the
partnership at the stage in which all the industrial designs had
already been completed. Having resigned from the Army by then,
İlmen accepted the offer, and the factory was established in 1915. In
the autobiography, we read that the German engineer left the partnership before the factory began to operate and, after a while, the
Armenian partner also sold his share to İlmen and left the venture.
These decisions to leave the partnership do not appear to be totally
voluntary, but from the Pasha's account of the situation—which is
the only one available—it is impossible to arrive at a clear judgement of the matter.

His story of this industrial venture does, however, give us an
idea about why it would have been extremely difficult for a German
and an Armenian to be successful without the connections of the
Pasha. There are certain incidents in the autobiography which

clearly show how significant these connections were under the particular conditions in which business had to be conducted. İlmen's friends and acquaintances accumulated throughout his and his father's military careers have proven to be useful, for example, right at the beginning of the venture when the necessary machinery was being imported from Germany. Given the upheaval in transports created by the war, it was decided to bring the machines via Rumania. In this process, the parcels were kept somewhere in Bulgaria and could be salvaged only by the intervention of several diplomates posted in Rumania and Bulgaria. As the shipment passed through the Turkish frontier, it became necessary to dissuade some military officials from confiscating the machines, a task which probably was easier for the Pasha than it would have been for his partners.

İlmen told the officers who wanted to confiscate the machines that they were for a factory which could cater to the needs of the military. In fact, as soon as it was established, the factory got an army contract to produce necessary materials for the national textile factory founded by the initiative of a prominent CUP member. İlmen insists that this particular deal was not really profitable but, as his Armenian partner thought wrongly, according to the Pasha, it was a guaranteed outlet for their products, eliminating the risk of insufficient demand from the outset.

İlmen's connections again became useful at a later stage in the war period when the Army decided to take over the factory buildings to use as stables. This incident—interesting in itself as showing the lack of sensitivity of the Turkish military about the continuity of industrial production—ended happily when İlmen found out that the officer responsible for the operation was one of his father's former aides-de-camp.

İlmen continuously complains about the difficulties of industrial enterprise throughout the book. He refers, in fact, to a small research project that he carried out in the early 1940s to find out the number of industrial establishments belonging to Muslims, and to document the cases of bankruptcy in the industrial sector. He writes that he was distressed both by the insignificance of the former in the industrial sector, and by the frequency of industrial bankrupcy cases.[54] Among his complaints, the instability of the economic environment has a central place. In this regard, he quotes, for example, a prominent member of the government who once told İlmen that he was crazy to waste his money in industrial activity in a country where there was no stability.[55] Discretionary intervention by the government and, in particular, arbitrary taxation are also mentioned as sources of business difficulty. In relation to this last problem, we see that a good dose of bargaining could sometimes be necessary for the reassessment of the tax burden.

Nevertheless, İlmen's factory became well-established, and his sons also assumed management functions in the enterprise after completing their higher education in Europe. By then, the Republic had been declared, and İlmen had become a member of the parliament. With his endless energy, he became involved in many social projects—troubling, in the meantime, some bureaucrats and politicians. These incidents are interesting in showing that political involvement of a businessman can be a source of difficulty as well as an asset in an environment in which the state is a crucial factor in business life. In fact, at some stage during İlmen's membership of the parliament, his sons had to tell him to stop making trouble if he wanted his enterprise to remain in business.[56]

In the early years of the Republic, İlmen undertook two other ventures as part of his activities for the improvement of municipal life. One of them was a movie theater which was opened in 1927. In the autobiography, this decision is explained with reference to the difficulties created by exclusively non-Muslim theater owners in renting space for public events organized by the Muslim-Turkish community.[57] Because İlmen often assumed the leadership role in such events, the establishment of the theater seems, in fact, to have been an appendage to his social activities—although it was, at the same time, a lucrative enterprise.

The same was true for the private beach and leisure center he established in the 1940s. This venture also seemed to be a quite profitable one, which benefitted considerably from the active encouragement of municipal authorities. The support of the mayor of Istanbul, who decided to construct a road to link the beach to a major municipal transportation network, was especially important.[58]

Among the ventures of İlmen there were also several mining concessions obtained before the foundation of the Republic. His firm belief in the importance of mining for the national development appears to have been more important than a strictly economic interest in İlmen's acquisition of these concessions. In fact, none of the mines were exploited. He writes that, in the 1930s, when there were wide-spread rumors concerning an eventual nationalization of mining activities, he sent to the government all the relevant technical reports "expecting nothing but the honor of serving the country in return."[59] He might, of course, have regarded the concessions as a good speculation, but the passages on the subject do not reflect any strong sentiment of disappointment. In general, İlmen writes more passionately and seems to be more involved in social and political projects than he does in matters pertaining to business. In fact, in the book entitled *My Enterprises and Presidencies*, business ventures take much less space than do social and political activities. Although in this regard İlmen is different from the other businessmen whose careers will be discussed here, the nature of his business ventures is interesting in anticipating an important characteristic of entrepreneurship in the Republican period. For example, in this particular case, one clearly observes the already mentioned trend toward a wide diversification of activity which does not follow a particular logic, but rather reflects the opportunities or interests that emerge at a given moment of time.

In the business career of the second entrepreneur-pasha— Selahaddin Adil Pasha—whose autobiography will also be discussed here, the concern for economic interest does not appear to be as insignificant as in the case of İlmen. Nevertheless, most of Adil Pasha's autobiography is also devoted to his political and military experiences as an active member of the CUP, his rather brief business career taking up only a small part of the book. After the war and the formation of the Republic, Selahaddin Adil resigned from the Army. Although it is not mentioned in the autobiography, he might have been forced to resign because of his deep involvement in Unionist politics. In fact, he refers to several actions taken against the former Unionists, and he even mentions some cases of business enterprises dismantled because of the Unionist background of their owners.[60] He reports that he had virtually no money and no business experience of any sort at the time of his decision to start a new life in the field of business. He had, however, certain connections formed in the CUP period which could still be valuable.

The first acquaintance of value that he remembered was the former representing agent of Krupp that he had met when he was in charge of the artillery department of the Turkish Army. Since the German defense industry was dismantled after the war, defense-related production units of Krupp were transferred to a Swiss enterprise. Relying both on his knowledge of the needs of the Turkish army, and on his friends and relatives in the army and in the Ministry of Defense, Adil Pasha attempted to enter into a partnership with these former acquaintances to work as the representative agency of the Swiss firm in question. Because he could realize this objective only after a certain period of time, he became involved in the meanwhile in several projects, mainly acting as an intermediary between the Army and the government on the one hand, and foreign exporters and investors on the other. He continued, nevertheless, to pursue his main objective of acquiring the representing agency of the Swiss firm. While he could not become the independent agency of the firm until 1929, he could establish a formal relationship with the latter after his successful intermediation in an important deal involving the importation of explosives. During the period between 1929 and 1939, we see him as the owner-manager of a firm offering services of intermediation between the Turkish government and foreign businessmen.

In 1929, Selahaddin Adil also ventured into the field of industrial production, especially considering the opportunities provided by the Law for the Encouragement of Industry. Having met two Armenians who ran a small industrial operation assembling imported material inputs for the production of electric cables, he decided to build a factory that would locally produce such cables. After forming a partnership with the Armenians in question who were familiar with technical aspects of the business—he built the factory and started production. We find, in the pages of the autobiography concerning this particular venture, several passages which are very similar to those in which Süreyya İlmen presents his views on the importance of industrialization for national progress. The Unionist emphasis of the need to establish a national industrial base forms a common ideological position shared by these otherwise quite disssimilar characters. Selahaddin Adil's cable factory became a successful operation. An important Army contract—which the enterprise managed to share with a foreign company offering a much lower price—significantly contributed to this success. The fact that Selahaddin Adil's factory managed to get part of the contract, in spite of the existence of foreign enterprises offering more favorable terms, shows that the political support given to indigenous entrepreneurs far exceeded the legal provisions of the Law for the Encouragement of Industry. We are not given more information about the role of the Armenian partners in the enterprise, but we are told about two Muslim partners who joined the enterprise at an early stage.

In the 1930s, Selahaddin Adil also became involved in the exploitation of a chrome mine operated by a Swedish firm. The Swiss firm, of which he was the representing agency, was among the shareholders of this mining operation, and it was through this connection that Selahaddin Adil assumed, first, a managerial position, and then became a shareholder of the enterprise. Although he complains that his involvement in the mining sector proved to be a financial burden, we are also told that, with the dividends he received in the 1940s, he could cover his losses.

Selahaddin Adil's business life was a rather brief one which ended in 1939 upon a parliamentary decision to eliminate intermediaries from the negotiations between state agencies and foreign businesses. Immediately after this decision, Selahaddin Adil was asked to return to the government his commission from a foreign firm that had recently concluded a deal with the Air Force. The intermediation was the major source of his income and, feeling that his relations with the government would no longer enable him to continue to be active in business, Selahaddin Adil decided to leave business life completely. He discontinued the agency and sold his shares in the cable factory, retiring, as he writes in the autobiography, with a very modest income. The role of the state was, therefore, the determining factor both in the development and the destruction of his business life. In the 1950s we see him in the parliament as a member of the Democratic Party, but we have no sign of his involvement in business after 1939.

These two entrepreneur-pashas—Süreyya İlmen and Selahaddin Adil—were among the best-educated individuals of their times. The military academy then offered an academic formation which far exceeded the requirements of a narrowly defined military life. This was a formation given to those individuals who were going to form the highest ranking elite of the society, representing the country not only in war but also in foreign diplomacy. When we compare the educational background of these two pashas with those of the founders of the two most important enterprises of the Republican era, the contrast appears to be surprisingly great. The latter, Vehbi Koç and Hacı Ömer Sabancı, are self-made men with no formal education, no knowledge of a foreign language, and no *savoire-vivre* of any sort. Although the contrast is interesting, it would be misleading to draw general conclusions from it. As the discussion presented in the previous section suggests, Koç and Sabancı appear to be exceptions among the modern Turkish businessmen who, in general, form a well educated group. One could perhaps venture into psychological speculations about why these most successful members of the Turkish business comunity are also the least educated ones, but this is not the line of discussion that I will follow. Rather, I will concentrate on those features of their career paths which highlight the areas in which the specificity of the Turkish business environment is to be sought. Relations with the state, with foreign capital, and with the minorities as well as the activity diversification patterns will thus form the points to be emphasized.

The story of Vehbi Koç provides an excellent illustration of the conditions under which a new group of businessmen was created after the foundation of the Republic. Son of a small grocery store owner and with a natural bent for commerce, he grew up in Ankara which had recently become the capital of the country. In his autobiography, he writes that, at the age of fifteen, he persuaded his family to let him leave high school and work with his father.[61] He was able to expand the family business in retailing, basically catering to the needs of bureaucrats as individuals and then by getting involved as a contractor in government projects. In the 1920s, he got involved in importing and distributing oil and gas and, later, of motor vehicles. The success of these ventures were closely related to the growth of Ankara as the capital of modern Turkey. Koç was, in other words, at the right place at the right time, and was able to form the right connections from the outset.

It is also important that he could become the representing agency of Ford motor vehicles. In this area, he benefitted from the cooperation of several Jewish businessmen of rather small rank but who were, nevertheless, better placed than he was to carry out relations with the foreign company and to handle technicalities of enterprise management. In the course of my interviews, I was even told by one elder businessman that "it is his Jewish associates that have made Koç what he is." What this businessman was referring to were the employees at the lower ranks of management, such as the accountants. There is, however, one Jewish businessman who joined the automotive branch of the firm as a partner in 1944 and has remained there since. This businessman, Bernar Nahum, is also a self-made man who has told the story of his business life in one of the autobiographies that will be discussed in this section.

The business of Koç grew on the basis of government contracts and, by its nature, it was quite similar to what Selahaddin Adil Pasha was doing. Commissions from import deals constituted a major source of capital accumulation and, in his case, there seems to have been no major impediments in this line of business. In his autobiography, Koç mentions, as one of the important points in his business life, the importation of trucks for the government during World War II with a commission of 90 percent on the retail value![62] He also relates similar projects undertaken for the government after the war and within the framework of the Marshall Plan.

In all these ventures, close contacts with government officials and the members of the Republican People's Party (RRP) were maintained. In fact, Koç remained a faithful member of the RRP until the late 1950s when he was forced to resign by the ruling Democratic Party (DP) government through continuous threats and bureaucratic obstacles. Some of the most interesting pages of the autobiography are the ones in which Koç relates this incident and the way he was affected by it. He was, by then, already the most important businessman of the country, and he shared with many other businessman of the era the concern for the highly uncertain business environment created by the discretionary economic decisions and highly erratic policy changes of the government in power. Although he probably appreciated the probusiness ideological stand of the DP, he had no desire to change his party to which he was attached by many ties of gratitude. Yet, he also knew—perhaps better than anyone else—the significance of the state support for business success and, consequently, could not resist in the face of open threats of the ruling party. In his autobiograhy, he acknowledges that his resignation was a cowardly act. He even writes that his wife and daughters refused to speak to him for some time after the event. He seems to have understood and even shared their sentiments.

We do not know what would have happened if Koç had refused to give up his RRP membership. We do know, however, that his business has continued to prosper during the DP government, after the military coup of 1960 that overthrew the latter, and in the subsequent reign of different civilian and military governments. His venture in assembly production in the automotive industry in the

1960s was a natural extension of his previous commercial activities in this sector. Yet, the overall activity diversification of his enterprise is difficult to explain with reference to particular relationships among different fields of activity. Rather, he seems to have responded to opportunities arising in different periods of time as many prominent Turkish entrepreneurs have done after him. The activity diversification patterns of big Turkish enterprises will be discussed in chapter 4. I would just like to mention here that, at present, the Koç group of companies has activities dispersed over many sectors with more than one hundred enterprises in automotive, household appliances, textiles, food processing, retailing, construction materials and mining, energy, and trade and tourism as well as in marketing, finance, and banking.[63]

In all these manifold activities, the final decision was always taken by Vehbi Koç himself, at least until the 1960s. The difficulties of this type of enterprise management, however, was becoming increasingly important with the expanding scope of activities and the advancing age of the founder. At the same time, by 1960, his children—a son and three daughters—had completed their educations and assumed managerial positions within the company. The daughters had married to close relatives of high-ranking employees of their father's. Their husbands, too, were now working for the company. The latter was thus expanding as a family venture, but it was clear that a serious organizational restructuring was needed. The recognition of this need has led Koç to seek an appropriate form of organization which would centralize decision making in a way to assure the continuity of the enterprise without compromising the family control over the business. The formation of a holding company was the solution found to achieve this objective. Consequently, Koç Holding company was formed in 1963 as the first company of this type in Turkey. After this date, a proliferation of such companies has been witnessed in the country, with most multiactivity firms adopting this form of managerial organization. The social context of the formation and the functioning of these holding companies modelled after the example of Koç forms the subject matter of chapter 4. That chapter will attempt to highlight the objective of reconciling the needs of professional management with the continuity of family control which dominated the formation of the Koç Holding as well as the adoption of this form by other big business firms in the country.

In his autobiography, Bernar Nahum, who has been a share-holding manager of Koç since 1944, gives a detailed account of the activity diversification pattern which has culminated in the foundation of the Koç Holding.[64] Independently of the information he gives on Koç, Nahum's book is interesting in presenting the career path of yet another successful entrepreneur who has entered the business scene with no capital, no formal education, nor even a background in craftsmanship. By the time he became a manager in Koç, he had acquired, however, a thorough knowledge of the automotive market accumulated in the course of his experience as a sales agent since 1928. In 1928, when he was 16 years old, Nahum's father made him leave the Jewish lycee in Istanbul, and placed him in a company specialized in the marketing of motor vehicles and car parts. He remained with this company until 1944 as a sales agent and participated in the successful completion of many deals including some important government contracts. Among the latter, he mentions the sale of several cars to the Ministry of Defense by successfully eliminating the Koç company that was competing for the same deal.[65]

Such successes of Nahum's as a member of a competing firm were probably instrumental in Koç's decision to hire him as a manager and small shareholder in the automotive branch of the company. Nahum writes that, just before his transfer to Koç, he managed to become, personally, the representative agency of the U.S. Rubber Co., and was, therefore, able to bring his new employer a small "dowry."[66] The two men—Vehbi Koç and Bernar Nahum—appear to be good merchants of very similar characters who have supported each other's decisions in a long lasting partnership. Consequently, the absence of certain important assets—such as the solid knowledge of a foreign language or good connections among government authorities—that Koç would probably have liked to see in a partner has not hampered the development of Nahum's career. In fact, in Nahum's autobiography, we see references to some Koç employees who had exactly these assets that he himself did not possess, but who nevertheless could not remain in the company because of their temperamental incompatibility with Vehbi Koç.[67]

The natural inclination of these self-made merchants was probably effective, to a large extent, in determining the development of the company mainly as a commercial enterprise in spite of its involvement in many industrial ventures. In Nahum's book, we have the full story of industrial ventures undertaken in the automotive industry. In the relevant passages, these ventures are mostly presented as the outcome of decisions reflecting the difficulties of limiting the operations merely to the realm of commerce. In the automotive sector, the first experiment with industrial production was undertaken in the 1950s when the company decided to build a factory, Otosan, for the assembly production of Ford vehicles. This experiment, for example, was clearly undertaken as a result of the acute foreign exchange shortages that characterized the period. As to the production of the first Turkish car—the Anadol, which would remain on the market only for short time—the decision was made in the 1960s, the early import substituting industrialization phase of Turkish economic development, as a response to the policy-induced difficulties of importers of final goods. Shortly afterward, Koç Company established a joint venture with the Army Mutual Aid Society (OYAK) for the local production of Fiat cars. After the commercial failure of Anadol cars because of their very low technical standards, Otosan mainly functioned as an importing agency until the 1980s when the company decided to put another car on the market produced under a Taunus license.

These decisions are explained by Nahum in the following words:

> The starting point of the Koç group was internal trade. This was shortly followed by import trade under the different forms of agencies, distributors, and general representing agencies . . . The long-lasting foreign exchange shortages which were felt in our country, and the import limitations, different trade regimes, and quotas implemented to deal with this problem have convinced the whole group, starting with Vehbi Koç, of the necessity of industrialization in Turkey . . . We have thus adopted the principle of national production for the saving of foreign exchange, starting with the assembly production of the goods that we were accustomed to import. It can be stated, therefore, that it was to guarantee the continuous and harmonious functioning of our commercial enterprises that our industrial enterprises were founded.[68]

This is clearly the approach to the industry of a born merchant, which says a lot about the mentality and motivations of the pioneers of industry in Turkey. In the case of Koç, this mentality does not only explain the origins of the industrial development, but it also sheds light on the actual enterprise management in which commercial concerns dominate the industrial ones. This particular characteristic of big business enterprises in Turkey will be further discussed in chapter 4. At this point, I wish only to refer to one manifestation of this general trend in Nahum's autobiography. Nahum mentions, with some emphasis, the acquisition of real estate as an important aspect of rational enterprise management in Turkey, and states that this is part of the managerial philosophy in the Koç group.[69] This approach suggests that enterpreneurship in Turkey involves a good deal of portfolio management along commercial lines. As the discussion in the following chapters will further clarify, this appears to be a highly rational strategy, given the uncertainties of the environment which call for a great deal of financial security and flexibility.

The concern for financial security and flexibility is also reflected, in a very clear fashion, in the diversification strategy of the Sabancı Group which, like the Koç, has a whole variety of activities dispersed over many different sectors as well as innumerable investments of a speculative nature in real estate. The founder of this group, Hacı Ömer Sabancı, was a half illiterate villager from the central Anatolian town of Kayseri.[70] In the early 1920s, Hacı Ömer went to Adana, a relatively rich town in the cotton-growing region of Southern Anatolia, to seek his fortune. At that period, there were many workers from Kayseri who, like Hacı Ömer, were attracted by the opportunities provided by cotton farming and industry. Among them there were also some rich merchants of Kayseri who had been led to Adana by the possibility of taking over the real estate as well as the commercial and industrial establishments left idle after the emigration of their Greek or Armenian owners. Such takeovers were encouraged by the government, and those who had connections with the government authorities could benefit greatly from these opportunities. Hacı Ömer was not an important man with such connections, but he benefitted from the same circumstances indirectly, through the ties of "fellow townsmenship" which can be very important in Turkey. Although he was too modest to be delegated a direct responsibility in the mission of indigenization of the economy, through acquaintanceship with families from Kayseri, he has taken some part in the takeover of old minority-run ventures in Adana.

Starting with small commercial dealings around the cotton industry and proving his aptitude and perseverance in this area, he could acquire some small artisanal production units. The first industrial enterprise of some significance that Hacı Ömer owned was a factory producing cotton-based vegetable oil. In this venture, we see him first attempting to purchase a factory owned by a Russian Jewish entrepreneur, and, failing to do so, building another plant right beside the first one. The factory started production just before the infamous Wealth Levy which was instrumental in ruining a large number of non-Muslim businessmen. In those difficult times, the Russian Jewish industrialist had to sell his factory to Hacı Ömer and his partners who could thus successfully eliminate their principal competitor. Eventually, Hacı Ömer also eliminated his partners and became the sole owner of this industrial enterprise.[71] Shortly afterward, he also became the founder and the major shareholder of a private bank.

In his autobiography, Hacı Ömer's son, Sakıp Sabancı, writes that, for those entrepreneurs from Kayseri who had started businesses in Adana, the typical career orientation was from commerce to land ownership, and finally to industry.[72] In conformity with this pattern, we see Hacı Ömer buying agricultural land around both Adana and Kayseri with the surplus accumulated in his commercial activities. In his case, this could easily be explained with reference to the aspirations of a landless peasant, who, while chosing to grow as an industrialist, could not, nevertheless, resist the attraction of large landownership. As Sakıp Sabancı writes, their group now appears as one of the largest landowners of the country.[73] While some of the land is used for agricultural production, it also represents a speculative investment of the type which most Turkish businesses undertake.

Hacı Ömer was already a landowner in the 1950s when the turning point in the industrial development of his enterprise was reached. The timing of the industrial development of the Sabancı group is closely related to the government's policy orientation in Turkey. The 1950s constitute a period when the entrepreneurs were actively encouraged by the probusiness DP government in power, and many enterprises were established on the basis of credits obtained from the Turkish Industrial Development Bank.[74] One of the largest industrial ventures of the Sabancı group, the BOSSA textile factory, originated in this period during a visit of Celal Bayar, then the president of the country, to Adana. The visit appeared to be partly planned to search for an entrepreneur to build a textile factory in this cotton-growing region. Identified as the right person for the project, Hacı Ömer founded this factory with a well-known family of Adana. The investment was financed by a very important credit from the Turkish Industrial Development Bank with the sponsorship of the World Bank. Eventually, as it appears to be the general trend in the evolution of Sabancı ventures, the partners were eliminated and the Sabancı family has acquired full ownership of Bossa.

The Sabancı Group has continued to develop by diversifying its activities over a wide variety of sectors from commerce, farming, banking, and insurance and, within the industrial sector, from textiles to tire production and finally to the automotive industry.[75] In this process of expansion, several joint ventures were formed with multinational enterprises and, starting with the late 1970s, the group itself has undertaken multinational activities abroad. In 1967, the company assumed the form of a holding, modelled after the example of Koç Holding, to centralize the management of its activities in these diverse fields.

Although the original capital came from commerce, the Sabancı group appears to be more firmly established in the industrial sector than, for example, the comparable group of Koç. After the foundation of Bossa, the family has founded many other enterprises in the textile industry and moved eventually to other sectors, sometimes with the direct suggestion and encouragement of the government. The production of industrial cord as an input used in tire manufacturing, for example, was undertaken in the 1960s with the initiative of Turgut Özal, then in charge of the State Planning Organization and, later, the prime minister and the president of the country.[76] In this venture, as in some others, the Sabancı group appeared as a threat to foreign multinational manufacturers of the final goods. For example, in this particular case, multinational firms producing tires for the local market had previously imported, from their home country branches, the materials that Sabancı began to produce. In such cases, the Sabancı group would also be confronting local partners of these foreign firms that included the Koç group with its many partnerships with foreign multinationals producing for the Turkish market.

In fact, there has been an undertoned animosity between the two groups which extended to areas ranging from competition in the industrial sector to the acquisition of shares in commercial banks, and even to the purchasing of art objects.[77] In most of these confrontations, we see the state as a principal actor assuming the role of the final arbitrator. We also see how official positions in the Chambers of Commerce and Industry are used to tilt the balance against the competitor. For example, as a member of the board of directors of the Union of Chambers, Sabancı could successfully prevent Koç from acquiring permission to establish a joint venture with a foreign company for the production of polyester fiber, when Sabancı already had a license to establish a similar enterprise.[78] In such stories of competition, told in the autobiographies of both Koç and Sakıp Sabancı, the action invariably takes place, not on the market, but in the relevant ministries and government offices in Ankara. It is, in other words, on the basis of the sovereignity of the state, and not that of the consumer, that such issues are settled.

Hacı Ömer and his five sons—there was another Sabancı brother who died at a relatively young age—seem to have understood this important characteristic of the business life in Turkey. Although they were not very well-placed to easily form the right connections with government authorities given the social background of the family, they could successfully compensate this disadvantage by the close relationships they formed with state employees of different positions. In his autobiography, Sakıp Sabancı tells about the importance that his father attached to the relations with two groups of individuals in particular—bankers and military officers. Hence, starting with the initial stages of development of their business in Adana, the family maintained a close relationship with the managers of state banks, and these relationships were used for different purposes such as the acquisition of financial advice or facilitating access to government credit. After the foundation of their bank—Akbank, which is currently one of the most important private banks in the country—and the launching of several enterprises in insurance and finance, these contacts were also used as a source of managerial personnel still in very short supply in the Turkish financial sector. As to the military officers, they were given prominent positions on the boards of directors of many Sabancı companies and have, undoubtedly, helped the smooth functioning of business operations in periods of military takeover, which are not infrequent in Turkey.

In general, the transfer of managerial personel from the public sector forms a very important aspect of the business development strategy in Turkey. In the case of the Sabancı Group, there have also been many prominent statesmen who became the company's employees at some points in their professional lives. Among these individuals, one finds, for example, Turgut Özal, who worked as a Sabancı executive after he had left the State Planning Organization and before he became the prime minister in 1983. The managerial personnel was also chosen, however, among the minorities who formed the most experienced businessmen of Turkey, at least in the early days of the Republic. In the autobiography of Sakıp Sabancı, we find passages about the significance of some Jewish and Armenian managers, mostly stolen from competitors, in determining the initial success in the textile sector.[79]

Social backgrounds of the three businessmen, whose autobiographies will also be discussed in this chapter, sharply contrast with that of the Sabancı family. In fact, these three businessmen conform more closely to the general pattern in Turkey where businessmen appear to be a very well-educated social group. Nejat Eczacıbaşı, the founder of the Eczacıbaşı Holding, comes from a well-established family in Izmir. His maternal grandfather was a fairly well-to-do merchant while his father, a chemist, owned a pharmacy and a laboratory. The family does not appear to be very wealthy, but they seem to have been quite close to some of the founders of the Republic—to Celal Bayar, in particular, who even paid a visit to their home in Izmir in 1950 when he became the president of the country.[80]

Nejat Eczacıbaşı received a very good education starting with his early childhood. He had a German governess at home, and was sent to American high schools, first in Izmir and then in Istanbul. After finishing high school, he studied chemistry in Germany where he completed his doctorate in this field. In his autobiography, Eczacıbaşı claims that his doctorate was of very little use to him in his business career and that it was mainly a waste of time.[81] Yet, this postgraduate diploma has probably played some role in the enormous respectability that he has always enjoyed in the social scene and in the company of politicians in particular.

When he returned from Germany in the 1940s, being the eldest son of the family, he was expected to run his father's business. However, thinking about similar small businesses that get divided among the heirs, he decided to start a new business in Istanbul. His first business ventures were the small-scale production of cod liver oil and baby food, both products whose importation was terminated with the start of the World War II. He also produced some drugs by using a very rudimentary technology, which was hardly anything more than mixing the ingredients in a kitchen. His third venture was undertaken upon the suggestion of a general when he was doing his military service. It involved the production of electrolytic copper for the needs of the Army. Eczacıbaşı's father provided the small capital needed for the venture, and the governor of Istanbul, a friend of the family, helped him to buy a piece of land in the outskirts of Istanbul for the establishment of the factory. Eczacıbaşı writes that neither he nor his father were very happy about this enterprise because they believed in acting with caution in business activities undertaken in close relationship with public authorities. This might well be an expost facto evaluation of the matter because the venture in question, in fact, failed when the general who was supporting the project had a confrontation with the Minister of Defense. The confrontation resulted in the minister's blocking the government credit promised for the establishment of the factory. This was Eczacıbaşı's first encounter with the state-related hazards of doing business in Turkey. The land purchased for the establishment of the electrolytic copper production unit was used to build a factory to produce porcelain cups, a venture that Nejat Eczacıbaşı started with a Greek shop owner selling such goods. The partnership ended in 1951 when the Greek associate decided to leave the country, in fear of the consequences of the tension between Turkey and Greece.

The turning point in Eczacıbaşı's business career took place in 1950, right after the establishment of the Turkish Bank for Industrial Development. Eczacıbaşı was among the first entrepreneurs who applied to the Bank for industrial credit. He wanted to build a factory producing drugs under foreign license. There were, however, two other applicants, both better established in the area than Eczacıbaşı. The latter could, nevertheless, get the credit partly as a result of a former high school teacher who happened to be among the board of administrators of the Bank. The factory started production in 1950 and has remained, since then, an important establishment in Turkish drug industry.

Eczacıbaşı's career path might, so far, seem to be conforming to the idea of "endogenesis" that Crouzet finds to be important in the British business history.[82] We see him, in other words, continuing a familiar line of business which is related to his father's field of activity. This particular trend in his early business life, however, soon began to evolve toward the typical pattern in Turkey where businessmen become involved in many unrelated fields of activity. Thus, he formed several enterprises producing ceramics, paper products, and bathroom and kitchen fixtures. Although these enterprises have little production or marketing related linkages with the original line of specialization, Eczacıbaşı justifies this pattern of diversification with reference to their hygiene-related character and offers an explanation which has to do with the public image of the company. The company also has, however, ventures in totally unrelated fields such as residential housing. In the 1980s, the group formed a foreign trade company like many other big holding companies that tried to benefit from incentives given to exporters in that period. These incentives were given not to producers, but to exporters—and only when the value of foreign sales exceeded a certain minimum. Hence, big holdings formed foreign trade companies and allowed smaller producers to market their export goods over these companies. This was, therefore, a strictly commercial operation undertaken also by Koç and Sabancı.

Different ventures of the Eczacıbaşı group were also centralized under the umbrella of a holding company in the 1970s. The company now appears among the most successful businesses in Turkey. Yet Eczacıbaşı's fame far exceeds his fortune. He is a well-known public figure involved in social projects. In this regard, he is quite similar to Süreyya İlmen, and, like the latter, appears to enjoy his social activities more than his strictly economic ones. He is, for example, the founder of the Conference Board on Economic and Social Issues which was quite influential in the 1960s and 1970s. The foundation of the Conference Board was a direct response to the increasing popularity of socialist ideas in Turkey. It was designed as a forum that would bring together academics, government authorities, and businessmen with a view to contribute to the development of an intellectual environment favorable to private enterprise without, nevertheless, adopting an attitude of crass anticommunism. As will be discussed in chapter 5, the foundation of the Conference Board anticipated, in fact, the social project later undertaken by a small group of entrepreneurs attempting to consolidate the social position of the business community as a class.

In the 1970s, we see Eczacıbaşı as the founder of a cultural foundation active in the organization of the annual Istanbul Festival. The latter is, at present, a well-established one attended by many musicians and performing artists of international reputation. These were genuinely exceptional enterprises in Turkey in the 1960s and 1970s, when businessmen ardently avoided the public scene and tried to make themselves as unconspicious as possible. In contrast to this general attitude, Eczacıbaşı has never sought invisibility. Much before the 1980s, when businessmen became very visible as public figures both in Turkey and elsewhere, he emphasized the importance of public activities that businessmen had to undertake both to promote the respectability of business activity and to consolidate a certain business ethic among the entrepreneurs. Not only as the founder of the Conference Board but also with his other social activities, Eczacıbaşı appears as a forerunner of those business leaders who, at present, try to get the business community actively involved in social and economic development of the country via a rigorous redefinition of the rights and responsibilities of businessmen. The nature of this project—as well as the difficulties it faces within the Turkish context—will be discussed in detail in chapter 5.

Another entrepreneur who is concerned with social and ethical questions pertaining to the rights and responsibilities of businessmen is Alber Bilen, who also published his memoirs in the 1980s.[83] Bilen has been active in the chemical industry for more than forty years. He comes from a middle-class Jewish family that had gone through some financially difficult times, first because of an unsuccessful industrial venture of Bilen's father, and then at the time of the Wealth Levy because of the arbitrary taxes imposed on them, as on many other Jewish and Christian taxpayers. Yet, the family managed to send their son to a French Lycee in Istanbul and put him through the university where he was trained as a chemical engineer.

In his autobiography, Bilen describes himself as someone more inclined toward academic research than toward a business life. Nevertheless, he entered the business field in the 1940s, after graduating from the university. His first businesses were partnerships with people who provided a small capital that they wished to combine with Bilen's technical knowledge in small-scale industrial ventures. These partners were either merchants or people with a stricly commercial outlook, and Bilen seems to have found it rather difficult to get used to their attitude toward business. His partners' lack of concern for matters pertaining to the quality of production, and their emphasis on quick and easy profit making as the sole end of business activity appear, in the autobiography, as a source of increasing uneasiness that he felt in these early partnerships.

He writes that he felt the same uneasiness when he began, in 1950, to work for a larger representing agency firm. The latter combined many unrelated lines of business in the marketing of different German products. "I was always against doing different types of business," writes Bilen. "I had had a specialized academic formation. My outlook was not a commercial one, and I also had an amateurish side, which largely explained my approach. I believe that it was the frequent changes in the economic conjuncture, especially in those years, which had led our businessmen to undertake activities in many different fields."[84] The previous discussion of different career paths suggests that Bilen is, in fact, depicting here a very significant feature of business orientation in Turkey, and tracing it to the instability of the business environment in the country. He shares, in this regard, the views that many other businessmen have expressed in different context.

Among the German enterprises represented by Bilen's employer was the famous drugs producer Böhme Fettchemie, an affiliate of Henkel. Bilen was responsible for the relations with this company, and eventually became its independent representative for the Middle East region. Later, in the 1950s, when the initial conditions of easy access to foreign exchange changed and an acute scarcity of foreign exchange became a crucial feature of business life, Bilen, like many other businessmen, began to explore the possibilities of local import-substituting production under foreign license. Having met a Turkish importer of drugs willing to provide some funding for local production, Bilen could establish a small factory in the chemical industry. This enterprise eventually formed the basis of a joint venture with Henkel.

Bilen's account of the completion of this joint venture agreement is very interesting in clarifying the attitude of the Turkish government toward foreign investment. The joint venture was formed in a period when a very liberal foreign investment law was in application, and the attitude of the government in power was also very favorable toward joint ventures between Turkish and foreign firms. Yet, the implementation of the law was governed by a very pragmatic attitude which consisted in limiting the period of the agreement with the objective of eliminating the foreign partner as soon as the technological know-how was acquired and the firm was established on the market. This obvious tactic was, of course, well-noticed by foreign investors who were driven away from the agreement as a consequence. There was, in other words, a clear discrepancy between the law and its bureaucratic implementation which Bilen strongly resisted in order not to lose his foreign partner. His resistance was successful mainly because he was able to find a high school friend, who was then the secretary general of the ruling DP, to explain his case.

After the foundation of the Turkish Henkel Company until his retirement, Bilen was not involved in any other business activity. He writes that the other Turkish partners have eventually left the partnership because of the basic incompatibility between their commercial mentality and the reality of industrial production in a modern enterprise. The latter, which, according to Bilen, consists in long-term committment to a given line of production undertaken with strategic planning, was also quite incompatible with the nature of the business environment in Turkey. Hence, the rest of the autobiography almost constitutes a treatise on the difficulties of modern industrial production in an environment of high political instability and rapid policy change, in an environment in which the state is the dominant actor affecting the course of the business life. Having remained as a part of a foreign partnership all through his business career, Bilen could, unlike most other Turkish businessmen, avoid adapting to the circumstances and conforming to the general pattern of activity diversification and enterprise management. Partly because of this, his autobiography highlights, much more clearly than the others so far reviewed, the peculiarities of entrepreneurship in Turkey.

The last autobiography that I will discuss here is by a very lucky man who has spent all his life doing what he most likes to do—building bridges, dams, and tunnels all over the country and, later, in other Middle Eastern countries.[85] In addition, he has begun doing all these things with a best friend who appears to be the most important person in his life. Although he does not elaborate on the insignificance of pecuniary gain as much as the other businessmen whose autobiographies were discussed so far, his material fortune genuinely appears as a by-product of the activities undertaken for another type of gratification.

An accomplished engineer with several international patents

registered to his name, Fevzi Akkaya is one of the two partners of a well-established contracting firm, STFA, which has been in business since the 1940s, although it was formally established only in the 1970s.[86] The second partner, Sezai Türkeş, is also an engineer. The two partners graduated from the same technical university in Istanbul in 1932, and have never been separated from each other since then. They both came from modest middle-class families, and had no capital to start a business. Their business career was based strictly on their technical knowledge, which was not a negligible asset in those years when the number of Turkish engineers was extremely limited.[87] Akkaya writes that the shortage of technical skills extended much beyond the engineering ones, and that there were virtually no Muslim-Turkish construction workers with the basic skills. According to him, after the emigration of Greek and Armenian artisans of this field, the skilled workers of Bulgarian origin dominated the field for a considerable period of time.

While the supply of technical skills was limited, the demand was quite high because of the infrastructure projects undertaken by the state after the formation of the Republic. It was in this environment that the two friends began their private business career, after having spent a brief period of time in the public sector. Virtually all of their business was with the state, and their major competitors were foreign engineering firms that dominated the construction industry well into the 1950s. Akkaya and Türkeş have naturally benefitted from the nationalistic sentiments of government authorities who were always inclined to give a contract to a Turkish rather than a foreign company. Although Fevzi Akkaya has little interest in engaging in nationalistic rhetoric, his relations with the state, as they are told in the autobiography, are of a nature to suggest that the private character of the business was often overshadowed by its being a part of a nation-building project.

Nevertheless, we see that, in the 1950s, projects undertaken jointly with foreign firms also began to play an important role in the development of the enterprise. During this decade, close relations between Turkey and the United States created many opportunities for Turkish engineering firms. STFA also had several contracts relating to World Bank-financed projects or NATO installations. Although from a strictly economic perspective, those were brilliant years determining the future success of the enterprise, Akkaya writes about the 1940s more enthusiastically. As it will be mentioned again in the next chapter, he points at a mutual understanding and goodwill between the engineers and bureaucrats who, in those years, were both interested in getting things done as efficiently as possible. According to Akkaya, this harmonious relationship was eventually replaced by a rigid and hostile one starting with the 1950s. Hence, as also emphasized by other contractors that I interviewed, after the 1950s the contractor's job became an endless struggle with the state, mainly to get paid on time. Inability to extract payment from the state—which is, by far, their most important client—seems to constitute, in fact, the most important problem of all the major contractors in Turkey.

It is impossible to learn much about the intricacies of these relations with the state from Akkaya's autobiography. In the division of labor between the two friends, he seems to have assumed the responsibility for technical hazards, leaving the policy-induced ones to his partner. We nevertheless get a feeling of the atmosphere created by unilateral changes in the clauses of contracts, by delays in payment, and, of course, by constant devaluations and changes in the trade regime. While the state is clearly an important hazard factor in the life of a Turkish contractor, it is unimaginable, for the latter, to seek a solution in the smaller state intervention in the economy. On the contrary, on the basis of his experience in Libya, where his firm often competed with East Asian firms for Libyan government contracts, Akkaya makes a distinction between those governments that support their businessmen and those that do not.[88] According to him, the fact that the Turkish state is unambiguously in the second category makes life extremely difficult for Turkish businessmen operating in another country. Akkaya clearly thinks that, in this day and age, business activity requires state support, and what must be discussed is the form, and not the extent, of the state intervention in business life.

The preceeding discussion suggests that the uncertainty inducing nature of state intervention in Turkey is depicted as a major source of business difficulties. It also suggests, however, that Turkish businessmen became adapted to policy hazards quite naturally, in such a way that this adaptation process appears as the most important aspect of business strategy and managerial policy. A complete analysis of the latter calls for, therefore, a more detailed discussion of state-business relations with a view to highlight the form of state intervention in business activity.

# 3. Political Context of Business Activity

## Economic Policy Process in Turkey

Sabancı Holding, whose development was briefly surveyed in the previous chapter, is, at the present, one of the most successful business enterprises in Turkey. In his attempt to account for the successful development of the family business, Sakıp Sabancı emphasizes two factors which form the dominant themes of his autobiography. These two themes appear to be quite significant in highlighting the societal characteristics of Turkish business life. The first one has to do with the overwhelming impact of state-induced uncertainty in business life. After presenting several striking examples of instability stemming from the role that the state plays in the field of business, Sabancı suggests that the success of their business strategy largely lies in accepting this particular difficulty as a constant in the life of a Turkish businessman, and going ahead with viable projects taking, at the same time, the necessary precautions to prevent the ruining of the enterprise by an unexpected policy change. He suggests, in other words, that the Turkish entrepreneur is in a position to learn to live with the destabilizing impact of the policy process, and the failure to do so almost unavoidably leads to business failure.[1]

In this uncertain business environment, Sabancı suggests that the businessman must rely on the support of his family. Thus, the significance of family support constitutes the second theme that he pursues in the autobiography. According to him, harmony and cohesion among family members is the key to business success, and he presents the solidarity of his own family as the major factor in determining the brilliant course of their business life. Also, in relation to this factor, we find, in his autobiography, references to the case of major business families ruined either because of discord among family members or as a result of the irresponsible behavior of the heirs after the death of the founder.[2]

These two factors emphasized by Sabancı, in fact, form the central components of Turkish businessmen's evaluation of their professional environment as presented, for example, in the autobiographies discussed in the previous chapter. In my interviews with Turkish businessmen, these two themes also frequently came up as the main determinants of business success and failure. The first one of these themes—the political sources of instability in business life—constitutes the subject matter of this chapter. The next chapter will then take up the role of the family in the organizational structure of the big Turkish enterprise in an attempt to explore the links between the sociopolitical environment and the form of industrial organization in the country.

In Turkey, the economic policy process has played a crucial role in shaping the business outlook in the country. In this regard, it is possible to make three interrelated observations concerning the basic features of the policy network. The first observation has to do with the strikingly pragmatic approach to economic process adopted by Turkish governments. This approach excludes any committment to a particular economic philosophy, or even to policy coherence. This is manifested both in the lack of clear-cut differentiation among different governments' economic programs and in severe policy turns taken during the office of the same government.

Second, and partly reflecting this pragmatic approach to economic policy-making, one observes a certain ambiguity concerning the boundaries of state intervention. Because of this lack of clarity about the legitimate domain of intervention, the policy-formation process in Turkey has, as a rule, engendered deep-rooted ambiguities concerning the legitimacy of business activity. These ambiguities have been further accentuated by a policy discourse, undertaken by most governments at some point during their office, in which the acceptability of business activity was presented as contingent upon its positive contributions to national goals. As a result, almost every major change of government has brought with it the potential for at least a partial systemic change. Businessmen, therefore, were often faced with doubts concerning the exact coordinates of their positions in society. Whether well-founded or not, these doubts were genuine and quite effective in shaping the business outlook and behavior.

The nature of the mechanisms through which state-business relations are mediated in Turkey has also contributed to the unstable business environment in the country. Here, one observes a situation in which the legal mechanism and the bureaucracy often become subordinated to the requirements of social and economic policy objectives set by the government in power. Since these objectives rarely present a coherent perspective, haphazard policy changes often become reflected in legal modifications and changes in bureaucratic rules which, in turn, enhance the instability of the economic environment. This is a situation, in other words, in which a clearly defined legal system setting the rules of the game for both actors—the state and the business community—is largely absent and the bureaucracy can only play a limited role in maintaining a stable policy network.

There are two types of uncertainty which emerge in this context. The first type prevails as regards to the exact coordinates of the businessman's position in society. In an atmosphere of doubt concerning the social legitimacy of business activity, the future of the private enterprise system could, at times, seem uncertain, especially in periods of rising antibusiness ideology. Nevertheless, during the office of governments contributing to the establishment of a pro-business ideology, businessmen have also often had to operate in a highly uncertain environment, this time because of the arbitrary policy moves leading to unexpected changes in the values of major economic indicators. In fact, as it will be discussed in this chapter, under the DP governments in the 1950s and the Motherland Party (MP) in the 1980s, both allegedly committed to the establishment of a free market economy, the second type of uncertainty reached unprecedented dimensions due to the extent of discretionary policy changes with an enormous impact on business activity.

Although the objective of the present discussion is to highlight the continuities in the policy process in Republican Turkey, a certain periodization seems indispensible to trace the underlying trends throughout the changes in policy discourse and orientation.

At a very general level, it seems useful to divide the economic history of the period into five stages corresponding to the changes in international and domestic factors influencing the economic policy environment. The periodization suggested here refers to the dominant themes which characterize the economic policy discussion in different periods of Republican economic history. In this context, the period of 1923–1929 appears to be an era when there were attempts "to lay down the foundations of a private enterprise economy." The next two periods—1930–1946 and 1946–1960—are then defined, respectively, as periods of "defining etatism" and "defining liberalism." "Experimentation with a planned economy" characterizes the period between 1960 and 1980. Finally, the 1980s is presented as a period when "economic liberalism is revisited."

### Laying down the Foundations of a Private Enterprise Economy

As it was briefly discussed in the previous chapter, the founders of the Turkish Republic were not fundamentally different from their Unionist predecessors in their economic outlook. Their emphasis, too, was on the creation of a national bourgeoise which was to assume the leading role in economic development of the country. Their project was, in other words, a nationalist one involving a major indigenization effort. The termination of the concessions given to foreign interests and the nationalization of foreign enterprises formed a part of this project.

Economic development of the country was a much emphasized objective shaping the nation-building efforts at this early stage. The organization of a National Economic Congress bringing together the representatives of major social groups in 1923, in fact, preceeds the formation of the Republic in the same year. The principles adopted in this Congress by more than one thousand delegates of merchants, industrialists, farmers, and workers clearly indicate a committment to the establishment of a private enterprise economy. These principles pertain to the preparation of a property regime and an institutional structure required for the functioning of a modern market economy, as well as to the special incentives to be designed for the development of indigenous entrepreneurs.[3]

The latter involved the maintenance of the provisions of the 1913 Law for the Encouragement of Industry which was to remain in application for twenty-five years—that is, until 1928. It was also agreed that the Law would remain in application for another twenty-five years after its date of termination. To promote national economic development, the Congress adopted several principles involving tariff protection of domestic industry and tariff exemptions in the case of imported inputs. However, given the provisions of the Lausanne Treaty which was signed later in the same year, Ottoman international trade regime had to remain unchanged until the end of the decade. Customs protection could not, therefore, figure among the incentives given to domestic enterpreneurs. The application of the 1913 Law—as well as its new version adopted in 1927—involved, under these circumstances, several tax exemptions; free allocation of land and buildings for the establishment of industrial enterprises; credit facilities; and provisions for the purchase of domestically produced rather than imported goods for the needs of the state. Industrialists could also purchase subsidized inputs from state enterprises. After 1929, tariff protection was also added to those measures. After its termination in 1942, the Law for the Encouragement of Industry was not extended. Thus, until the implementation of the development plans of the 1960s, domestic industry was not supported in a systematic fashion. It was mainly the protectionist trade regime and, especially in the 1950s, ad hoc favoritism which have contributed to the development of the Turkish business community.

In the 1920s, the Lausanne provisions against tariff protection eliminated one important source of revenue for the new Turkish government. Besides, the traditional tithe on agricultural output was abolished in 1925, partly as a political gesture indicating the repudiation of the Ottoman past. The government was, therefore, in a position to find new sources of public revenue. While new types of indirect taxation were also used, state monopolies constituted the major source of public revenue in these years. The burden of foreign debt inherited from the Empire also exercised a significant pressure on the government budget. Under these circumstances, it was not at all easy to deal with inflationary pressures and to maintain the stability of national currency. Toward the end of the decade, the significance of a balanced budget policy and the need to maintain monetary stability appeared as the main themes of the public policy discourse.[4]

In this environment, government authorities were, quite naturally, looking forward to 1929 when the limiting clauses of the

Lausanne Treaty would expire and the foreign trade regime could be organized in such a way so as to alleviate the pressures on the public budget and balance of payments. A certain change in policy orientation was therefore expected. However, the end of the decade was marked by two developments which were probably instrumental in an unexpectedly radical modification of the policy environment and state-business relations. One of these developments was, of course, the world economic crisis. Perhaps more important than the direct impact of the Great Depression on Turkish economy was the intense questioning of the viability of the market system brought along by the crisis. Early attempts at the formation of a modern economy and the accompanying institution building efforts were therefore marked from the outset by significant doubts about the ability of self-regulating markets, organized around the principle of private interest, to ensure the optimal allocation of resources, especially in a developing country. Furthermore, World War II shortly followed the Great Depression and enhanced the extraordinary character of the international conjuncture in which the formation of the modern Turkish economy was to take place. Under these circumstances, it becomes natural to assume that modern Turkish economic institutions as well as the economic policy processes would exhibit certain characteristics likely to be different from those in other developing countries whose nation-building and institution-forming efforts have taken place in a different conjuncture in which the faith in the private enterprise system was more solid. Given the general economic and political environment of the 1930s and 1940s in Western market societies, it was quite natural, in other words, for Turkish policymakers to seek an alternative path in which the organization of the economic activity would not be entirely left to the market. State-business relations in the country were thus formed in an environment in which the necessity of a substantial degree of interventionism was taken for granted without much questioning.

This, in itself perhaps would not have been so problematic as far as the state-business relations are concerned. Nevertheless, the 1920s ended with another development which has engendered a certain hostility between Turkish businessmen and government authorities. This hostility—which has, at times, become a significant part of the policy discourse in Republican period—first emerged in 1929 with rampant speculative activities undertaken in anticipation of a major change in the foreign trade regime. Toward the end of the decade, businessmen, or rather most holders of liquid assets in Turkish currency, tried to protect themselves against trade limitations and capital controls that would follow the termination of the limiting clauses of the Lausanne Treaty. This implied a massive speculation of imported goods and foreign exchange which enhanced the already present difficulties of balance of payments and accentuated the pressure on the value of the domestic currency. As a result, Turkish economy entered a period of crisis before the impact of the Great Depression was felt elsewhere.

### Defining Etatism

Etatism—which remained a crucial concept in policy discourse until the end of the 1940s—thus appeared as a policy orientation before the advent of the Great Depression.[5] The policy orientation in question was characterized especially by the government's committment to the stability of the foreign exchange rate. In this regard, government authorities clearly voiced their faith in the gold standard as a major component of macroeconomic policy. Their committment to a balanced budget and to the equilibrium of the balance of payments was equally clear.

These objectives were to be attained by interventionist measures, and it was explicitly stated that the private sector could not be entrusted with the task of leading a smooth process of development. The Law for the Protection of Turkish Currency adopted in early 1930 presents an important benchmark in this regard. This law was first adopted for a temporary period of five years, but remained in application until the 1980s as a government policy tool of crucial significance. Characterized by the extreme ambiguity of its text, this particular law clearly demonstrates some of the most crucial characteristics of the policy process in Turkey. It assigned the government the responsibility to assure the stability of the exchange rate, but the nature of the measures the government could take to fulfill this task was not stated. The text incorporated, instead, the type of sanctions to be imposed against those who act in a way to hamper the currency stability. As indicated by some researchers, it was partly the ambiguities in its text which have made the law so popular with successive Turkish governments who could liberally define the boundaries of the domain of intervention through numerous bylaws adopted according to the reguirements of the day, in conformity with the pragmatic nature of the policy process.[6]

In the 1930s, with the enactment of the Law for the Protection of Turkish Currency, the allocation of foreign currency was centralized, and a total control of international capital movements was institutionalized. Consequently, issuing import licences became an important prerogative of the state, and largely restricted the activities of importers, who, as a consequence, became totally dependent on the discretionary decisions of government authorities for the importation of every single item. Import controls were, in theory, beneficial for domestic producers. However, this group, too, was unsatisfied with the new trade regime to the extent that provisions for imported inputs were far from being clear at the initial stages of its implementation. A possible elimination of tariff exemptions for the importation of raw materials and intermediary goods given by the Law for the Encouragement of Industry, in particular, constituted a significant topic of discord between the state and industrialists. They formed, in fact, one of the major problems leading to the resignation in 1932 of Mustafa Şeref, the "etatist" Minister of Economy.

The replacement of Mustafa Şeref by "liberal" Celal Bayar has received a lot of attention by the economic historians of the early Republican era. It is often presented as the landmark of a decisive policy turn taken by the Republican government and is interpreted as an indication of both the hostility of the private sector toward the etatist policy orientation of the government and the power of the business community to impose their own policy choices upon the government.[7] A closer look at the developments of the period in question could, however, challenge both contentions of this particular evaluation of the state-business relations in the 1930s. Rather, developments in the policy process tend to highlight two characteristics of this decade concerning the relations between businessmen and their state. First, businessmen of the era were faced with a situation in which the stability of basic macroeconomic variables were thought to be contingent upon the increasing state intervention in the economy. Given this choice between intervention and instability—which was, rightly or wrongly, taken as inevitable—businessmen seem to have opted for the first alternative. When the type of complaints that businessmen had in the 1930s are considered, one sees that these complaints had less to do with policies that enhanced the role of the state than with policies introducing an element of instability in the system. In this period when macroeconomic stability was largely assured, the main source of business uncertainty was related to the boundaries of intervention. In this regard, businessmen were not questioning the extent of state intervention, but were seeking reassurances within the area left to the private sector. What they wanted was the continuation of their rights and privileges within the frontiers of this area and, more significantly, a clear definition of these frontiers. There was, in fact, an important degree of state-induced uncertainty as regards this concern. As it will be discussed later in this chapter, it was this type of uncertainty which marked state-business relations in the 1930s.

The second widely established contention concerning the ability of businessmen to change the policy orientation also seems unfounded in the light of the economic policy choices made in this decade. The new Minister of Economy replacing Mustafa Şeref could have seemed much more acceptable to the private sector. His policy decisions were, however, far from being totally satisfactory from a businessman's point of view. The latter continued, in fact, to voice their complaints against many of these decisions without much success in reversing them. That the Turkish state had a considerable degree of autonomy can hardly be challenged with reference to the critical stand of the business community in economic policy-related issues. The fact that these criticisms were continued to be voiced until the end of the decade indicates, rather, that the business community was far from being able to dictate its choices on policymakers, even when a Minister of Economy often described as a liberal was in power.

What triggered the opposition of the business community—and of the National Union of Industrialists in particular—against the Minister of Economy in the beginning of the decade was a decision aimed at redefining the instruments of government intervention in the economy. In 1925, the Republican government had formed an Industry and Mining Bank responsible both for the financial management of State Economic Enterprises (SEEs) and the allocation of credit to industrial establishments. In the beginning of the 1930s, the Minister of Economy prepared an alternative model involving the foundation of a State Industrial Office responsible for the first task, and of an Industrial Development Bank for the second. This alternative approach to the organization of state intervention in industrial development was strongly opposed by industrialists. The main source of controversy had to do with the way in which the capital of the Industrial Development Bank was to be raised. Because there were few other sources of funding, the necessary capital was to be raised mainly by the limitation of tariff exemptions given to industrialists through the provisions of the Law for the Encouragement of Industry of 1927 which was enacted for a period of twenty-five years and, consequently, was supposed to remain in application until 1942.

It was against this arbitrary termination of their privileges that the businessmen were reacting. In the report prepared by the National Union of Industrialists to voice their dissatisfaction as regards the formation of the Industrial Development Bank, the central point of emphasis is clearly the instability created in the business environment by the proposed change in the provisions of the Law for the Encouragement of Industry.[8] Whether the changes proposed by the Minister of Economy really constituted a more etatist orientation remains, however, highly doubtful. Mustafa Şeref attempted, for example, to reduce the rate of effective protection by imposing tariffs on imported raw materials. Ironically, the "etatist" Minister thus seems to have been trying to follow a trade policy along the lines of the country's comparative advantage as a producer and exporter of agricultural raw materials. His attempts to implement a differential protection policy via the preparation of lists of protected items might also be interpreted as a reflection of a desire to distinguish the areas in which Turkish industry could be competitive from those areas which could only be protected by totally overlooking all market signals.[9]

Şeref's successor, Bayar, who was successful in calming the private sector's fears, was, in no ways, more liberal in his policies. The latter modified Şeref's model by reintegrating the functions of the State Industrial Office and the Industrial Development Bank under the newly founded Sümerbank, which largely constituted a return to the Industry and Mining Bank model. Yet, the real expansion of the state sector took place when Bayar was in office. A large number of SEEs were established with the aid of Soviet experts under the First Five-Year Development Plan which was also prepared in cooperation with the latter. In some ways, the new strategy reflected a much more etatist orientation than what Şeref had in mind. Şeref had wanted to elaborate a strategy involving what was then called "key plants" (*santral fabrikalar*)—that is, state-owned factories which would supply private firms with cheap materials. The idea seems to have been developed mainly with a view to encourage small industries in the textile sector. In contrast, the public sector development policies during the Bayar era were directed at the establishment of "integrated plants" (*koordine fabrikalar*)—that is, self-sufficient state enterprises with few links with the private sector. Prominently absent in this second period were policy efforts to encourage the development of small industry. Competition in general was viewed as a wasteful and harmful process, and explicit measures were discussed to limit competition in the industry. The preparation of a bylaw against overproduction (*Sürprodüksüyon Kararnamesi*) in 1933 constituted an important illustration of the government's attitude in this area. This measure was actively supported by the Union of Industrialists.[10]

Other, extremely nonmarket oriented policies were also endorsed or even proposed to the government by the business community in this period. Concerned with the decline in domestic demand they proposed, for example, that the government impose on civil servants the obligation to consume only domestically produced items. The upward pressures that such a measure could exercise on prices could, according to business representatives, be checked by extensive price controls. We are thus faced with a very interesting situation in which businessmen actually endorsed and supported price controls which constituted one of the most etatist aspects of the economic strategy implemented in the 1930s.

So far, state-business relations in the 1930s were discussed mostly in relation to one particular group of businessmen, namely the industrialists. Although the latter constituted a somewhat more vocal group than the rest of the business community, they were much more limited in number and economic significance than were the merchants, especially the ones involved in import and export activities. Throughout the 1930s, these foreign trade activities were subjected to extensive state control, especially after 1932. In fact, it was after the resignation of Şeref that the government's role in the regulation of external trade was considerably enhanced. The adoption of a clearing system based on bilateral agreements was accompanied by the implementation import quotas periodically adjusted by government authorities.[11] Bureaucratic red tape involved in the implementation of the trade regime was enormous, and the importers greatly suffered from the restriction of imports. The government tried to encourage exports with little success partly because of the circumstances in international markets. It is also interesting, however, that tax incentives were not used for the promotion of exports. For the government that was strongly committed to a balanced budget policy, all taxes were, first and foremost tools for public fund raising. Their allocative function was largely ignored, and the imports and exports were subjected to equal rates of taxation. The exporters were encouraged only through tariff exemptions on their imported inputs, and this measure was implemented along with extensive bureaucratic measures taken to prevent the marketing of these privileged imports on the local market.

As previously stated, it was not interventionism nor protectionism per se which was instrumental in shaping the business attitude and outlook in the country. It was rather the uncertainty concerning the rights and priviledges accorded to a given line of business which was the dominant factor in determining the nature of the business environment. While still in the initial stages of his office, Bayar was successful in assuring the business community of the continuation of the provisions of the Law for the Encouragement of Industry. However, this promise could hardly be kept given the fiscal pressures generated by the committment to a balanced budget policy in the environment of the Great Depression. Hence, a series of extraordinary taxes continuously eroded the priviliges accorded by the law in question. Even when they were imposed on wage and salary earners, their market-limiting impact appeared as a continuing source of complaint by the business community. Taxes, in fact, constituted one area in which policy-induced uncertainty was especially important in the 1930s. Yet, the main uncertainty characterizing the era had to do with the boundaries of the legitimate domain of private enterprise. Businessmen were mainly uncertain, that is, about the coordinates of their social position and about the limits of government intervention in the economy.[12]

This ambiguity was, in fact, explicitly discussed by a prominent politician of the era, Necmeddin Sadak, known to be close to the less etatist group within the RPP. Sadak stated in 1945—that is, toward the end of the etatist period—that the problem with etatism in Turkey was the failure of the government authorities to clarify the boundaries of the state sector and to specify the area left to the private sector.[13]

The significance of this type of uncertainty for the course of an economic development stratetegy in which private investment was to play some role seems to have been understood by certain intellectuals of the period. We find the latter expressing their views on this subject within the context of analyses on the causes of economic backwardness in the Ottoman Empire. In many of these analyses, two major causes of underdevelopment are underlined. The absence of protectionist policies appear as one of these causes. It is thus argued that the Ottoman Empire had remained underdeveloped because the rulers were unable to capture the logic of economic development. This implied, in the 1930s, not the inability to understand the subtleties of the liberal economic model, but those of the mercantilism.[14] What was needed to reverse the historical trend, therefore, was to adopt a mercantilist policy. Such a mercantilist policy package—involving a committment to the protection of the domestic industry and the domestic industrialist—was necessary to effectively deal with the constraints imposed by the international economy. The suggested policy package thus required an unambiguous committment to the continuing support to domestic producers, and it had to be coherent enough to introduce an element of long-term stability to the business environment.

The second principal cause of the historical backwardness of the country was depicted as the precarious nature of private property rights in the Ottoman Empire.[15] The insecurity of property was often underlined as a factor blocking the accumulation of capital and the development of a self-confident business community. The emphasis placed on this question of the legal basis of private enterprise is of a character to suggest that it was mainly there, as part of the analysis, for the benefit of the politicians in power. It seems to exist, in other words, to make the latter see the importance of dismantling the ambiguities concerning the meaning of etatism and its implications for the legitimate domain of private enterprise as defined by the legitimate boundaries of state intervention. In this decade of defining etatism, possible interpretations of the concept had, in fact, a central place in the discussions concerning the uncertainties in the business environment.

Everybody in Turkey seemed to believe, in those years, that liberalism was dead and buried everywhere. Not only the Great Depression, but also the noncapitalist economic models experimented in Russia on the one hand, and in Italy and Germany on the other, seem to have greatly influenced Turkish policy circles. For most of the politicians and even the intellectuals of the era, the lessons to be derived from Italy and Russia—or, as the title of a book by a famous party intellectual describes, from *Rome and Moscow,*— were not too different.[16] These lessons had to do with the necessity of an etatist orientation. Yet, the meaning to be given to etatism was far from being unambigious.

In the beginning of the decade, we find both Atatürk and Prime Minister İnönü talking about the etatist mentality of the Turkish population and the conformity between the inclinations of the population and the policy orientation of the government. Later in the decade, the same statesmen expressed somewhat stronger views on the nature of Turkish etatism, emphasising, on the one hand, its differences with liberalism and referring, on the other, to the failure of the private sector to successfully assume the leading role in the process of development and industrialization. In the meantime, certain members of the RPP used the term "state socialism" with reference to the economic regime of the country. "Socialism of an advanced type" is another description of etatism given by a leading politician who was the Prime Minister of the country during the period 1942–1946.[17]

There were, at a more general level, two dominant views on the subject. One of these was formulated with reference to the necessity of state intervention in those areas in which the private sector could not be successful. Summarized by the statement that "the state does what the individual can not do," this view represented a mild approach to the problem of interventionism. This was, for example, the approach adopted by Celal Bayar who has, nevertheless, explicitly denied allegiance to a liberal outlook. In 1936, for example, he was quoted as saying that "liberalism is such an alien concept that I have difficulties even pronouncing the word."[18] Among the intellectuals, those who were labelled as liberal or pro-private enterprise also assigned a signiicant role to the state in the formation of social overhead capital, regulating industry, controlling foreign trade and taking necessary measures for improvement of social inequalities.[19]

The second view was more radical than the first, and its advocates implied that there might be areas in which public enterprise would be more desirable than private sector activity regardless of the desire and the ability of the latter to enter into the areas in question. Certain strategically important fields of economic activity should, therefore, be left to the state, and advocates of this view implied that the scope of public sector activity could be expanded according to national goals. Certain leading figures of the RPP— such as İsmet İnönü and Recep Peker—endorsed this approach, as well as did the editors of *Kadro* magazine and independent intellectuals such as Ahmet Hamdi Başar.[20]

Both approaches were marked by a strong element of pragmatism, with all parties emphasizing that the notion of etatism did not have a doctrinaire character, and that the economic philosophy of the Republic was essentially a pragmatic one. Also underlined by all parties was the idea that Turkish etatism had nothing to do with "bolshevism." While this was probably reassuring for the private sector in an environment in which Soviet experts were actively involved in the preparation of the First Five-Year Development Plan of the country, the reassurance given by the emphasis of the pragmatic element in the policy orientation was not a very solid one. What the alleged pragmatism implied was, more than anything else, the significance of the scope of discretionary state involvement in the economy. Under these circumstances, the state could expand the domain of intervention in the economy whenever the circumstances required it. Of course, it was the public authority that was to judge whether such an expansion was required or not.

Given their inherent pragmatism, none of the views on the nature of Turkish etatism could totally eliminate the doubts of the private sector. The second approach involved, however, additional elements of hostility toward the private sector. It was marked, first, by the impatience of many late-industrializing country governments with the discrepancies between the actuality of private sector development and the desired objective of a modern industry. Hence, certain politicians and intellectuals close to governmental circles expressed their doubts concerning the reliability of the private sector as the key agent of economic development. These doubts were mainly voiced in relation to the primitive, technologically outdated industrial enterprises benefitting from the provisions of the Law for the Encouragement of Industry, with the advocates of radical etatism stating that these enterprises had surely nothing to do with the industrial development model adopted by the new Republican state.[21]

Furthermore, largely under the influence of the speculative

activities of 1929 and their impact on the national economy, most of the advocates of radical etatism had a tendency to see the business-man as a potential outlaw, if not traitor. Hence, many government authorities were convinced that there was an ever-present potential for legal abuse in commercial activity. This was reflected, in partic-ular, in the foreign trade policy of the 1930s which required an intricate maze of bureaucratic mechanisms, both for its implemen-tation and for the prevention of its violation or abuse by importers and exporters. In this regard, it clearly reflects one major charac-teristic of the policy process in Turkey, in which one policy measure is immediately followed by another designed to prevent the busi-ness community from circumventing the legal provisions of the first one. Hence, the formulation of the import quota system of 1931, for example, was accompanied both by certain clauses which enabled the government to periodically modify the list of items with a view to control speculation, and, also, by the enactment of another Law for the Prevention and Punishment of Smuggling.[22] As in most protectionist trade systems with such intricate bureaucratic mecha-nisms, the room for abuse was ample. Moreover, the external trade regime of the 1930s was instrumental in shaping the business atti-tude in the country in a significant way. Largely necessitated by the international conjucture, this regime was, nevertheless, imple-mented in the formative years of the modern Turkish business community that has derived an important lesson from it. It has taught the business community the significance of flexibility of adjusting business operations to a changing policy environment. Hence, in the 1930s, importers have launched some industrial enter-prises to maintain their import activities without really becoming industrialists, while the exporters have sought ways of marketing their privileged imports.[23] Rent-seeking activity, in this conjunc-ture, naturally became a significant component of business life as a birthmark. It became, in other words, a dominant preoccupation of a business community in which the classical distinctions between merchants and industrialists, and between exporters and importers were already becoming blurred.

The hostility of radical etatists toward the business com-munity was, thus, instrumental in fostering certain undesirable business attitudes and, at the same time, it was reinforced by these attitudes. Bayar shared—at least in part—the impatience of radical etatists toward the industrial development in the private sector.[24]

He was also concerned with the dishonesty of certain merchants, who, especially in the area of foreign trade, created important problems for the country's economy. He thus voiced his committment to the implementation of effective sanctions against such dishonest merchants.[25] As previously mentioned, both the expansion of the public sector and the control of private business activity continued when he was in office as the Minister of Economy.

Yet, the mutual distrust between the business community and politicians could be kept under control during the office of Bayar. In 1937, certain steps were taken for the elimination of the quota system, and the objective of further liberalization of the trade regime was announced. That year—1937—was also the one in which Bayar replaced the radical etatist, Recep Peker, as the Prime Minister of the country. It seems highly plausible, in the light of some developments that had taken place earlier in 1937, that the replacement of Peker was a reflection of Mustafa Kemal's position against the radicals in the RPP.

In the beginning of 1937, two important changes were made in the constitution of 1924. With one of these changes, the principle of etatism entered the constitution as a constituent part of the country's political regime. The second change involved a modification of constitutionally given property rights with a view to introduce a countrywide land reform project. Certain members of the parliament strongly reacted to these changes. It was asked, for example, whether it would constitute a violation of the constitution to profess belief in liberalism or socialism.[26] Radical etatists who had pushed for the change in question answered in the affirmative. They also resisted those politicians who drew attention to destabilizing elements inherent in a change of the property regime at such an early stage of economic development. They were, nevertheless, unable to enforce the implementation of an effective land reform program. In fact, throughout Republican history in the 1940s, 1960s and 1970s, land reform periodically came into the agenda. Each time, it created a considerable degree of unrest and confusion—not only among large landowners, but also among other elements of the business community which were sensitive to any infringement of legal property rights of which they could never be totally certain. One could suggest that, if the government had been successful during the 1930s in reforming the agriculture, development of the market economy could have proceeded on more solid grounds, with agricultural productivity improved and the problem of income distribution alleviated. Moreover, questions about the legal basis of property rights would have been settled once and for all.[27]

With these constitutional changes indicating a shift of the pendulum toward a more etatist orientation, the replacement of Peker by Bayar could indeed be interpreted as an indication of Mustafa Kemal's dissatisfaction with the developments in question. However, shortly after the latter's death in late 1938, Bayar had to resign, and the tendency toward an ever-increasing state intervention over the economy was reaffirmed.

The Second Five-Year Development Plan, which was supposed to be put in application in 1939, had a less etatist outlook than did the first one. It involved provisions to limit the scope of the state intervention, and promote the importance of private sector activities.[28] However, with the change of government and the outbreak of World War II, a totally different policy orientation was taken in the beginning of the 1940s, and the business community found itself in a radically different environment than the one anticipated during the premiership of Bayar.

The cabinet formed after the resignation of Bayar included a newly established Ministry of Commerce, mainly responsible for controlling illicit profits which were presumed to have recently increased in importance.[29] This was a prelude to the increasingly hostile state-business relations of the 1940s. In the 1930s, bureaucratic control mechanisms on the one hand, and regime-related uncertainties on the other had already begun to form the business attitude and business outlook in a highly unpleasant manner. As to the experience of the following decade, it can best be described as traumatizing and corrupting.

The decade began with the discussions around the preparation and enactment of the National Defense Law which would accord the government extensive powers to interfere in economic activities to face the special circumstances created by World War II. The nationalization of export/import activities was being discussed, but there were strong implications that the scope of nationalizations could be much larger. For example, as the Minister of Commerce "gently" put it, "[The government] is convinced that merchants have a function in society and in economic life. Since it is impossible to clearly predict the economic form which would emerge at the end of the war, it is not possible, for the moment, to have a clear idea about the uselessness of this group." [30]

Such rather ambigious statements about the future of private commercial activity were followed by some high-ranking government officials' less ambigious threats addressed to those businessmen engaged in socially harmful activities, but extended, at the same time, to cover the whole business community. In December 1940, the Prime Minister R.Saydam stated that, "We consider the merchant as a necessary element in national life. If this element determines and assures, by itself, its normal [sic] existence, it will receive the support of the state and the government . . . But, if the merchant does not understand this as such, we are determined to see him as an element which should be totally eliminated and to act accordingly."[31] After having thus made it clear that the survival of the private commercial sector depended upon the merchants' behaving themselves, the Prime Minister addressed the importers in particular and stated that, "If I can make myself understood to importers, fine. If not, I will nationalize import activities."[32]

Foreign trade activities were not nationalized, but they were— as was the rest of the economic life—extensively controlled, regulated, and restricted by the government. The controls, however, were ineffective in preventing the decline in total production and in increasing net exports. There were increasingly acute shortages of basic necessities. Inflationary pressures on the economy, which the government tried to deal with through price controls, could not be contained. These were, in part, wartime difficulties encountered by many other countries. However, in the formative years of the modern Turkish business class, they had a determining impact on state-business relations and, consequently, on business attitudes and business outlook.

Unable to control the economy, the government had become increasingly hostile toward the business community. Wartime profiteering was used as a proof of the unreliability of private business in general, and enhanced the element of distrust which was already an established feature of the relations between businessmen and the radical etatist wing of the RPP then in power. A general survey of the newspapers of those years clearly shows the atmosphere of hostility and fear characterizing the period in question. From 1942 to 1945 in particular, not one single day passed without a first-page report on charges of speculation and marketeering against merchants of different size and importance. Former civil servants then in business were especially under attack, while the cases of abuse of governmental positions against those still holding such positions were also ample. During the parliamentary debates of the budget of 1945, certain members of the parliament even asked for the establishment of special courts, such as the notorious ones formed in the 1920s after an unsuccessful conspiracy against Mustafa Kemal Atatürk, for the trial of illicit deals between civil servants or politicians, and businessmen.[33]

In this period—when a large number of state employees became businessmen (see table 2.6)—the accusations in question were probably not unfounded. What was unusual, however, was the reaction of the government which, instead of punishing the guilty under the existing legal provisions, chose to take extrordinary measures which affected the whole business community. The political authority was unable to control the rampant profiteering of the war years, and the ever-increasing regulation of the economy had, as its main outcome, the ever-increasing scope of rent-seeking activity. In the meantime, there were pressures on the government budget, and the inability to tax those individuals—who were obviously getting richer in the midst of general poverty—was very frustrating for the authorities.

Extraordinary taxes imposed in this period did not only constitute an economic necessity, but were, at the same time, the end results of this frustration and the ensuing hostility toward the business community. The infamous Wealth Levy enacted in 1942 as one of these extraordinary taxes was, in many ways, the epitomy of the state-business relations of the 1940s. Officially, the Wealth Levy had three purposes: (1) to tax part of the incomes derived from wartime profiteering, (2) to force the speculators to market the stocks and thus curb black market activities, and (3) to secure funds to eliminate the pressures on the government budget. In practice, it has mainly led to a total shattering of the economic position of minorities—not only of businessmen of a certain importance, but also of small craftsmen and shopkeepers. It constituted an abominable act of discrimination, but its harmful effects on the respectability of the legal system, on the bureaucratic process, and on business ethics were probably much more serious.[34]

Legally, it was an aberration, partly because the tax burden was determined in a totally arbitrary and discriminatory fashion, and also because it included clauses preventing the the taxpayer from demanding a court settlement. There were three different rates of taxation corresponding to three types of tax payers: (1) Muslims (M for *müslüman*); (2) non-Muslims (*G* for *Gayrımüslim*); and (3) converts (*D* for *Dönme*).[35] The tax burden was, therefore, determined by the religious faith of the taxpayer with Muslims paying lower taxes than did converts and non-Muslims.

From the point of view of the bureaucratic process, it both placed impossible demands on bureaucrats who were left in a position to prepare files for thousands of taxpayers in very short time on the basis of almost nonexistent data and, at the same time, accorded them extensive discretionary powers that could be easily abused.

As far as the business morality is concerned, it was totally corrupting. Muslim businessmen took ample advantage of non-Muslims' difficulties, and, in certain cases, settled their own internal conflicts by informing the government authorities about each others' hidden wealth. For example, in his autobiography, Sakıp Sabancı writes about a prominent businessmen of Adana who informed the local tax authority about the value of the timber stocks owned by his father, which apparently led to a significant increase in the wealth levy which the latter had to pay. This, however, does not seem to have generated a significant animosity because one of the Sabancı brothers later married a girl from the informers' family with the full consent of his father.[36]

In spite of the material gain realized by some of the Muslim businessmen during the episode, it would be impossible to state that the Wealth Levy left them in a happy state. In other words, the episode was not only corrupting, but it was also traumatic. First, Muslim businessmen who were partners with minorities had significant difficulties. Second, all businessmen were negatively affected by the slowing down of market activity after the imposition of the tax. Finally—and, more significantly—some Muslim businessmen who were not on good terms with Ankara for one reason or another, had to pay substantial taxes and, consequently, found themselves faced with important financial difficulties. It seems highly implausible that even those who could get away without much difficulty would not have been psychologically affected by the scope of arbitrary state action which totally disregarded the legal foundation of private property.

In fact, it was nothing less than an act of state terrorism with which the whole business comunity, including very small businessmen, were faced. Those who could not pay their taxes—often even after the sale of all their property—were sent to work camps in

Eastern Anatolia. Although the figures for the causalities are not available, it is known that some of these individuals actually lost their lives or contracted fatal illnesses in those work camps. One Muslim businessman, Fevzi Akkaya, whose autobiography was discussed in the previous chapter, upon receiving a tax statement which he could not possibly pay, decided to go and work with a friend who was involved in an engineering project not far from the work camps in question. This, according to Fevzi Akkaya, was the most rational thing to do because government authorities were unlikely to look for an individual around the work camp to which they were going to send him! Akkaya briefly refers to the living conditions in these work camps, without making any comments about their economic, political, or moral implications.[37]

The Wealth Levy episode appears, in fact, as a bad dream that the Turkish business community—especially its Jewish members—has chosen to forget. Some of the businessmen whom I interviewed were from families that were deeply affected by the Levy. Yet, neither they, nor the others who were in a position to remember the episode, were willing to talk about it. The only interviewee who talked about the Wealth Levy at some length was a Muslim professional manager who later published a novel on the subject.[38] Although, at the present, there are several researchers working on the subject, the only extensive source of information on the preparation, implementation, and the socioeconomic impact of the Wealth Levy is still a book published in 1950. It is a most interesting source because it is written by an individual who was, at the time, the highest ranking bureaucrat in Istanbul tax department.[39]

The Wealth Levy was enacted in 1942, and was abolished 16 months later, in 1943. The government could not obtain the results that it expected from this unusual tax, but the whole episode undoubtedly had a great significance in affecting state-business relations in the country.

The hostility of government authorities toward the private sector continued until the mid 1940s, and started to gradually peter out afterward. For example, in 1945, we see the Chambers of Commerce holding a general conference in Izmir and preparing a list of their requests from the government. There were seven requests of main importance in the list:

1. The elimination of barter arrangements in foreign trade,

2. Dismantling of the Unions of Exporters and Importers which were formed to control foreign trade along government dictated lines,

3. Modification of some of the particularly restrictive clauses of the National Defense Law,

4. Dismantling of some of the governmental bodies controlling the channels of distribution of certain commodities,

5. Provisions for marketing products of State Economic Enterprises by private merchants,

6. Termination of the expansion of the realm of the public sector, and

7. Restructuring of the Chambers of Commerce as autonomous organizations that can chose their administrative personnel.[40]

Apart from these specific demands, representatives of the Chambers demanded the formation of special councils in which government authorities and private sector representatives would participate to determine the boundaries of the public sector and the scope of state intervention in the economy.[41] The government agreed to study the requests in question and, in December, representatives of the Chambers were received by the Minister of Commerce. Although some of the requests—such as the autonomy of the Chambers—were rejected from the outset, and, in other areas, the outcome was mainly promises and encouraging statements rather than specific results, the newspapers reported that the delegation of the Chambers was happy to have been received by the government.[42] After years of mutual distrust, this meeting with the Minister of Commerce probably seemed to be an important sign of change in the general atmosphere of state-business relations.

The change in the government's attitude toward the private sector was also observed in the evolution of the policy process in two particular areas: land reform and industrial planning. In January 1945, a land reform bill was prepared and brought to the parliament. It was not the first time that the issue was being debated in the parliament, but it still did not fail to generate a good deal of unrest and discontentment. In the general atmosphere of the 1940s, it was not surprising to see it interpreted as a potential infringement of property rights, especially because the objective of the reform was presented by some of the spokesmen of the government as weakening of the economic and political power of landlords and strengthening the hand of the state.[43] It was not only the large landowners who were nervous about implications of the reform project. All the propertied groups were carefully following the rumors around the issue. According to some of these rumors, expropriation was going to be without indemnification and it was not going to be limited to agricultural land holdings. City property over a certain size, was also going to be expropriated.[44] In a country where real estate speculation traditionally constitutes an important form of savings, the psychological impact of such rumors would not be difficult to see. The Land Reform bill was accepted by the parliament in June.[45] In the following year, however, a new cabinet was formed, and the person chosen as the Minister of Agriculture who was to implement the reform project was a wealthy landowner. This was generally interpreted as a sure sign that the land reform law was a stillborn child. In fact, it remained largely ineffective even during the period when the RPP was still in power.[46]

Another stillborn project of the 1940s was the 1946 Development Plan. Some of the members of the radical etatist Kadro movement assumed important roles in the preparation of this plan, which constituted the first comprehensive planning attempt beyond previous attempts which were not much more than a few sectoral development projects brought together. Reflecting the convictions of the Kadro members actively involved in its preparation, the 1946 plan gave a central role to the public sector. This was explained, in the plan document, not only as an economic requirement given the insufficiency of private capital accumulation and entrepreneurial talent, but also as a socially desirable choice aimed at preventing class conflicts likely to appear as a result of the development of capitalism.[47]

Nevertheless, the international conjuncture of the post–World-War-II era, as well as its reflections in the Turkish political scene, were inappropriate for the adoption of the approach advocated in the plan. Turkey wanted to be among the beneficiaries of the Marshall aid program. It could, however, only convince the aid donors to consider its application by giving more weight to the agricultural sector and by assuring to the private sector a more important and safer place in the economy than the plan did. Especially after the formation of a new party—the DP—by some of the less etatist members of the RPP, the latter was under pressure to adapt to the new circumstances. The RPP government thus decided to replace the 1946 plan with a new one giving more emphasis to the agricultural sector, and much less emphasis to etatism. The 1947 plan also remained largely as one of the several unimplemented development plans in Turkey. It constitutes, however, an important manifestation of the decision taken by the RPP authorities to compete with the DP in leading a major economic policy reorientation.[48]

Neither the DP, nor even the National Development Party founded by a big businessman, had a clearly liberal approach to economic matters.[49] Hence, in the late 1940s, the difference between the approaches of these two parties and the RPP, committed to the repudiation of its etatist legacy, was indeed marginal. Clearly reflecting the pragmatic approach of Turkish politicians in the realm of economic policy, the antibusiness discourse of the RPP authorities had given way to a totally different style in the atmosphere of the postwar-era. In 1946, the government formed by Recep Peker—perhaps the most ardent etatist among party members—made a declaration stating that most of the restrictive wartime measures would be eliminated. The declaration involved several statements which were obviously included to please the private sector and to send the right message to doners of Western aid. It was stated, for example, that

> We are determined to benefit from private entrepreneurship and private capital in our economic activities, not to allow any discrimination between public and private enterprises, to contribute to the security and development of the private sector activities, to assure the cooperation between public enterprises and private capital, to prevent the expansion of public enterprises in the areas where [the] private sector can successfully operate, and to eliminate the cases which do not conform to this objective . . .[50]

In spite of this radical change in policy discourse, the probusiness discourse of the RPP—with its still too-close historical legacy of interventionism—could hardly be convincing. Although there was little difference between the economic programs of the two parties,[51] it was the DP that was elected, in 1950, to guide the economy away from etatism.

*Defining Liberalism*

The 1950s began with an extremely friendly atmosphere in state-business relations. In July 1950, the Minister of Commerce and Economy met with a delegation of leading businessmen, announcing to them that his ministry would hitherto take all major economic decisions in collaboration with the business community. He asked the members of the delegation to openly present their views concerning necessary conditions for the development of trade and industry, regardless of the nature of the policies presently in application. It was implied that any economic law considered to be detrimental to the development of private enterprise could be modified, changed, or abolished. As the journalists covering this meeting indicate, "The official attitude in this regard was so liberally formulated that the members of the delegation found it almost strange."[52] The government seemed to be firmly committed to the encouragement of the private sector, but also to a tight budget policy and monetary restraint to assure economic stability. In fact, in the late 1940s, when the party was in opposition and, in the early 1950s when it had recently formed the government, the leaders of the DP criticized the previous RPP governments not so much for their irrational committment to etatism as for their fiscal irresponsibility, monetary mismanagement, and the policy-induced uncertainties negatively affecting the private sector.[53]

Subsequent economic developments, however, were of a totally different nature than the principles adopted in the DP program. Throughout the decade, it became increasingly clear that the policies implemented by the DP government were leading to a certain strange phenomenon which could be called "the paradox ot Turkish liberalism." This phenomenon, which—as will be discussed later in this chapter—also appears as a crucial characteristic of the country's second experiment in liberalism in the 1980s, consists of a particular type of economic policy process in which a promarket and probusiness government restricts the realm of the market through a series of extremely intricate mechanisms of intervention. By endless modifications of this interventionist policy package, life became extremely difficult for the business community. In such a policy environment, the traditional love and hate relationship between the state and the business community reaches its most significant dimensions. In spite of the magnitude of illicit wealth accumulation in the hands of certain segments of the business community, the latter feels uncomfortable with the instability generated by frequent policy changes and the ensuing uncertainty. While the latter appear to be a continuous subject of criticisms directed against the government by the business community, the businessmen, at the same time, oppose any possible change in government. This is not only because of the profitability of rent-seeking activity in an interventionist environment of this particular type, but also because they appreciate the impact on their social status of the probusiness discourse of these allegedly liberal governments. In fact, after the suffocating atmosphere of the World-War-II years, it seems natural that Turkish businessmen would prefer to live with the economic chaos generated by the DP government than to go back to a RPP rule—this in spite of the changes that had taken place in the discourse of the latter. Or, as it will be discussed later, it seems understandable that, in the 1980s, the business community preferred the policy induced economic uncertainty to the political uncertainties of the late 1970s.

To summarize the general character of state-business relations in the 1950s, we can make three interrelated points. First, although the successive DP governments were undoubtedly committed to the encouragement of private business, their efforts in this direction were of a nature to foster not "the spirit of entrepreneurship," but rather "the spirit of profit."[54] Or, as one of the businessmen whom I interviewed put it, "The DP was out to create millionaires, not businessmen. Their slogan was 'A millionaire in each neighborhood.' Note it carefully, *not* a businessman in each neighborhood."

Second, the policy process, which deliberately excluded the notion of strategic planning, has led to increasingly severe economic problems. The government tried to deal with these problems by increasing the intensity of economic controls. Third, the rent-seeking activity encouraged by the unsystematic interventionism of the policy process has enhanced the spirit of profit, and the already present economic problems were aggravated by speculation and profiteering. As a result, the government designed further measures of economic control to punish the guilty as well as to deal with the intensified problems of the national economy. In this atmosphere, businessmen and government authorities criticized and accused each other, but were helpless to break the vicious cycle of "liberal interventionism" in which the economy was caught.

As was mentioned earlier in this chapter, the 1927 Law for the Encouragement of Industry expired in 1942 and was not replaced by a new one until the 1960s. Yet, both the 1940s and the 1950s constitute periods of significant wealth accumulation and new business development. In fact, most of the big enterprises currently in business were founded in the 1950s as we mentioned in the preceeding chapter. There were, in this period, several mechanisms of promoting entrepreneurial activity. It is possible to depict, in particular, three such mechanisms: (1) the allocation of preferential credit, (2) government contracts, and (3) foreign exchange allocations to importers. The final mechanism came later, after the return to a protectionist foreign trade policy following a brief experiment with trade liberalization.

In the allocation of preferential credit to entrepreneurs, the Turkish Industrial Development Bank, which was founded in 1950, played an important role. As mentioned in the previous chapter, TIDB credits were instrumental in the development of some of the prominent industrial enterprises in the 1950s. Credits provided by state banks also constituted an important support mechanism provided to businessmen. It also constituted, however, an area which was a continuous source of dispute and discontentment. First, never ending rumors about the cases of abuse in the allocation of public funds found their ways to newspaper columns. The discussions around this issue were instrumental in the intensification of the controls by the Central Commission for the Organization of Credit Allocations, one of the many bureaucratic mechanisms designed in the 1950s against the illicit deals between businessmen and state authorities.[55] Second, the business community was increasingly discontented with the scope of available credit, which they thought was limited by the needs of the public budget. In fact, throughout the decade, the share of the public sector in total credit has continuously increased, and the conditions of credit has remained less advantageous for private sector borrowers.[56] The complaints in this regard were implicitly drawing attention to significant crowding out effects through the expansion of government borrowing which eroded the supply of funding to the private sector and increased the price of credit. During the parliamentary debates around the 1955 budget, it was stated, for example, that the issuing of government bonds had become a common source of funding with highly detrimental effects on the private sector borrowing conditions.[57]

Here, we see an interesting aspect of the paradox of liberalism which, both in the 1950s and the 1980s, instead of limiting the scope of the state involvement in economic activity, has led to substantial increases in government spending resulting in inflationary pressures on the economy. In the 1950s, as in the 1980s, budget deficits were seen as a major cause of inflation.[58] In this regard, the burden of the SEEs on the budget was a much-discussed issue of the DP period. The government had, in fact, attempted to sell the SEEs to the private sector in the early 1950s. The private sector, however, did not seem very willing to take over these industrial enterprises. Some business representatives suggested unrealistically privileged conditions of transfer, making the purchasing of the shares of state enterprises almost less risky but more profitable than the purchasing of government bonds.[59] Even under such conditions, there were, as Prime Minister Menderes stated in 1954, too many profitable investment opportunities in the country for the private sector to show any interest in taking over the industrial establishments under state ownership.[60]

There were, in this period, two other sources of pressure on the government budget. The committment of the government to policies favorable to the agricultural sector, hitherto neglected by the successive RPP governments, was one of them. In fact, agricultural support policies constituted a major item in total government spending. Also important were the large infrastructure projects undertaken in his period. As government investment increased in social overhead capital, as well as in industry, the private sector could benefit extensively from government contracts. Contracting was, in fact, one of the most profitable businesses of the period, especially for engineers. Most of the contracting firms whose owners or professional managers whom I interviewed had either started in the 1950s with a state contract, or had the turning point of their business success in this period, again thanks to a state contract. Big holding companies—such as Enka, Tekfen, Alarko, and Doğuş—are among the prominent examples in this regard. It was not only engineering firms, but also foreign trade companies that benefitted from such business deals with the state. The fact that the import needs of state enterprises or other governmental bodies were contracted out to private businessmen constituted an important mechanism of government support for the private sector. Obviously, this was an area particularly open to favoritism through the abuse of political authority. There were many well-founded—as well as unfounded—rumors about wealth accumulation through illicit deals with politicians or bureaucrats, and many businessmen have been rightly or wrongly marked by such accusations for the rest of their business lives.[61] In general, foreign trade appears as an area in which doubtful sources of profit accumulation were especially important. Underinvoicing for export goods and overinvoicing for import goods with a view to maximize the foreign exchange left abroad or transferred abroad were among such sources of profit. Also important was the false identification of the traded commodity to overcome the barriers against the imports and exports of certain products.[62] As the trade regime became an increasingly important source of uncertainty with the intensification of protectionist measures, the importance of rent-seeking activity also has intensified.

Foreign trade regime, in fact, constituted an area in which the state-induced uncertainty was especially severe in the 1950s. As soon as it came to power, the DP government announced that the trade regime was going to be fully liberalized. Yet, for several months, the nature of the liberalization in question was totally unknown, and the business community as a whole remained in a state of suspended animation during this period. The experiment with the liberal trade regime which started later in the year was a rather short-lived one, with the changes toward a protectionist system already beginning in 1952, and becoming increasingly important thereafter. Throughout this second change, business activity was also paralyzed in anticipation of the new trade regime.

The change in policy orientation in this area was largely necessitated by the pressures on the economy. The balance of trade which could be maintained throughout the etatist period had shown a deficit starting with 1946. Yet, in the early 1950s, with the favorable conjuncture created by the Korean War, there were no serious difficulties in this regard. These were also good crop years for Turkey, and the country could benefit greatly from the favorable terms of trade for agricultural products associated with the impact of the war. In general, the period between 1948 and 1953 was a period in which there was rapid growth of investment and production. The pressures that rapid growth and increasing government spending exercised on domestic prices and on the balance of trade were felt after 1953, especially with the impact of the postwar changes in the international conjuncture. Moreover, Turkey's relations with the international organizations was becoming increasingly tense because of the rather strong reaction of the DP government toward the criticicisms directed by organizations such as the IBRD and the OECD against the inflationary policies in implementation. Such conflicts were of a nature to endanger the influx of foreign credit necessary for the smooth functioning of the economic activity.[63]

These pressures on the economy and the ensuing policy reorientation toward more protection and intervention were instrumental in generating a wave of speculative activity. The cases of speculation and marketeering—along with rumors about the illicit deals taking place in the allocation of import licenses—began to dominate newspaper columns as early as in the 1950s. The government retalitated both by taking court action and by intensifying controls, but it was quite helpless in controlling the situation. In this atmosphere, Prime Minister Menderes was quoted as saying that "They steal, I know that they steal. But what can I do? I am the Prime Minister, not an inspector!"[64] Yet, the measures taken by the government involved the inspectors more than the economists. In 1954, the tone of state-business relations for the rest of the decade was already set by several measures anticipating reactivation of the National Defense Law in 1956.

In the first half of 1954, an army of supervisors—consisting of the employees of the Ministry of Finance, Customs and State Monopolies, and the Ministry of Economy and Commerce—were actively involved in stock controls in Istanbul, Ankara, and other big cities of Western and Southern Turkey. Importers were subjected to strict antispeculative controls, and there was a wave of arrests for illegal stock building.[65] Later in the year, the Law for the Regulation of Profits was enacted, and the controls over supply and supply price became more systematic. They seem, however, to have been rather ineffective in controlling either the speculative activity or the escalating inflation. The frustrations of the government over economic issues were translated, as in the previous decade, in the intensification of economic controls as a sign of hostility toward the private sector. A certain bill debated and voted on in the parliament in 1956 is interesting as an indicator of the nature of state-business relations in the mid–1950s. The bill in question called for the death penalty for speculators. It was rejected by 102 votes against 88.[66] A few days later, a new version of the 1940 National Defense Law was reactivated.

The business community had violently reacted against the reactivation of this notorious law of the war years with a large number of provisions according the government extensive powers of control over the market. The only problem the law generated was not, however, the extent of the state control that it made possible. The main source of complaint seems to have been the impossibility of having a clear idea about the regulated areas and the nature of the regulation. Businessmen complained that economic life was almost paralyzed in a maze of intricate and detailed mechanisms of control, and they demanded the repeal of the law with an increasingly strong voice. The government heeded these complaints, and this made things worse for businessmen, as well as for the economy in general. Several attempts were made to modify the law, and rumors about the nature of these modifications enhanced the economic uncertainty.[67] Then, several provisions of the law were repealed, and doubts about the procedures concerning the areas thus left unregulated led to a slowing down of economic activity.[68]

Worse still, the government began to prepare another law to replace the National Defense Law. The Economic Measures Bill proposed as an alternative antiinflationary measure with provisions against speculation and marketeering accorded even more extensive and arbitrary powers to the government. At the end of the decade, the business community was in a position to ask for the implementation of the National Defense Law rather than suffering through its modifications or getting adapted to a new set of even more intense and intricate controls.[69]

During a conference of the Union of Chambers, economic policies implemented by the DP government were criticized in these words:

> In order to be able to plan their future activities and to organize their businesses on the basis of certain assumptions, businessmen desire stability more than any other social group. While the accelerating inflation of the last few years has ruined the market stability in the country, unplanned, discretionary controls of the government have covered the whole market. The businessman has found himself in a straightjacket as a result of credit and quota allocation procedures, and price and profit controls. Since these extremely extensive controls are not products of a coherent perspective, they lack a rational basis.

As a result, they change every day, are continiously modified, abolished, and reintroduced. This situation leaves the businessman in a state of total confusion.[70]

With particular reference to the instability generated by the modifications of the National Defense Law, a report published by the Izmir Chamber of Commerce refers to "the impossibility of understanding the procedures related to the Law given its 12 modifications, 1135 (!) coordination decisions pertaining to its application, and the numerous procedural statements issued by the ministries involved in its implementation."[71]

As emphasized by certain critiques of the economic policies implemented by the DP, in the second half of the 1950s, the government was engaged in a futile attempt to control the economy through "threats, punishments, accusations, advice, appeals to sentiments of morality and good citizenship"[72] The stabilization program adopted in August 1958 was, in part, a response to the failure of the previously implemented policies to control inflation and to deal with balance of payments difficulties. Yet, perhaps more significantly, it was a step taken to please the international aid donors—a step, in particular, enabling the government to conclude the negociations for a $190 million credit package with the OECD.[73]

The program involved a de facto devaluation through a system of multiple exchange rates for different export and import items. This, in itself, was a positive measure settling, at last, the uneasiness generated by the expectations of devaluation. However, it could not eliminate the long-lasting uncertainties concerning the trade regime and the determination of the prices of traded commodities. In principle, with the adoption of the stability program, the provisions of the National Defense Law were supposed to be abolished. Yet, they were not—or at least they were eliminated, not as a whole, but only in a piecemeal fashion. Hence, in the area of foreign trade, businessmen were more confused than ever.

In other areas—such as the prices of state-produced commodities—there was also a good deal of confusion. The program called for increases in the prices of some materials produced by the SEEs. The timing of the price adjustment was, however, not indicated. Once again, the government was quite powerless to control the ensuing wave of speculation.

The business community was particularly dissatisfied with credit restrictions involved in the program. These restrictions pertained only to credits given to the private sector. There was no restriction for the credit sources open to the public sector. As a result, the relative share of the public sector in total credit used increased considerably in the final years of the decade, and the private sector suffered from a shortage of funding which was much needed in an environment of declining economic activity.

One year after the adoption of the stability program, it was quite clear that, first the program was adopted, not so much for a genuine restructuring of the economy, as it was to satisfy the country's creditors. It was also clear that the economy was in a greater state of chaos than before. In this unstable environment, the demand for a planned approach to the economy was becoming increasingly widespread. The attitude of the DP authorities—and of Prime Minister Menderes in particular—had, in the meantime, undergone several changes. During his early years in office, Menderes had a rather hostile attitude toward the idea of planning, identifying it almost with communism. Later, he referred to the difficulties of planning, and to the failure of the previous RPP governments to prepare viable development plans. He then suggested that his government had a planned approach to the economy, giving budgetary provisions as examples of planning. Finally, during his last year in office, he took certain steps toward the preparation of a development plan, but these initiatives were kept as a secret. It seems that the plan in question was being prepared largely upon the suggestion of the OECD, concerned with the chaotic development of the Turkish economy.[74]

Within the country, too, there was an increasingly articulate diagnosis of the economic problems as the natural consequences of the confusing zigzags of the policy process. In the final year of the DP rule, a famous economist summarized such views in the following words: "We still do not have an established economic system, a set of rules and institutions whose permanent character we are sure of. We are wavering between different systems, changing direction every day. This wavering and this chaos result from the absence of a basic philosophy."[75]

The same diagnosis was also present in the recurrent demands for stability of private sector representatives. The modifications of the National Defense Law, rumors about its replacement by the Economic Measures Bill, and the uncertainties caused by the implementation of the economic stability program of 1958 created a highly unstable business environment and generated a considerable degree of business discontentment at the end of the decade. We also observe, in the same period, certain attempts at reconciliation with the business community undertaken by the increasingly weak DP government. Legal modifications to extend the powers of the Chambers might be considered as just such an attempt.[76] The atmosphere of the March 1960 visit of the Prime Minister to the Istanbul Chamber of Commerce, for example, clearly reflects an effort to appease the concerns of the businessmen. In this visit, Menderes was quoted as saying that "the demands of the business community only concern simple problems which could be solved in a couple of hours."[77]

In the same period, the government also tried to win some of the prominent businessmen to the ranks of party members through the intermediation of some ardent supporters of the party among the community. This wide-spread DP propaganda among businessmen was a recurrent theme of criticisms directed against the government by the opposition. In the discussions around this issue, it was also mentioned that very few businessmen could resist the pressures to join the DP, and there were several analyses of this inability of Turkish businessmen to take a firm stand against the government. In one of these analyses, the meekness of the business community vis-à-vis the government is explained with reference to three societal factors. It is mentioned, first, that, trying to function in an overwhelmingly unstable environment and facing an unpredictable future, businessmen try to maximize whatever gains they might realize in the short run. Because these short-run gains depend largely on the discretionary moves of a dubious legality of the government in power, businessmen do not dare to oppose government authorities in any area. Second, the absence of a well-rooted habit of long-term strategic business planning in Turkish business culture enhances the reluctance of businessmen to risk short-term profits by taking a critical stand against the government. The third factor mentioned in this analysis of state-business relations in the late 1950s has to do with the precariousness of business ethics in Turkey, where businessmen often fail to realize the significance of their social status and the social responsibilities the latter involves.

This situation in Turkey is then contrasted with the situation in Western democracies where the business community plays a crucial role in checking the power of the government and in preventing the abuse of political power.[78]

These factors were undoubtedly important in shaping state-business relations at the end of the 1950s. One could also suggest, however, that the key factor affecting business attitudes in this period was lack of confidence about the changes that a new government would introduce. In other words, one could suggest that the fundamental uncertainty about the future of the private enterprise system dominated the uncertainty induced by the arbitrary policy changes of the government in power. Businessmen were obviously not very happy with the actual state of policy-making. They were probably more concerned, however, with the potential for a systemic change which could threaten their position in society.

In any event, at the end of the 1950s, the business community tried to avoid open confrontation with the government and was careful not to appear to be flirting with the opposition. In March 1960, for example, the Istanbul Chamber of Commerce turned down the demand of a RPP delegation to visit the chamber for an economic discussion with the members.[79] There were also certain expressions of business solidarity with the government, which turned out to be rather embarrassing for the business community after the military coup of 1960. The few months before the coup constituted a politically turbulent period when there were several student demonstrations. After such a demonstration of the students of Ankara University, the Ankara Chamber of Commerce and Industry sent a telegram to Menderes to express the regrets of its members. After the military coup which took place approximately one month later, the board members decided, in panic, to change the minutes of the meeting in which the decision to send the telegram in question was taken, with a view to dissimulate the gesture. The whole episode was unveiled by the revolutionary committee responsible for examining the records of the chambers in order to reveal the cases of abuse of chamber functions in areas such as the distribution of import licenses. [80] Such incidents indicate that the atmosphere of the period immediately following the coup was a rather tense one in spite of attempts of the authorities of the new regime to appease the fears of the business community concerning the future of the private sector.[81]

*Experiments with Planned Economy*

Throughout the two decades between the military interventions of May 1960 and September 1980, periods when such reassurances were not needed were extremely rare. During these two decades—which witnessed three military interventions, two aborted military coups, two reform cabinets, eight very short-lived coalition governments, several ministerial crises, and escalating terror and violence toward the end of the 1970s—the political uncertainty of the business environment was at its peak. Moreover, the two decades in question constituted a period when the Turkish economy underwent a genuine economic restructuring with the implementation of an import-substituting-industrialization strategy. Problems of structural change, accompanied with the usual problems of import substitution, introduced additional elements of instability to an already turbulent business environment. The planned approach to economic development, which was adopted in the 1960s could, of course, have alleviated the economic instability in question. Nevertheless, given the way in which they were implemented—or could not be implemented—the five-year development plans have enhanced the economic uncertainty rather than alleviating it. Development planning could not change the fundamentally pragmatic—and, hence, unprincipled and unreliable characteristic—of policy formulation and the implementation process. Yet, it introduced new questions concerning the domain of government intervention and the area left to the private sector.

The private sector has, nevertheless, further established itself in this period. By the end of the period, it had a crucially significant presence in the industrial sector, and the big private enterprises had achieved a highly sophisticated organizational structure. The two decades in question have also witnessed a process whereby the social position of big business was being shaped. In this regard, there were two interrelated developments. First, the cleavage between big business and the rest of the business community, consisting of small- and medium-sized firms, was becoming increasingly clear. Big businessmen seemed to be increasingly concerned with the long-term economic strategy, as opposed to short-run developments affecting their immediate interests, and were increasingly articulate in their demands to take an active part in the formation of public policy. Starting with the early 1960s we observe, second, an increasing distancing of big businessmen from the organizations grouping together all elements of the business community. Consequently, the demands of the big business community have been increasingly voiced by prominent businessmen in individual visits to government authorities without the intermediation of the Chambers. The formation of the Turkish Industrialists' and Businessmen's Association (TÜSİAD) in 1971 was largely the result of these developments whereby big businessmen have dissociated themselves from the rest of the community in an attempt to assume a quasi-public function in determining the economic and social orientation of the country. The formation of the TÜSİAD was preceeded by the rise of particularism in state-business relations. As will be discussed in detail in the final chapter of this book, this particularist tendency could hardly be overcome, even with the increasing public significance of the association.

Certain writers have interpreted the economic policy orientation in post–1960 Turkey as presenting a new model of accumulation based on the alliance between the developmentalist state and the big bourgeoisie.[82] In light of the preceeding discussion, however, the model in question does not appear as representing a rupture within the legacy of state-business relations in Turkey. It appears, rather, as the natural outcome of a historical process whereby a state-created big bourgeoisie is assigned a somewhat more important responsibility in the economic development of the country. While the social position of big businessmen was increasingly consolidated in the post–1960 period, state-business relations continued to be characterized by the tension generated by state-induced uncertainty of the atmosphere.

At a certain level, it would be possible to depict a similarity between the social and economic developments characterizing the business environment in the two decades between 1960 and 1980. Both decades—the 1960s and the 1970s—started with a military coup that brought along the idea of economic reform and restructuring. The political turbulance was thus accompanied with questions pertaining to the nature of the reform project and to changes it could imply concerning the social position of the private sector. Both in the 1960s and the 1970s, such doubts were quite rapidly eliminated in the beginning of each ten year period. What followed then was instability generated by the nature of macroeconomic policy-making and of the institutional framework of policy implementation. At the end of both decades, the secular and conjunctural problems of the economy constituted a major concern for the business community.

I have suggested that system-level concerns pertaining to the nature of economic reform projects were eliminated in the beginning of each decade. The fear of systemic change, however, has remained, albeit assuming a society-emanated form rather than a state-induced one. In the second half of the 1960s, Turkish businessmen discovered anticommunism, with a considerable lag compared to their Western counterparts. After the 1971 military intervention there was a return to earlier patterns in which the state again constituted the locus of the business concern about systemic change. However, starting with the mid–1970s, with political unrest and the rise of terrorist activity, such concerns were once again expressed with reference to societal actors rather than the state itself. The latter, of course had also remained as a significant actor, with the business community voicing its discontentment about the ineffectiveness of the state in dealing with political turbulance. As it will be argued in this chapter, during this period, political preferences of big businessmen were mostly formed in relation to the potential of any given political party to control social unrest and violence.

In the politically tense atmosphere of the early 1960s, after the initial shock of the military coup, businessmen began to ask for clarification of their status in the new regime. As in the earlier periods, such demands were voiced by the Chambers. However, news coverage of this issue indicates an emerging development in this regard. In this period, individual businessmen with no representative function also began to take part in the negotiations with government authorities. In the beginning of 1962, for example, a group of businessmen, including Vehbi Koç and Nejat Eczacıbaşı, visited İsmet İnönü, then the head of one of the four coalition governments of the first half of the 1960s. After the visit, Vehbi Koç informed the journalists that "I told the Prime Minister that the most important issue was that of the establishment of peace and stability, and especially of political confidence which constitutes 80 percent of all our problems."[83] Throughout the decade and after, one periodically finds references to similar meetings between politicians and businessmen as well as to declarations of individual members of the business community concerning what they perceived to be the main economic problems of the country. While initially most of these statements were made by one single member of the community—Koç—at later stages other prominent businessmen have also begun to appear as public figures, a phenomenon which had hardly existed in the pre–1960 period.

It is clear that Turkish businessmen shared Koç's view that 80 percent of their problems had to do with political confidence. Businessmen's common attitude in this regard was clearly expressed in the course of the discussions around the preparation of the First Five-Year Development Plan.[84] In these discussions, businessmen firmly expressed their conviction in the necessity of a planned approach to development[85], yet they also emphasized their desire to see the meaning given to planning clearly defined, put on paper, and settled once for all. As indicated on the first page of the Union of Chambers report on the issue,

> It is necessary to explain more broadly that the plan is of an indicative type like the plans implemented in the free world and to put special emphasis on this issue. Although there is a passage, on page 690 of the text of the plan, where it is mentioned that the plan is of a nature to support and to guide the private sector, it is still necessary to state in more detail that its implementation would be based on an approach which relies on the market mechanism, that free decisions of the entrepreneur would not be hampered, and that the private sector is expected to contribute to the realization of the objectives set in the plan only through encouragement, persuasion and motivation. It should be clearly explained that this type of indicative planning, which has been implemented for years in countries such as France, Japan and Italy belonging to the free world of which we are also a part, is, by its nature, different from imperative planning.[86]

What businessmen were asking was, therefore, not the modification of certain specific issues which did not conform to business interests, but explicit reassurances about the boundaries of the private sector activity. In this regard, they raised several questions pertaining, not only to the nature of the planning process, but also to certain concepts used in the plan, such as "equality" "social justice," and "mixed economy." Businessmen wanted to hear from the planning authority that the first two terms did not suggest a social-ist orientation with drastic redistributive measures. They also em-phasized, however, the need for a modern labor legislation with extensive union rights. Labor problems and radical social move-ments did not yet constitute a problem for the business community that was mainly concerned with the state activity in the realm of redistribution. What was not yet settled almost forty years after the foundation of the Republic was the legitimate domain of state inter-vention.

Hence, with reference to a state communique to the general secretariat of the OECD where it was mentioned that the Turkish economy is a mixed one where the private and the public sectors coexist side by side, a Union of Chambers' report stated that

> The private sector wishes to know which economic activities would be undertaken by the state since it is hardly possible that a private sector which does not know the area it is to operate, or will have the opportunity to profitably operate, would engage in economic activities. This is because the entre-preneur is a being who is infuenced by psychological factors as much as economic and legal factors, and he plans his activities accordingly.[87]

Other than elimination of the uncertainties about their social position, private sector representatives asked the state authority to participate in the economic decision-making process through the formation of bipartite councils. While there were several promises—and even certain experiments—in this regard, the forma-tion of business councils could never be institutionalized. Until the present day, the business community has continued to put forward the same demand after the formation of each new government.

The exclusion of the business community from the economic decision-making process did not imply that the latter did not con-form to private sector interests. Governments have, in general, been cautious not to harm business interests, and they have provided many incentives to persuade the business community to act in conformity with social and economic goals. That the policies adopted after 1960 were conducive to business interests was gener-ally accepted, and there were frequent references to the increase in the number of millionaires during the first half of the decade.

"Creating millionaires" was, as it will be remembered, a motto of the DP years, and, in 1962, Prime Minister İnönü had stated that "in a period of planned economic development, the government can not be expected to make promises about the creation of millionaires." The critiques of the probusiness nature of the economic policies implemented in the same period have later pointed to the contradiction between İnönü's statement and the statistics about the increasing number of millionaires.[88]

Turkish businessmen were, in fact, getting rich under the import substituting industrialization strategy, implemented with heavy protectionism. The first FYDP had reintroduced, for the first time after the expiry of the Law for the Encouragement Industry in 1942, a set of systematic incentives to encourage the commercial interests to move to the industrial sector. Industrial investments were encouraged by several types of incentives such as tax rebates on income taxes and customs duties, and credit facilities provided by the TIDB as well as by the newly founded Industrial Investment and Credit Bank and the State Investment Bank. The incentives as well as the legal arrangements contributed to the emergence of large industrial enterprises organized in the form of holding companies. As will be discussed in detail in the following chapter, it was in the early 1960s that the legal basis for the formation of holding companies was prepared upon the demands of certain big businessmen, Vehbi Koç in particular. These demands were put forward, along with others concerning the modification of legal provisions in a way to make the formation of family foundations easier and more attractive for businessmen. One sees in these demands an emerging concern for the continuity of family business and fortune, a concern, in other words, for the consolidation of the institutional basis of business activity.

The Turkish business class was, therefore, consolidating its presence in the industrial sector and its position in the society, but it was doing it in an extremely unstable environment. The doubts about the character of Turkish planning were settled to the satisfaction of the business community, but the implementation of the plan was of a nature to create a significant degree of confusion. First and foremost, neither the exact nature of the incentives nor the governmental body to be contacted in order to benefit from them were well-known. The rules determining eligibility for subsidized investment credit were especially ambigious, and politicians and bureaucrats had a considerable degree of discretionary power in their allocations. These factors were reflected in the actual distribution of credits, with big businesses that enjoyed easy access both to sources of information and to decisionmakers, getting the bulk of the available funds.

However, big business, too, did not seem to be happy about the orientation of economic policy. A report prepared by the Union of Chambers to be presented to the concerned ministries, for example, begins with a discussion of the problems generated by the differences between the declared objectives and the actual implementation of economic policy. Pointing to changes that frequently take place in economic decisions, the report states that "Since the foremost objective of the government should be to maintain the confidence the people has in the state administration, it is absolutely necessary to avoid decisions which create confusions detrimental to the objective in question."[89] Big business had complaints, in particular, about the ambiguities of the import regime.[90] There was, in general, great confusion concerning implementation of the plan. In this regard, the unsettled character of the bureaucratic apparatus constituted a central problem. Each attempt at reforming the bureacracy brought with it additional doubts concerning the powers and responsibilities of different ministries and other governmental bodies.[91] The confusion around the nature of and ways of access to existing incentives has led to the incorporation of certain provisions in the Second FYDP to deal with this problem.[92]

The second FYDP, apart from introducing new incentives, attempted to reduce bureaucratic red tape by centralizing the implementation of the incentive system. It also introduced a system of selective incentives depending on the conformity of the investment project to plan objectives instead of the across-the-board support hitherto provided to all investments. Both these changes, however, were short-lived. The Supreme Court ruled out the system of selective incentives because of the possibility of its abuse in illicit deals between bureaucrats and bussinessmen. As to the centralized approach to the implementation of the system, it has largely failed to serve its purpose through numerous changes in the bureaucratic structure in which the Central Bureau responsible for the determination of access to different incentives was to function. Each new FYDP introduced new provisions for the restructuring of the bureaucratic apparatus, but very few of those could be permanent. The responsibilities to be assumed in this area by the State Planning Organization, the Ministry of Finance, and the Ministry of Industry could not be well defined. In a seminar held in 1978 at the Istanbul Chamber of Commerce, businessmen, planners, and representatives of the ministries involved were still discussing the nature of the bureaucratic channels to be used for obtaining investment certificates necessary to benefit from incentive measures. Businessmen still did not know whether they were supposed to contact the State Planning Organization, the Ministry of Finance, or the Ministry of Industry within the bureaucratic process involved.[93]

It was not only the unsettled nature of the bureaucratic procedures which contributed to the instability of the business environment. In 1965, after four coalition governments succeeding each other, the Justice Party (JP) of Süleyman Demirel, mostly a reincarnation of the DP, formed a government with a large popular support. Demirel was, in no way, a firm believer in development planning, and he had no intention of losing his popular support. These two factors together have contributed to the emergence of an economic atmosphere in which plan provisions were largely ignored in the economic decision-making process, in which the tension between bureaucrats and politicians was substantial, and in which inflationary finance was rampant. The instability generated in the process of planned development under a government which was hostile to the idea of planning was, in fact, the subject matter of many economic analyses in the second half of the 1960s.[94] The problem of inflation was also a much discussed issue, and the business community was also referring to this problem in the criticisms directed against government policy.[95]

Nevertheless, in this period, businessmen also seemed to be quite concerned with the danger of communism. The instability of economic environment was underlined as a factor contributing to the rise of antibusiness sentiments. Hence, business demands from the government included both the creation of a stable environment which would not be conducive to the rise of communism, and, also, propaganda activities to publicize the merits of private entrepreneurship.[96] In fact, certain members of the business elite led by Nejat Eczacıbaşı had already taken initiative for the formation of an organization to fulfill this purpose in 1961. The Conference Board for Social and Economic Issues was founded as a tripartite organization bringing together the members of the business community,

university professors, and government authorities to organize semi-
nars and conferences on social and economic problems.[97] It was a
very shrewd attempt to meet the challenge of the liberal constitution of 1961, which would inevitably lead to the spread of socialist
ideas and popular movements in a country where intellectual and
political activity had long been severely repressed. As Eczacıbaşı
said in a personal interview, it was also a step taken to bridge the
distance between businessmen and members of the political and
intellectual elite. Business participation to the activities of the Conference Board was not very wide, with most businessmen adopting a
much cruder anti-Communist stand. In the course of our interview,
Eczacıbaşı, in fact, told me about the resistance he met from the
business community when he invited a famous British Labour Party
member to give a talk on socialism. However, the Conference Board
undoubtedly fulfilled an important purpose as an elite organization.
As will be discussed in chapter 5, it constituted an important aspect
of the social process in which big business was dissociating itself
from the rest of the business commununity in an attempt to assume
a role in the orientation of public policy.

A more significant step in the same direction was taken with
the establishment of the TÜSİAD in 1971, soon after the military
intervention of March 1971. More will be said on the activities of
both the Conference Board and the TÜSİAD in the last chapter of
this book. For the moment, it suffices to say that they were the
products of a politically turbulent environment in which the business community did not fully trust the ability of the government to
maintain popular unrest. Rather than forming a forum to promote
short-term economic interests of the business community, they
constituted the expression of a desire to contribute to the creation of
a social environment in which the legitimacy of business activity
was assured.

Big business wanted economic stability for its economic and
social interests. Hence, it was very much against the JP government's unplanned, pragmatic approach to economic policy, which
aimed at the daily management of different popular demands and
interests. Hence, businessmen welcomed the military intervention
of March 1971 and the ensuing attempts at economic reform. It was
even stated that the failure to immediately implement the reform
program would endanger the private enterprise system.[98]

The way in which the reform cabinet approached the problems

of industrialization was, however, found to be unsatisfactory by businessmen. The latter group was especially uncomfortable with discussions about tax reform and the role of the public sector in the economy. Debates over a land reform project also appeared to be a source of anxiety for even those members of the business community who had no interests in landed property. In less than a year, tension between the government and the private sector had led to a stagnation of investments. In September, the president of the Union of Chambers confirmed the decline in private sector investments and explained it with reference to the government's distrustful attitude toward the business community. Soon afterward, radical members of the government resigned, and the same Prime Minister, Nihat Erim, formed another short-lived government. The first and the foremost demand of the Chambers from the new government was, as in the early 1960s, clarification of the meaning of the term *mixed economy.*[99] Once again, the private sector wanted to be reassured of its social status.

Throughout the decade—including the periods when the new, social democratic RPP of Bülent Ecevit was in power—it became increasingly clear that it was not the parliamentary governments that were going to tilt the balance against the private sector in the distribution of economic power between the latter and the public sector. Yet, the tension between the business community and the state has continuously increased. The former was dissatisfied with the increasingly chaotic economic policy process under successive governments, and the inability of the latter to deal with mounting political unrest and terrorist activity. Among the several coalitions and interim governments formed in the 1970s, only the two formed by Bülent Ecevit in 1974 and 1977 were received with some hope by the private sector. Yet, as it is often emphasized by Turkish social scientists, TÜSİAD was actively involved in events leading to the fall of the second Ecevit government in 1978.[100] This strange relationship between the first Social Democrat party leader in Turkey and the big business elite is indeed interesting in shedding light on the political and social positions of big businessmen.

In the course of my interviews with some of the former presidents of TÜSİAD, the conversation naturally led to these brief experiments with social democracy. My interviewees did not regard it to be at all strange that the big business community supported a Social Democrat party instead of the probusiness, right-wing JP. Two of them explicitly stated that the natural political inclination of an industrialist is social democratic. The same two have also said that Ecevit is a man like themselves, meaning "Westernized," "cultured," and "civilized." "He sits, talks, and eats like I do. Of course, I would have liked to see a man like this as my Prime Minister" one of them said. The other referred to unimplemented economic programs and continuously reversed economic decisions of the governments which preceeded the first and second Ecevit governments. They both stated that they were then hoping that a Social Democrat government would be committed to a planned strategy of industrial development and would be able to control the radical left which was becoming increasingly powerful, both in the union movement and out in the streets.

Why had they turned against Ecevit then? The first government was doomed, according to my interviewees, because of the presence of the Islamic fundamentalist National Salvation Party (NSP) as the coalition partner. Moreover, when he was in office both times, Ecevit performed as a populist and not as a Social Democrat leader. As one of the former TÜSİAD presidents put it, "Populism was exactly what Turkey did not need at that period. Populism is exactly what Turkey does not need."

One could perhaps see an element of populism in the reluctance of Ecevit to implement the IMF-suggested stability program in 1978. He did not, indeed, have a Social Democrat alternative to deal with the problems of balance of payments deficits, rampant inflation, and rising unemployment. A planned approach to economic policy which could eliminate the usual policy-induced uncertainties o the business environment was totally absent. Besides, the government introduced certain retroactive policy changes which had devastating effects on business activity. One of these policy reversals was mentioned to me by several businessmen in the course of interviews as an example of the state-induced uncertainty as the central problem of business activity in Turkey. The example has to do with the foreign exchange regime. In 1976, the right-wing National Front coalition led by the JP issued a decree which provided exchange-rate guarantee for the credits which businessmen obtained for importing capital goods. Businessmen thus expected to pay back the credits negotiated after 1976 at the rate prevailing at the time when credit was obtained. In 1978, the Ecevit government retroactively abolished the exchange rate guarantee, and businessmen who had negotiated import credits found themselves in a situation in which they had to tackle a substantial exchange rate difference.

The business community—TÜSİAD in particular—soon turned against the second Ecevit government and was engaged in a massive public-opinion campaign which was at least partly responsible for the fall of the cabinet in October 1979, after the defeat the RPP suffered in partial elections. In January 1980, the JP minority government adopted the IMF stability package, but did not have the chance to implement it. In September 1980, the Army took over, and what followed was probably the most sinister period of the modern Turkish political system, with the most striking violations of democratic freedoms and human rights.

### Liberalism Revisited

For the private business sector, however, the 1980 coup did not bring along the fear of systemic change that was associated with the two previous military interventions, at least in their early stages. This was in spite of the fact that TÜSİAD was closed after the coup, as were other associations, for a brief period. It was clear from the outset that the military had come to assure a politically stable environment in which the IMF package of 1980 could be implemented. It was indeed surprising to hear the leader of the junta mentioning, among the objectives of the new regime, successfully implementing an outward-looking development strategy in his first public speech on television on 12 September 1980. Like all elements of the civilian population, the business community was not trusted and respected by the military, but the latter now seemed to recognize the private sector as an integral part of the economy and society. Moreover, the military was coming in, not to implement an ambigious reform project with etatist or socialist overtones, but to simply follow an IMF-sponsored stability program. The promarket orientation of the military—as well as of the following Motherland Party (MP) governments after the general elections held in 1983— was clear enough to eliminate system-level uncertainties from the business environment for the rest of the decade.

The second type of uncertainty associated with the unexpected policy changes reached, however, unprecedented dimensions in the course of the decade. This situation, in which an unambigiously probusiness government plays a significant role in destabilizing the business environment, was highly reminiscent of DP rule in the 1950s. As in this early attempt at the establishment of a market economy, the MP rule led to a chaotic development at the level of the economy and economic institutions. As in the DP era, the government was instrumental in the creation of huge fortunes and also considerable difficulties for different elements of the business community. Toward the end of the 1980s, as in the late 1950s, the animosity between the government and the business community had reached a very high level, with, however, certain attempts at reconciliation and peacemaking always present. There was, however, an important difference between the two periods which had to do with the presence of an already well-established business community in the second period. The confidence that big businessmen in particular had in their positions in society modified the nature of state-business relations, and also introduced new elements in the political arena.

Notwithstanding this change, the political framework of business activity remained marked by the historical legacy of state-business relations in the country. Although the form of government intervention in the economy has changed, the overwhelming presence of the state in the economy has remained, with businessmen more preoccupied than ever with what the government would or would not do. The well-entrenched tendencies to engage in rent-seeking activity were unleashed by the manner in which supposedly market-augmenting and export-promoting policies were implemented. As some Turkish researchers have highlighted, it was indeed interesting to see a standard policy package—which had already led to entirely different consequences in other countries—leading, in the Turkish context, to usual rent-seeking activities because of the nature of the policy networks in the country.[101]

A few words must also be said, however, on the nature of the policy package in question. The policy package that military and civilian governments tried to implement in the 1980s aimed at the establishment of a liberal market economy in a country where the price mechanism was severely distorted as a result of the hitherto followed import-substituting-industrialization strategy. It aimed, in other words, at "putting the prices right" in order to leave resource allocation to market signals. As the experience of several other countries where there were similar policy reorientations has shown, this type of market-oriented economic restructuring does not necessarily imply a "retreating state." On the contrary, there were cases in which the increase in the degree of centralization of the economic decision-making process has actually contributed to the success of the liberalization strategy.[102] In Turkey, too, what was experienced was a step toward the elimination of political distortions of prices in certain areas, namely in the determination of the exchange rate, the rate of interest, and the prices of the products of the SEEs. What was observed in these areas was an increase in the flexibility of the prices, but not the elimination of state control over price determination. Governmental decision, in other words, was still dominant, but the government was now more sensitive to market forces in the decision-making process.

The state has not gotten smaller in the 1980s. There was, in fact, a decline in the share of the public in manufacturing output. Yet, the share of the public investment in total investment has continued to increase until 1988, because the public investment in infrastructure has increased considerably. We see that, in 1979, relative shares of the public and private sectors in total fixed investment were 49.7 and 50.3 percent respectively. In 1980, the balance shifted against the private sector with the public share exceeding that of the private sector until 1988. In 1987, relative shares of the public and private sectors were 53.5 and 46.7 percent. In 1988 the same figures were 47.6 and 52.4 percent respectively. There has, in fact, been a decline in total fixed investment in the period following 1988 which is because of significant cut backs in public infrastucture projects imposed by the fiscal crisis of the state.[103]

The crisis in question also reflects the expansion of the state in the 1980s. Public debt has continiously increased in the 1980's, hence the presence of the state in the market for loanable funds. The budget deficit, which was TL 117.2 billion (1.8 percent of the GNP) in 1981, reached TL 14,202.3 billion (5 percent of the GNP) in 1990.[104] In internal borrowing, the government heavily relied on government bonds and short-term treasury bills, which, unlike the common practice in developed industrialized countries, had very high rates of interests making them more attractive than bank deposits or the securities issued by private firms. Partly because of this reason, public sector issues constituted around 90 percent of the securities issued in the Istanbul Stock Exchange at the end of the decade.[105]

Public sector domination of the financial system is also reflected in the increasing share of public sector banks in total bank deposits which has reached 55 percent in 1990 (with private sector banks receiving 44 percent and the foreign banks about 1 percent of total deposits).[106] In the meantime, the significance of the share of the public sector in Central Bank credits remained very high until the end of the decade, showing a slight decline in 1990.[107]

Perhaps more significant than these indicators of state presence in the economy was the centralization of decisionmaking power in the area of economic policy. Throughout the 1980s, there was a substantial increase in the power of the executive branch i general, and of the Prime Minister in particular. The extension of the prime ministerial power was realized through a series of organizational changes which have served to create, within the office of the Prime Minister, a number of key agencies responsible for strategic decision making and policy implementation.[108]

As regards the expansion of centralized executive power at the expense of the legislative branch, extrabudgetary funds—one of the most ingenious post–1980 innovations—appear to be of particular significance. These extrabudgetary funds were created through the diversion of tax resources from the parliament-controlled consolidated budget, as a source of revenue which the government could freely use without going through the approval of the parliament. They constituted, in other words, an institutional device which was in perfect conformity with the MP's strictly pragmatic approach which involved a clear disregard for the rule of law whenever there was even the slightest conflict between legal provisions and the reguirements of goal directed action. While there was no parliamentary control over the off-budget funds, there was also a general lack of transparency as to their nature, magnitude, and use. It is indeed interesting that the coalition government that replaced the MP rule in 1990 had to spend a few months before it could have an idea about the resources each fund had.[109]

In the late 1980s the number of funds in existence was estimated to be around one hundred with, however, about eleven important funds accounting for two-thirds of the earmarked revenues channelled toward this type of extrabudgetary spending. The sum of these revenues was estimated to range between $3.5 and $5.7 billion in 1987–1988, with the single largest extrabudgetary fund—the Mass Housing and Public Participation Fund accounting for more than half of this sum. The latter was created in 1984 to assume a series of different functions, including direction of the privatization program. It was under the direct control of the Prime Minister and was instrumental in significantly enhancing Prime Ministerial power in economic decisionmaking process.[110]

These organizational developments increasing the discretionary power of the Prime Minister were amply used in the course of the decade in a series of pragmatic decisions which were often not only unexpected, but also conflicting and contradictory. In fact, the presence of the state in economy was felt, more than anywhere else, in this type of discretionary meddling introducing an overwhelming degree of uncertainty in business environment. In other words, the state was important mainly because the businessmen were in a position to watch every single move of the policymakers in order to be able to form at least a vague idea about the highly unpredictable changes in the values of the key macroeconomic indicators. Therefore, the state formed, more than ever, the center of the businessman's daily concerns.

In the 1980s, the policy-induced uncertainty had to do, first and foremost, with the ways in which basic policy objectives were defined. According to all formal policy statements, the mission of the MP government was the implementation of a standard IMF stabilization program. The Prime Minister (now the President) Turgut Özal was presented to the public as an economic wizard, and the proof of the statement was going to be the success of the program in question. During the first few years of his rule, his opponents almost exclusively directed their criticisms toward the appropriateness of the standard IMF recipe in general and for the Turkish economy in particular. There were hardly any doubts about the conformity of the government's program to this recipe. Later, it became quite clear that the program implemented in the country— at least between the general elections of 1983 and 1987—was an expansionist program with heavy state investment in infrastructure acting as the main engine of growth.

The ensuing budget deficits and an accelerating rate of inflation appeared as the end result of the economic strategy in question.[111] The basic uncertainty of an inflationary environment presented a major obstacle to the smooth functioning of the market. A government which had repeatedly declared its determination to fight the etatist tradition in Turkey in order to establish a real-market economy was, thus, instrumental in bringing about a highly uncertain environment inimical to its allegedly market-augmenting orientation.

What was even more significant than the government's inability to assure price stability is the central place that the objective of controlling inflation continued to occupy in the official discourse. Thus, businessmen found themselves facing a doubly uncertain future. Price fluctuations resulting from government policy were only one element of uncertainty. A second, and perhaps more significant, factor was the possibility of a major policy reorientation. At any moment, the control of inflation could appear as a real concern in conformity with the declared policy objectives. The business community simply did not know the basic parameters of the system and, like farmers in a simple peasant community watching the clouds to predict the weather changes, they kept track of the signals to guess the future course of events—that is, the future moves by the government.

One implication of the growing budget deficit had been the significant pressures that the rising public debt exercised on interest rates. In fact, members of the private sector voiced their complaints in this area, pointing at the crowding-out effect of government operations whereby private business firms found themselves in a position to compete with the government for loanable funds.[112] However, it is interesting that, with regard to the interest rate policy, business complaints were directed more at the uncertainty about the rates than at their levels. At a panel discussion on television in 1988, for example, the president of TÜSİAD mentioned that the interest rates were changed nineteen times in the course of the previous year which made irrelevant all discussions about the rate of interest as a tool of economic policy.[113]

It is important to note here that what was being changed by the government was not only the level of interest rates, but the rules of the game in relation to the determination of these rates. In February 1988, for example, interest rates were raised to 65 percent. This decision generated many complaints on the part of businessmen who were adversely affected by the high costs of credit. Then, in September 1988, the rates were reduced. A few months later, the government discontinued interest rate controls, and announced that they were going to be determined by the market. The banks immediately raised their borrowing rates, ferociously competing with each other to attract deposits. On the next day, the government announced a new decision fixing the highest legal deposit rate at 85 percent. This rather confusing development toward interest rate liberalization was generally interpreted as an act of punishment against certain private sector banks which were heavily involved in foreign exchange speculation. This interpretation is in perfect conformity with the nature of the legal framework of state-business relations in Turkey, as will be discussed later in this chapter. In any case, the whole episode left the business community with certain uneasy questions of legal rather than economic natures. They found themselves in a position to decide whether, in Turkey, foreign exchange speculation constituted a crime or not.[114]

Such erratic economic policy changes of the 1980s were especially severe in two areas: the tax system and the foreign trade regime. In the first area, frequent changes as well as ambiguities in the text of the law contributed to the unpredictability of the future tax burden as well as to the difficulties of figuring out the exact amount of taxes to be paid. These ambiguities naturally represent a perfect incentive for tax evasion which, in its turn, often leads to government retaliation with more changes enhancing the arbitrary character of the taxation system. The late 1988 changes in the tax system provide a good example of this process. It was mainly the failure to realize the level of tax revenues expected in the 1988 budget which was instrumental toward the changes in question. With modification of the tax law, the power of the government in changing the tax structure was considerably enhanced at the expense of the legislative responsibility in the area. Hence, the government was given the power to impose new taxes and to alter existing rates on certain revenues and transactions by decree rather than by legal changes approved by the parliament. The uncertainty that the possibility of such changes introduced into business life was emphasized by several writers critical of expansion of the executive's discretionary power.[115] Nevertheless, the imposition of a new so-called temporary business tax, in less than a month after the modification of the tax system, was realized through the usual, parliamentary channels. This new tax was based on the previous year's declarations as well as an estimate of the taxpayers' "standard of living." It was a tax in which the payment preceeded the actual earning of the taxable income, and it was especially detrimental to newly established small businesses whose tax burden would be estimated in a rather arbitrary fashion, on the basis of the declarations of comparable establishments. While economists and legal experts were highly critical about the overall economic and social implications of this new tax, the latter considerably enhanced the already strong tension between the government and the business community.[116]

The nature of the foreign trade policy followed in the 1980s was an important factor contributing to this tension. The stated objective in this area was the promotion of export activity and the liberalization of the import regime. Comparing the foreign trade performance of Turkey in the early and late 1980s, it would be possible to state that there were, in fact, important steps taken in this direction. The percentage of imports financed by export revenues considerably increased throughout the decade, and the import regime was liberalized to a significant degree by the elimination of most of the nontariff barriers and by the considerable decline in tariffs especially after the decisions of August 1989. Yet, the overall development of the trade regime was hardly compatible with a healthy restructuring process associated with a manufacturing export-led growth strategy.

The promotion of exports largely relied upon the establishment of Foreign Trade Companies, inspired by the East Asian development model. The Law on Foreign Trade Companies stated that companies which surpassed a certain prespecified export target would be eligible for certain incentives, mainly export tax rebates and a privileged position in trade with Eastern block countries subjected to special bilateral arrangements. These companies also had some advantages in the importation of materials used in export production. The rationale behind the establishment of Foreign Trade Companies was the restructuring of the export activity in a way so as to take advantage of the increasing returns to scale in marketing and, thus, to enhance the competitiveness of Turkish exports on international markets. At the initial stages, this arrangement led, in fact, to a considerable increase in exports. It had, however, certain disadvantages which soon began to undermine this initial success. First, as several economists underlined, the system was based on incentives given to exporters and not to producers.[117] Consequently, it could mainly be instrumental in the marketing of the existing surplus production through a mechanism reminiscent of the Smithian idea of the vent for surplus, rather than leading to a genuine restructuring of productive activity with strengthening of the export goods sector. Second, the incentives system was quite easy to abuse through rent-seeking activity. Hence, it soon led to the emergence of the notorious phenomenon of fictitious exports based on overinvoicing practices. In a few years, these fictitious exports reached a considerable part of total exports,[118] and the social discontment that they caused was largely responsible for the elimination of most of the incentives given to Foreign Trade Companies in 1988 and 1989.

The export regime underwent several transformations in the course of the 1980s. Export tax rebates, which were the main instrument of export promotion during the period of 1980–1984, were significantly reduced in 1985 and 1986. These reductions reflected a policy decision according to which the exchange rate was to be the main policy instrument for export promotion. Nevertheless, negative export growth in 1986 resulted in a reversal of this decision, and, in 1987, tax rebates were again reinstituted. They were then gradually reduced and finally abandoned in 1989. This was followed by the introduction of new incentives such as subsidized credits and energy inputs.

Throughout this period, the frequency of changes in the list of commodities benefitting from different types of export promotion measures simply makes one feel dizzy. Equally confusing were the changes in the percentage of premiums and tax rebates as well as the terms of repayment of export credits. As in the uncertain environment prevailing in other areas of business activity, these changes, which constantly gave rise to and destroyed rents, created an ambiguity as to the acquired rights of businessmen. The final dismantling of the export promotion system based on the privileges given to the Foreign Trade Companies also resulted in considerable losses for those businessmen who had planned their investments on the basis of the continuity of the incentives system in question. As the manager of one of the Foreign Trade Companies put it, the organizational structure designed to carry out export activities in the policy environment of the early 1980s was very costly and time-consuming to eradicate. Hence, it was quite a shock to the concerned exporters to see it becoming largely redundant at a point when its establishment was hardly completed.[119]

The liberalization of imports also involved similar uncertainties with the industrialists unable to forma clear idea about either the timing or the stages of the process. Hence, the radical liberalization package of August 1989 arrived quite unexpectedly, with the industrialists insisting that they were not against the policy move but against the way it occurred in a manner which made all strategic planning impossible for the local producer. Government authorities responded by evoking unjustifiably high profits made behind the walls of protectionism, and, as one of the top level managers of a prominent holding company put it, the whole policy decision seemed to be taken in anger.[120] The debate around the issue took a rather strange form with irrelevant accusations, insults, and threats directed against local producers by the Prime Minister.[121] This type of discourse was, in fact, quite characteristic of state-business relations in the last few years of the 1980s. For example, in August 1989, we again hear the Minister of Finance threatening businessmen by confiscating their houses if they insisted on paying their taxes on the basis of a gross undervaluation of property. By the end of 1990, politicians both within the MP and the opposition had gotten quite used to addressing the business community through similar threats.[122]

This type of discourse reflected, more than anything else, the government's inability to discipline the business community to act in ways conducive to economic stability and development. The reason for this inability, in its turn, lay in the nature of the policy process which, in varying degrees, characterized the entirety of Republican history, but which appeared in its most striking form in the 1980s under the MP governments. It was this policy process which was instrumental in the creation of a business mentality directed both at survival and rent-seeking in an environment in which policy-induced uncertainties hampered the development of an industrialist's outlook. What prevailed in Turkey in the 1980s was a policy environment ideal for the utilization of already well developed talents of Turkish businessmen in zero-sum entrepreneurship. It was an environment where the rich could easily become richer, but where the wealth was not established on a solid ground.

Most of the policy moves toward the establishment of an outward-looking market economy—such as the import liberalization, export promotion, establishment of the stock market—contributed to easy profits via rent-seeking activity. Moreover, centralization of economic decision making with greater Prime Ministerial powers enhanced the particularist tendencies in the business environment. As it will be discussed in more detail in the next chapter, big businessmen could often enter into direct contact with the highest level policy makers who led them into certain activities by giving assurances and making promises. The implications of this particular type of state-business relationship for individual businessmen were not uniform. First, there were cases in which specific policy changes, by law or by decree, directly contributed to the enrichment of particular individuals. Second, there were decisions specifically designed to harm certain individuals with the wrong political affiliations. Finally, there were cases of certain entrepreneurs who put themselves in a difficult position because they had undertaken certain activities following the advice of top-level politicians. In this last group, one finds, in particular, those businessmen on especially good terms with the leaders of the MP harmed, in a paradoxical way, by their very closeness with state authorities.

The extremely intricate and frequently changing character the export promotion measures provided, in the 1980s, an excellent medium for state-supported wealth creation. The lists of the commodities benefitting from a particular type of incentive—as well as the percentage of premiums to be received in the exports of particular commodities—could be changed by different governmental bodies, such as the Prime Minister's office, the State Planning Organization, the Ministry of Finance, or the Central Bank, with a substantial impact on the export revenues of particular firms or individuals. Two of the many such changes caused a particularly strong reaction from public opinion. One of these cases had to do with the decrease from twenty-five to fifteen cents of the payments made to a particular fund by the exporters of dried figs. The decision for this change was taken at the end of the export season for this commodity, and the only person likely to benefit from it was a particular exporter who still had a certain amount of this export commodity to be shipped abroad. This exporter happened to be a close friend of the Minister of Finance and the future father-in-law of Turgut Özal's son.[123] The second similar case involved the neglect to erase a particular commodity, plastic slippers, from the list of commodities whose export premiums were reduced. Hence, for a period of about two weeks, exporters of plastic slippers received premiums which could often well exceed the cost of production of the commodity. Although the incident received a lot of press coverage, the lucky exporter for whose benefit the scheme was designed could not be discovered.[124]

In the same period, the changes made in the import regime with a view to support certain industries also served to benefit particular individuals. The decision to encourage the development of the automotive industry taken toward the very end of the MP rule, for example, was mainly beneficial for the Sabancı group that immediately announced its decision to invest in this industry through joint venture arrangements with the Toyota group. Other groups that were formerly distributing agencies of foreign firms also began to negotiate with these foreign firms for local production in the automotive industry after the policy change affecting this sector. In the meantime, those businessmen who had already settled in the industry claimed that they were unable to understand the decision given the extremely limited size of the market. The members of the Sabancı group ardently defended the policy move in question, while, in the public opinion, the incident was received with a suspicious attitude given the briefness of the period between the policy move in question and the Sabancı initiative to enter into the industry.[125]

The new institutional arrangements of the 1980s were also instrumental in promoting the particularist relationship between the state and individual businessmen. For example, off-budget funds outside the control of the parliament were used to give credits at preferential rates to certain individuals. In this regard, it was argued that the resources accumulated in the largest one of these funds— the Mass Housing and Public Participation Fund—were mainly channelled toward a few firms.[126]

The overwhelming presence of the state in the financial system was instrumental, yet in another way, in the increasing importance of particularism as a major factor behind business success. In the newly established stock market in which public securities form 90 percent of the traded securities, there were few rules and regulations preventing the use of inside information by individuals close to government authorities. The case of Turgut Özal's son who made a fortune on the stock market is notorious in this regard. It is not surprising that many similar cases, in which the functioning of an insufficiently regulated stock market was instrumental in illicit wealth creation, were witnessed throughout the decade.[127]

The state, however, was not only instumental in creating wealth for particular individuals. It was also the major factor in business difficulties of out-of-favor individuals. As a prominent businessman put it in the course of an interview by a journalist, in Turkey, a Prime Minister has the power to destroy a whole sector if he wishes to do so.[128] The MP governments—or Özal as the Prime Minister—have not really destroyed a whole sector or even a whole enterprise. Government authorities have deliberately acted, however, to make trouble for certain businessmen who had supported the political opponents of the MP before the general elections of 1983. For example, the business community in general shares the opinion that the decision taken in 1984 to prohibit the advertisement of beer on television was a deliberate act against two major holding companies, Yaşar and Anadolu Endüstri, that were, among their many other activities, important producers of beer. Both companies had openly supported the National Democracy Party which was the principal rival of the MP in the first general elections held after the 1980 coup.

Yet, the businessmen who ended up with substantial government-generated difficulties were not only the enemies of the ruling MP. On the contrary, in many cases they were individuals especially close to ruling circles. The cases of Enka Holding and Ercan Holding provide excellent examples to this process whereby state authorities encouraged a particular firm to invest in designated areas, and then rendered those investments unprofitable by not providing the promised support.

In the case of Enka—a well-established holding company whose main line of activity is construction projects under state contracts—the owner/managers were personally encouraged by Turgut Özal to undertake industrial activities in those fields of the manufacturing sector related to construction activity. Hence, Enka established several industrial firms in the early 1980s which were largely unsuccessful. As one of its managers told me in an interview, the company could survive only because it had sufficient flexibility due to its widely diversified structure of activity. The new industrial ventures were eliminated, and the difficulties were largely overcome.

In the case of Ercan Holding, the difficulties stemmed from the same source, but they were not as easily overcome as in the case of

Enka. In 1987, Tevfik Ercan, the owner/manager of the holding, was encouraged by the government and by military authorities to enter into the production of municipal buses and military trucks upon the promise that he would be the main supplier of these commodities to the state. The sales were to begin in 1989. Then, state authorities reversed their decision, and both the buses and the trucks were imported from Germany. As for Tevfik Ercan, he is still trying to redress a virtually collapsed business enterprise.

These two cases frequently came up in the course of my interviews with different businessmen. Yet, as one of my interviewees explicitly stated, there was nothing very unusual about them. "What happened to Enka and Ercan," this particular interviewee said, "also happened to the whole community of exporters and is about to happen to investors in tourism, both groups that were first encouraged by very attractive incentives and then left alone with important investments and profitability that considerably declined with the change in policy priorities. The state, in other words, threw a bait to these businessmen and they swallowed it."

The reason behind this seemingly pointless luring of people into business difficulties has remained unexplained by my interviewees. They seemed, nevertheless, to be quite used to this particular type of policy process, and most of them could adjust to unexpected changes by compensating for losses in one area by profits made in another, by relying on wealth accumulated through real estate speculation, or by shifting from one line of activity to another, from industry to trade or vice versa. They behaved, in other words, just as they were described as behaving by business historians who, as discussed in the previous chapter, find these behavioral characteristics quite detrimental to a healthy development process. However, one can see after this discussion of the policy process in Turkey, why Turkish businessmen act the way they do, and how the nature of the policy process and this particular form of behavior reinforce each other and accentuate each other's impact on the course of economic development. The big multiactivity firm, the Turkish holding company, constitutes an area in which this particular interaction between state policy and business behavior is most clearly reflected. Strategy and structure of these multiactivity firms will be discussed in the next chapter. Before proceeding to this discussion, however, it seems necessary to say a few words on the nature of the mechanisms of intermediation in state-business relations with a view to complete the picture of the policy environment in which business activity takes place in Turkey.

## GOVERNMENTS AND STATE INSTITUTIONS IN TURKEY

The preceding discussion of the policy process throughout Republican Turkey somehow anticipates the nature of the roles that the bureaucracy and the legal system play in Turkey as mechanisms of intermediation in state-business relations. It would not be difficult to see, for example, that, in the presence of a rule-bound, autonomous bureaucracy and a set of clearly defined legal principles that could not be violated by the political authority, the latter could hardly indulge—at least to the extent that it has been traditionally done in the country—in discretionary meddling with the economy. Similarly, it would be natural to assume that the overwhelming pragmatism that characterizes the policy process and rules out serious committment to a planned development strategy would also be reflected in bureaucratic and legal institutions, which would thus acquire a certain malleability to be easily adjusted to politically set economic and social objectives. The haphazard policy changes would thus become reflected in legal modifications and changes in bureaucratic rules which, in turn, enhance the instability of the economic system.

The nature of legal and bureaucratic mechanisms through which government-business relations are mediated in Turkey, therefore, reflects the policy formation and implementation process in the country. As underlined by several writers who trace its origins to the Ottoman state tradition, one of the most distinct characteristics of this process is the tendency of the government to regard its political power as absolute.[129] In Republican era, this tendency is manifested in the emphasis on "national well-being" by nonelected governments and of "national will" by elected ones. Consequently, all of the governments, to varying degrees, felt that they had the right to monopolize state power and disregard structures of intermediation between the government and the people. In any event, in the social setting of Republican Turkey, where economic development became the foremost national objective and the absence of committment to a particular social philosophy the most significant component of the official ideology, it would, in fact, be unrealistic to expect either the bureaucracy or the legal system to manifest unchanging and stable norms that could be used as reference points in the settlement of potential or actual disputes between the government and different social groups.

While referring to the continuity between Ottoman and Republican periods, one should not overlook the fact that there were several attempts to reform and restructure the bureaucracy in the latter period. In spite of these attempts—or perhaps partly with their contribution since they have introduced more change into an already unstable system—the powers and responsibilities of bureaucrats, the criteria for appointment to and promotion in bureaucratic positions, as well as the decision rules pertaining to different procedures remained quite ambigious throughout the Republican era. As several studies on the subject have indicated, this state of affairs led to the emergence of timidity, lack of initiative, and overrespect for hierarchy as the determining characteristics of the Turkish bureaucrat.[130]

Such ambiguities and the ensuing behavioral deformations seem to have been less important in the single-party era than in the following period. During the RPP rule as the single party, one observes a certain fusion of the political and bureaucratic elite joined to fulfill the task of transforming the society.[131] Bureaucrats were, thus, a significant part of the mission led by the political leaders, and they did not have any difficulty in adapting to changing requirements of this mission. The almost legendary position in the early Republican period of the bureaucratic cadres of the Ministry of Finance—chosen from among graduates of the Faculty of Political Science in Ankara—indicates the significance of the bureaucratic elite in the social transformation project undertaken by the RPP.[132]

Yet, even in the single-party period, the bureaucracy was not important as a neutral and autonomous institution. Its importance lays, on the contrary, in its willing subservience to the political leadership, to the highly personalized political power structure in the country. The infamous Wealth Levy of the World War II years, for example, presents an episode in which committed bureaucrats had some difficulties in accepting the arbitrary decisions of the politicians in power.[133] Moreover, certain modifications of the bureaucratic system, already undertaken in the single-party period, were of a nature to suggest that the possibility of confrontation between bureaucrats and politicians were not totally excluded even in that period. Hence, certain legal provisions of the bureaucratic system—which were adopted in 1924 and 1926 and which assured the security of the bureaucrat vis-à-vis the politician—were modified in 1936 as a means of enhancing the power of the ruling government over careers of civil servants and hence, limiting the autonomy of the latter.[134]

Steps taken in this direction were especially important in the 1950s. While the DP government took several initiatives to reform the bureaucracy and even invited several foreign experts to serve as consultants to the government on this issue, its main achievement in this area was a radical limitation of the bureaucratic autonomy. This was realized mainly by a law enacted in 1954 which gave the government the power to dismiss civil servants judged to be incompetent or politically involved.[135] Their job security thus hampered, civil servants found themselves in a position in which the failure to comply with the political decision-making process could result in the disruption of their bureaucratic career.

After the 1960 military coup—which largely represented interests of the civil and military bureaucracy—there was an attempt to remedy this situation by new legal modifications assuring the security of bureaucratic careers. After 1960, there were also attempts to realize an overall restucturing of the bureaucracy and, to serve this purpose, a comprehensive research project on the totality of the Turkish bureaucratic apparatus was commissioned by the government. As in similar projects submitted to the government in the 1950s, these researchers also pointed at the ambiguities in the way in which rights and responsibilities of the civil service personnel were defined, and emphasized the negative impact of these ambiguities on bureaucratic efficiency and productivity. They also underlined the significance of limiting the scope of political interference in the remuneration and career-path development of civil servants. Although the project was an important one in diagnosing the problems of the bureaucratic apparatus in its totality, it made little impact on the bureaucratic system in general, and on relations between bureaucrats and politicians in particular.[136]

The unsettled and unstable character of the bureaucratic apparatus, as far as its role in business activity is concerned, was greatly accentuated by a very significant development of the 1960s. The establishment of the State Planning Organization (SPO) in 1961 was especially important in affecting the role of the bureaucracy as a mechanism of intermediation in government-business relations. Somewhat paradoxically, instead of introducing an element of stability in business life by providing some indication about future trends in the values of basic economic variables, the SPO contributed to the basic uncertainty of business environment. This was because it failed to develop as a neutral bureaucratic body, but became, instead, a politically manipulated agent of ruling governments. Furthermore, the prerogatives of the SPO were not clearly defined and could thus expand to areas in which other bureaucratic bodies also claimed to have responsability and decision power.

The ambiguities in the way in which the functions of the central planning body were defined were, in fact, instrumental in enhancing the confrontation with the planning bureaucracy and the ruling government. As highlighted by several writers, the establishment of the SPO was realized in an atmosphere in which those in power had a great faith in the planning mechanism and wished to see it rule out the political authority in matters pertaining to economic policy. Consequently, the SPO was born endowed with certain powers which well surpassed its natural status as a technical advisory body and extended into the realm of the executive. At the same time, the mechanisms of sanctions to enforce the executive's compliance with the guidelines set by the plan were not at all well-defined. The outcome of this contradiction was a continious political interference in the planning body and highly successful attempts to politicize the organization.[137]

The nature of the political interference in the planning process was such that it prevented, according to some writers, the full implementation of any one of the FYDP's except the first one (1963–1967).[138] Even the implementation of the first plan was interrupted with the formation of each government during the plan period. In fact, the lack of coincidence between the date of general elections and the date of preparation of each new plan invariably led to discontinuities in the planning process.[139]

Perhaps more important than these discontinuities were changes in the planning personnel that took place with each change of government. Such changes—which sometimes led to a total transformation even in the basic principles of the organization's approach to the planning process—could be observed in the extremely high rate of turnover in top bureaucracy. Hence, in the first two decades of planned development in Turkey, the SPO had eleven different presidents. The Economic Planning Section had thirteen different directors. There were eight directors of the Social Planning Section, and the Section for General Coordination had nine different directors. Most of these changes took place in the 1970s when the average life span of each government was less than two years, and where the bureaucracy was more politicized than ever.[140]

Another outcome of the politicizing of the bureaucracy in the 1970s was the overgrowth of civil service personnel. The SPO was also affected by this phenomenon. We see, for example, that in 1980, 183 new planners were hired, which constituted more than 50 percent of the existing staff. This hiring took place, moreover, at a time when the stability program adopted in January 1980 had rendered the Fourth FYDP largely redundant and the future of planned development highly uncertain.[141]

In fact, throughout the 1980s, development plans increasingly became functionless documents. Yet, the SPO remained as an important body of the public bureaucracy which continued to enter into conflicts with other governmental bodies, especially with the Ministries of Finance and Industry with regard to the boundaries of its domain of responsibility. Conflicts between the SPO and these two ministries were especially severe with regard to the administration of the incentive mechanism, and they often left the business community in a state of utter confusion. Especially in the 1970s, there were periodic shifts in the distribution of responsibilities in this area with certain governments increasing and others decreasing the respective responsibilities of the SPO on the one hand and the two ministries on the other. In 1979, there was even one episode in which the Minister of Industry told a group of businessmen not to take very seriously the annual program prepared by the SPO and to take any problems related to plan provisions directly to his ministry.[142]

In the 1980s, with the massive centralization of economic power in the Prime Minister's office, such conflicts were largely reduced. However, there were still complaints about the confusion prevailing in the administration of the foreign trade regime. Turkish Foreign Trade Companies, for example, had to deal with the SPO in matters concerning subsidies and tax rebates, and with the Undersecretariats of Treasury and Foreign Trade concerning export and import permits. Moreover, the Central Bank was responsible for currency transfers and the disbursements of export tax rebates and export credits, while the Ministry of Finance was responsible for exchange and customs matters.[143] In the course of my interviews, the managers of several Foreign Trade Companies bitterly complained about the confusion created by the number of government agencies responsible for different phases of export procedures.

Apart from the problem of bureaucratic fragmentation, an ever-increasing tension between bureaucrats and politicians characterized the policy environment of the 1980s. This might, in fact appear to be quite difficult to understand, given the significant steps that the MP government took in dismantling the established bureaucratic structures and hierarchies to give more power and flexibility of movement to the executive in economic matters. Some of the bureaucratic positions of crucial significance were filled with young graduates of American universities who had not followed the usual bureaucratic channels of promotion. These "princes," as the media referred to them, were supposed to work in harmony with MP politicians, and especially with the founder of the party, Turgut Özal. The princes were not spared, however, in the politicians' assault on bureaucratic cadres. Especially under attack from the members of the executive and the parliament were general managers of some important public banks, the Export Credit Bank (Eximbank), and, quite naturally, the director of the Central Bank. The manager of the most important public bank, Ziraat Bankası, also had to launch a real battle against some members of the parliament fighting for his replacement by a more "understanding" bureaucrat who would be less rigid in considering the demands for credit of the important individuals among the MP constituency.[144] Another one of the princes, the manager of the Eximbank, was accused by one of the ministers in charge of the economy for having the main responsibility for the country's declining exorts. Around the same period, another minister, also in charge of the economy, claimed that the director of the Central Bank was surpassing his limits by getting involved in the macroeconomic management process. This was a reaction to the Central Bank's resistance to increase the money supply to meet the requirements of deficit finance.[145] In the meantime, several ministers—all responsible for the economy—had increasingly severe confrontations among themselves, which were reflected in the media especially toward the end of the MP rule.[146]

This disarray at the level of economic policy implementation was an increasing source of concern for the business community.[147]

In a rather surprising fashion, the latter quite clearly sided with the bureaucracy in its conflicts with politicians.[148] This interesting attitude of businessmen toward the bureaucracy was also highlighted in the course of my interviews. My original expectation was to hear a lot of complaints about bureaucratic impediments and difficulties of dealing with bureaucrats. Contrary to such expectations, the interviewees seemed to be highly conscious of the conflicts between politicians and bureaucrats, and tended to sympathize with the latter. In general, they shared the following view expressed by Nejat Eczacıbaşı in his autobiography: "A public administration, which is deprived of all standards of value because of the inadequacies of personnel payment policies, and because of the doubts about job security that emerge with each change of government, have left the country in the hands of a timid, indecisive, and oversized army of bureaucrats."[149]

The role of the bureaucracy as a mechanism of intermediation in government-business relations also appears as a crucial factor in older businessmen's evaluation of the business environment in different periods of Republican history. For example, as it was mentioned in the previous chapter, even Fevzi Akkaya, whose business success could clearly be traced back to the 1950s, writes more favorably about the bureaucratic process in the 1940s. According to him, the mutual understanding between bureaucrats and businessmen was, in the 1940s, an important factor contributing to the creation of a stable business environment. He relates, for example, two episodes in which understanding bureaucrats agreed to pay contractors ahead of the official schedule in order to speed up the construction activity, which would have been considerably delayed had the installement been made on time.[150] According to Akkaya, this type of mutual goodwill eventually gave way to a rigid and hostile one starting with the 1950s. Although he does not attempt to analyze the reasons behind this change, the atmosphere of the 1940s and of the subsequent periods conveyed in the book points to two major developments which could have been instrumental in destroying the harmonious relationship between the two parties in question. One of these developments has to do with the diminished power of the bureaucrat in the multiparty era. While bureaucrats could no longer make use of discretionary decision-making powers in order to facilitate the contractors' job, the second development— namely the increasingly clear separation between the realm of the state and that of the private sector as a result of the growing importance of the latter—might have also reduced the incentive to do so. In fact, several analyses of the evolution of the public bureaucracy in Turkey deal with these two factors which jointly create a situation in which a frustrated and insecure army of bureaucrats adopt an increasingly hostile attitude toward the members of the private sector that has been gradually taking the place of the bureaucracy in the higher echelons of social hierarchy.[151]

The frequency of turnover in bureaucratic positions, as a factor largely instrumental in shaping the bureaucratic mentality, is also depicted as an important problem by businessmen. Sakıp Sabancı, for example, writes in his autobiography about an incident which is directly related to this problem. The incident takes place at the headquarters of the State Organization for Agricultural Equipment where Sabancı was visiting with an American representative of the Ford Motor Company with a view toward reaching an agreement for the joint production of farm machinery. Ford Motors, Sabancı and the Organization for Agricultural Equipment would form a partnership for this purpose. The visit was one of many that had already taken place in the highly complicated course of the negotiations with the bureaucy, and Sabancı and the Ford representative waited for a long time to see the director of the Organization. While they were waiting, the Ford representative asked Sabancı about a number of photographs on the wall. When he learned that they were those of the past directors of the organization, he wanted to know when the latter was formed. According to Sabancı, after having divided the age of the organization by the number of directors, he jumped up and announced that he was leaving immediately since it was utterly impossible to make a healthy deal with an organization whose directors spend an average period of less than nine months in office![152]

In general, among the businessmen that I interviewed, even the ones who referred to bureaucratic impediments as a major source of their business difficulties did not elaborate their point in reference to the bureaucratic process, but to the frequency of policy change and the ambiguity of policy content. According to them, it was these changes and ambiguities which enabled bureaucrats to create obstacles for businessmen.

One of my interviewees referred to another factor which, in his view, tends to paralyze the bureaucracy. This factor has to do with the extent of particularism in state-business relations in Turkey. As my interviewee put it,

> He who manages to explain his case to the Prime Minister or the minister concerned solves his problem. You go to Işın Çelebi [one of the ministers responsible for the economy], you cry on his shoulder and he says 'O.K., I'll find you the necessary funds.' When the Central Bank says that the funds are not available, the minister orders the transfer of funds from one budget to the other. This leads to interferences at all levels of the bureaucratic process. And, of course, you are very happy because your problem is solved. You tell others what a nice, understanding person the minister is, and how nicely he has solved your problem. But the institutions cannot function under these circumstances, the State Planning Organization cannot function, the Treasury and the Central Bank cannot function. Institutionalization becomes impossible.

The disregard for the established course of bureaucratic process was, in fact, a typical aspect of the period when the MP was in power. Also typical of this period was the ease with which the legal system was modified to conform the requirements of economic and social policy objectives, or, simply, the interests of the ruling politicians. While the self-serving behavior on the part of politicians could not, of course, be publicly justified, economic wealth of the nation was unscrupulously presented as the ultimate social goal to which the state institutions should serve even at the expense of the violation of existing legal provisions. This particular attitude of the MP governments toward state instititions could be best described as part of a process of "economizing the bureaucracy and law." In this process, both the bureaucratic rules and the existing legal code were seen as means to an end—namely to the development of the economy. It therefore seemed natural that modifying, reinterpreting, or circumventing legal and bureaucratic rules should be regarded as perfectly legitimate acts when economic circumstances so dictated. Consequently, it was totally out of place to make a big fuss about violations of law. As Prime Minister Özal put it in a much quoted speech, "No harm would be done by violating the constitution once."

Many individuals, especially those in the legal profession, were quite justifiably shocked by this attitude which became an integral part of the official ideology in the 1980s.[153] However, it should be admitted that the attitude in question is not entirely peculiar to this period of MP rule, and it can be found reflected in many decisions throughout the Republican period in which the unsettled character of main social institutions and a strictly pragmatic approach to policy-making have marked the political process. Hence, not only in the 1980s, but in the post–1923 period in general, the legal system could not form a stable framework in which state-business relations could take place according to a well-defined and unchanging set of rules. Even the fact that Turkey had four constitutions (1921, 1924, 1961, and 1982) and four constitutional changes (1923, 1928, 1937, and 1971) in the course of the last eighty-year period, and that a major constitutional change is currently on the agenda is probably a sufficiently strong indication of the limitations of the legal system in contributing to the establishment of a stable policy network.

Concerning the role that the legal system plays in state-business relations in Turkey, one could make six observations . The first observation refers to the weakness of the legal basis of property in Turkey. In this regard, it would be interesting to note that, until 1982, private property rights were not included in the section on individual rights of the Turkish constitution, but were among the social and economic rights.[154] The ambiguities in the boundaries of property rights mainly pertain to landed property, but are of a nature to create similar ambiguities in other areas. This seems to be one of the reasons why businessmen, even when they have no interests associated with landed property, have repeatedly opposed the recurrent land reform projects which have periodically come into the agenda with no results obtained.

City property has also not been immune to similar legal ambiguities. Confiscation of land and buildings in cities for the purposes of municipal development has always been a largely arbitrary process, especially as regards the settlement of indemnization payments. Especially in the 1950s, one could hardly find a single day when the newspapers did not report a case involving the settlement of disputes over confiscated property. A guite amusing advertisement that appeared in a newspaper is interesting as it shows the extent of such confiscations in the 1950s. The text reads, " Do not despair because your house is confiscated. Our company has many parcels of land in close vicinity to the city center and offers you a hand to construct your new home"![155] Around the same period—as an indication of both the significance of and the legal and administrative confusion around the same issue—a question asked in a final examination given to the students of the Faculty of Law appeared as a news item . The question had to do with the powers of the Prime Minister in decisions pertaining to the confiscation of city property.[156]

The issuing of building permits for construction projects also has always remained a process in which both the rules and the office determining the rules continiously change, creating or destroying rents for the individuals involved. These uncertainties about property rights in real estate appear to be particularly important if one considers the magnitude of the rents involved, and, as will be discussed in the next chapter, the extent of businessmen's involvement in real estate speculation.

The second observation refers to legal changes which accord extraordinary powers to the ruling government, and which thus modify the domain of legitimate government intervention. The National Defense Law of 1940 and the Economic Measures Bill of the DP government constitute prominent examples in this area. Changes made by the MP government to extend the scope of policy decisions which can be taken by prime ministrial decree without parliamentary approval can also be evaluated under this category. There were also unsuccessful attempts to similarly extend the scope of government intervention which failed because as a of popular reaction. One such aborted attempt was undertaken after the military coup of 1960 to include in the text of the new constitution certain provisions enabling the government to make full use of the objects of private property or to take over private enterprises under extraordinary circumstances.[157]

Third, Turkish governments have a tendency to pass retroactive laws which sometimes exercise a devastating effect on business activities. Still more important than this effect is the impact on the business mentality of the possibility of retroactive legal changes.[158] Implications of the DP's electoral victory in 1954, for example, was discussed by some writers in reference to such retroactive changes and already mentioned extensions of the legitimate domain of intervention. "If such a political victory took place in one of the European democracies," wrote Şerif Mardin, "the only concern that might emerge would pertain to the ability of the ruling party to implement its already known program without any checks from the opposition. In our country, on the contrary, the changes that would be made in an unknown area becomes a matter of concern. Will the government pass retroactive laws? What kind of limitations will it impose on the acquired legal rights of individuals?"[159]

A fourth tendency of Turkish governments is to disregard legal provisions for practical purposes. A typical example of this tendency is presented by a 1959 decree enabling importers to make foreign currency payments for goods imported without being given an import permit and without using the officially allocated foreign exchange. It was quite clear at the time that the source of funds to be thus used by the importer was the foreign exchange illegally transferred and kept abroad through the violation of the then prevailing Law for the Protection of Turkish Currency. The government in power had not felt the need to amend the Law, but had just decided to overlook its violation in order to channel the much needed foreign currency into the country.[160]

Another important characteristic of the legal framework of state-business relations in Turkey is the incapacity to mobilize law for the settlement of problems engendered by policy implementation. The same incapacity extends even to cases in which the government simply does not honor a contract concluded with a businessman. In the course of my interviews, I have heard many complaints about such cases, but have not come across any attempt to take legal action. In fact, most businessmen seemed to be genuinely surprised when I asked them whether they had considered such a possibility. It is interesting that a lawyer whom I interviewed on the subject also appeared to regard court action by businessmen against the government to be quite unusual. "Whom would they sue?" he asked. "The state?[161]

A final observation about the legal system as a mechanism of intermediation in government-business relations has to do with the tendency of the government to have recourse to policy change when it fails to punish those who legally abuse a given policy. The rather abrupt elimination of export tax rebates in 1988, for example, was in part, a result of the incapacity to effectively mobilize law to prevent overinvoicing practices. A related problem is the lack of clarity between illegal acts and behavior which is simply not conducive to the fulfillment of national economic goals. A particular policy discourse in which the whole business community is implicated in accusations directed against those engaged in criminal acts is a distinct characteristic of state-business relations in Turkey. Equally frequent are the declarations of government authorities denouncing perfectly legal acts which are simply not in conformity with policy objectives as if they constitute a crime. There were times when this type of policy discourse was so frequent and so strong that it led business representatives to ask the government authorities "not to treat them as thieves wearing ties"![162]

The problem here is not, of course, the hurt feelings of businessmen. This particular nature of the legal system through which government-business relations are mediated has highly negative implications, first and foremost, for the business morality in the country. Given the characteristics of the legal framework of their relations with the state, businessmen, as do their governments, begin to regard law as something which can be manipulated, circumvented, or even violated. It becomes, in any event, a debatable subject whether it is stupid or not to abide by law even when it is possible to do otherwise for one's business interests, and without much risk. In this situation, the dividing line between honesty and incompetent entrepreneurship could indeed become quite shady.

In a country where rumors about wealth accumulation through illicit deals with state authorities are frequent—and, at times, well-founded—the significance of this ambiguity for business ethics is quite clear. In this setting, the ambiguities concerning the legal basis of business activity complement the widely shared idea that business success is, more than anything else, contingent upon the manipulation of political and bureaucratic decision-making processes. Business activity thus acquires a rather unpleasant social image. The most important problem in this regard appears as the internalization of this social image by businessmen themselves, with the decreasing significance attached to the adherence to a sound business ethic as its likely consequence. Moreover, given the prevailing social image of business which is partly internalized by businessmen, the latter often try to dissociate themselves from their peers and avoid showing an allegiance to their professional group. This was reflected, for example, in the attitudes of the businessmen that I interviewed. I have found it quite typical that in the course of these interviews most of the interviewees referred to the business community in the third person plural as "they," rather than in the first person plural as "us."

With their outlook and behavior thus shaped, as isolated individuals without much community spirit, Turkish businessmen try to maximize the opportunities and avoid the risks that stem from the policy process, relying more on relationships of personal trust than on their professional organizations to overcome their difficulties. The organizational form of Turkish holding companies, in fact, closely reflects these characteristics of business activity. The structure of activity diversification within these companies can be largely explained with reference to instincts for survival in a turbulent environment, as well as to shrewd strategies designed to make the best of the opportunities created by frequent policy changes. Both the launching and management of these activities, in turn, requires the maintenance of close and amicable ties with the state. On the other hand, given their importance for the national economy, holding companies have a considerable ability to have access to special favors in direct contact with government authorities without the intermediation of associations.

These companies are generally managed by members of the family of the owner rather than by professional managers. This appears to be quite logical in an environment where the ambiguities concerning the social legitimacy and the legal basis of business activity render the personal confidence factor to be very important. As it will be discussed in the following chapter, in the Turkish context, one also finds other societal factors which accompany the desire to maintain the family character of holding companies and which contribute to the ability to do so. With the general characteristics of its strategy and structure, the Turkish holding company, thus, appears as a social institution in which many features of the business environment in the country are manifested.

# 4. The Turkish Holding Company as a Social Institution

Multiactivity firms organized in the form of holding companies constitute the typical big business unit in Turkey. In this chapter, the Turkish holding company is analyzed, first, as a response to the requirements of late industrialization. As such, it shares many common features with multiactivity firms found in other late-industrializing countries. Yet, the Turkish holding company forms, at the same time, an integral part of the Turkish society and reflects the typical characteristics of the social and political framework of entrepreneurship in this country. The chapter approaches this particular form of business organization with reference to the characteristics both of late industrialization and of the societal context of enterpreneurship in Turkey. This discussion addresses itself to certain issues which pertain to the relationship between entrepreneurship and industrial organization on the one hand, and industrial organization and the social structure of the country on the other.

It is, of course, possible to find, in history of economic thought, a fairly extensive body of analysis on entrepreneurship and the centrality of the entrepreneur in capitalist development. Nevertheless, this literature—which includes the path-breaking contribution of Joseph Schumpeter as well as the post–World War II analyses of the role of entrepreneurship in economic development—largely neglects the relationship between entrepreneurship and the structure of the business enterprise. A prominent exception to this neglect is Alfred Chandler's *Strategy and Structure*, in which strategic decisions concerning the growth and activity diversification of the business enterprise are studied in relation to organizational changes affecting the entrepreneurial function.[1] In fact, some of the theses put forward in Chandler's study forms a significant part of common wisdom in the area of business organizations. For the purposes of this chapter, it would also be useful to revisit these theses and explore their relevance for a study of the institutional context of business activity in a late-industrializing country.

In his approach to American business history, one of the points that Chandler underlines is the crucial significance of market forces in affecting the strategic business decisions concerning growth and diversification. Hence, he explicitly states that antitrust laws, tax regulations, or labor and welfare legislation had much less impact on the historical development of the American business enterprise than the nature of the market forces determining the supply of inputs and demand for final products.[2] Given the type of concerns central to the present study, this constitutes a statement which must be qualified in relation to the market-forming role of the state in late-industrializing countries. When the state appears as a crucial factor in determining the boundaries of private sector activity, enterprise growth and business activity diversification could hardly be analyzed by placing the emphasis on the market on the basis of a conceptual dichotomy between the market and the state. In the context of late industrialization, it becomes necessary, therefore, to consider the nature of the policy process as a key variable in determining the business strategy—either directly or indirectly—via its market-shaping impact.

The second thesis which has a central place in Chandler's study has to do with the stages of structural development of businesss enterprises. According to Chandler, ownership and control of business enterprises pass through a historical transition process in three stages. In the first stage, one finds "personal enterprises" in which both management and investment decisions are taken by the owners. In the second stage, there are "entrepreneurial enterprises" in which strategic decisions pertaining to the long-term growth of the enterprise are taken by the owners while the managers are now in a position to take routine management decisions. The final stage is characterized by a situation in which the ownership is widely diffused, and the founding family has little say in the management of the enterprise which is largely carried out by salaried managers.

In this last stage, the latter make routine managerial decisions and also assume long-term strategic planning functions. What Chandler has in mind is, therefore, a process in which ownership is increasingly separated from management, and the role of the founding family in enterprise management gradually becomes negligible.

This particular thesis also needs some qualification with reference to the actual state of enterprise management, not only in late-industrializing countries, but also in developed industrialized countries. More specifically, one needs to first ask whether the role of the founding family in controlling the business enterprise is really as negligible as the Chandler thesis implies. Much more significant than this question is, however, questions pertaining to the societal factors which hamper or promote the professionalization of management and the decline of family control. Therefore, rather than taking Chandler's stages as given, it would be more interesting to dwell upon the environmental factors which determine both the ownership and management structure of the business enterprise, and the implications of this particular structure for the overall economic development performance of the country.

In fact, an analysis of the group phenonenon in late-industrializing countries calls for such an approach that would explore both the reasons behind the significance of economic concentration in late-industrializing countries, and the implications of a particular type of concentration on economic development. In this area, one must make a distinction between two different aspects of economic concentration. Economic concentration has to do, first, with the market share of a given number of enterprises. However, it also has to do with the control exercised by certain groups of affiliated enterprises in different markets. It is particularly this second type of control by multiactivity enterprises that forms a particular characteristic of many developing countries. Consequently, the second dimension of the problem of economic concentration appears as an interesting issue to be explored in development studies.

Groups of affiliated enterprises hold a considerable proportion of industrial and commercial assets and play a significant role in the economies of many late-industrializing countries of different levels of development such as Brazil, Mexico, Malaysia, Kenya, Nigeria, Pakistan, India, and South Korea.[3] The Indian managing agency system—which emerged in the nineteenth century and was abolished in the 1970s—probably constitutes one of the first institutional forms designed to respond to the same needs that lead to the significance of the group phenomenon in many late-industrializing countries. More specifically, the Indian managing agency system appears to be a response to the shortage of entrepreneurial talent and venture capital. As such, it forms a type of industrial organization in which the operations of several apparently independent enterprises is controlled by a single agency firm. While this control might be exercised on the basis of a management contract, a form of financial holding, or different share-holding and voting arrangements, regardless of the instrument of control chosen by the managing agency firm remains as *the firm*—that is, the institutional setting in which entrepreneurial decisions are made.[4]

This type of centralized organization of highly diversified activities is also observed in other late-industrializing countries which today form part of the developed world. Germany and Japan constitute typical examples in this regard.[5] In both countries, one observes that the historical emergence of activity diversification as an enterprise growth strategy preceeds the appearance of the same growth strategy in earlier industrializers such as the United Kingdom or the United States. This suggests that it is the state of the domestic and international markets under conditions of late industrialization which are partly instrumental in the emergence of the diversified conglomerate. The centralized organizational structure of the latter responds, in turn, to similar factors which have led to the emergence of the managing agency firm in India, such as the shortage of entrepreneurship and venture capital. One observes, in the case of both Japanese and German multiactivity firms, that financial requirements are met through a group bank which also performs the function of coordination. Both countries have a long experience with bank-coordinated activity, and the part of enterprise financing that comes from the sale of equity shares is still much lower than it is in the United Kingdom or the United States.

Compared to Chandler's account of the strategic growth of American enterprises, the pattern of growth and development of Japanese and German firms show some divegences. Unlike the situation in the United States, where growth has preceeded diversification, in Germany and Japan, the activity of diversification has taken place at a relatively low stage of enterprise growth and has led to further growth of the enterprise. Moreover, the policy environment reflected, for example, in the absence of American style antitrust laws or tax regulations affecting the formation of joint stock companies, has exercised a nonnegligible impact on enterprise strategy and structure.[6] Nevertheless, to the extent that the phenomenon of late industrialization is reflected in the size and structure of domestic and international markets, as well as in the supply and demand conditions prevailing in factor markets, the two cases in question could be said to conform to the first Chandler thesis on the predominance of market forces over political factors. A real challenge to this thesis is presented, however, by the circumstances under which multiactivity firms emerged in some developing countries in the post–World War II era. In this regard, the case of South Korea—where the state has actually encouraged and led the process whereby a few giant firms, the chaebol, expanded their control over many unrelated fields of activity—is quite striking.[7] As it encouraged the strategy of diversification a few decades ago, the South Korean state is today exercising an equally significant impact on enterprise strategy by forcing the chaebol to limit their activities to three sectors of their choice. While it has been reported that the enterprises show some resistance to this particular move of the state in favor of specialization, the incident is important to show the extent to which political factors could be significant in shaping the patterns of enterprise growth in a developing economy.[8] As it will be discussed in this chapter, the case of Turkish multiactivity firms also constitutes an example in this regard.

In these examples, state policy also reflects the same factors concerning the supply of capital and entrepreneurial talent that leads to the emergence of multiactivity firms. There is, nevertheless, another factor of crucial significance which should be taken into account in explaining this wide-spread group phenomenon. In many contexts, the organizational form of the diversified enterprise, in which the control functions are highly centralized in a managing agency firm, a bank, or a holding company, reflects an attempt to assure the continuing dominance of the founding family over many divers fields of activity. In fact, in spite of the individualistic approach generally adopted in theoretical studies on entrepreneurship, historical analyses of business enterprises often highlight the crucial significance of the family as the relevant unit of analysis. These enterprise histories provide many examples in which the collective ownership of the family property is maintained through rules defined in the family code. The Krupp code, for example, was based on a type of primogeniture with the shares of the other children held in the inheritance of the eldest who, thus, ceased to be the sole owner of the property which he inherited. The Du Pont code, on the other hand, involved a partnership among three male members of the family. When a partner died, his children did not inherit his share. Instead, a new partner was chosen among the the young members of the family.[9]

In many instances, these family codes continue to be effective in determining the pattern of inheritance, even when they conflict with the legal code prevailing in the country. As they have resisted legal changes taking place in society, entrepreneurial families have also not yielded easily to new financial and managerial requirements which were often incompatible with the maintainance of family control. What Landes writes, for example, about the stubborn refusal of the French entrepreneurial families to use easy credit resources which would alleviate family control over business operations[10] may not be a peculiarity of the French society. Many entrepreneurial families in different societies seem to have acted similarly and have tried to maintain the family control often by refusing to yield to economic necessity. When traditional family structures have eroded, novel mechanisms of sustained family control were found. The formation of holdings in which a centralized management structure was eradicated with a view to assuring optimal use of the entrepreneurial resources available to the family was one of these mechanisms. The increasing organizational complexity of the firm and the ensuing managerial requirements were confronted by the transfer of only nonstrategic decisions to professional managers while fostering managerial skills in talented family members.

As suggested by the preceeding discussion, activity diversification appears at an earlier stage of enterprise growth than elsewhere in an environment in which markets are limited and resources are scarce. In such an environment, a centrally managed multiactivity firm contributes to the optimal use of scarce investment funds and entrepreneurial talent. This is true for both the resources available to the economy as a whole, and to those held by the founding family. Hence, the Indian managing agency firms, the Japanese zaibatsu (and later keiretsu), the Korean chaebol, or the Turkish holding companies form ways of extending family control over the enterprises. It is stated that, not only in late-industrializing countries but even in England, many of the multiunit enterprises, to the extent that they existed—albeit to a much limited extent than in late-industrializing countries—in certain sectors at the turn of the nineteenth century adopted a loose holding form and remained essentially as federations of family firms.[11] The formation of financial holdings constitute, along with other arrangements such as family trusts and preferential shares, the ways in which the French family firms attempted to hold on to their past organizational structures.[12] The same devices were also used to sustain family control over the management of large Italian enterprises.[13] As a result of such sustained attempts of the founding families against the separation of ownership and control, the advent of the managerial enterprise appears as a much slower and less easily completed process than as implied by in the second thesis of Chandler concerning the stages of industrial organization. Such arrangements delay the advent of the joint stock company, or render possible its coexistance with the continuing significance of the managerial role played by the family.

Some recent studies show, in fact, that this role is still much more important than it is implied by Chandler's analysis or by the extensive literature on the so-called "managerial revolution." It is widely accepted today that family majority shareholdings or different forms of family control in the absence of majority shareholding are more common than the earlier research had suggested, both in Europe and in the Anglo-Saxon world. One currently observes, moreover, an increasingly significant questioning of the hitherto accepted relationship between professionalization and successful management.[14] At a more theoretical level, it is argued that the entrepreneur is more likely to be the owner of investment resources than a simple professional because the typical entrepreneurial attributes of originality and risk-taking are not widely shared, and a noncapital owning individual with these attributes would find it quite difficult to convince potential investors of the likely success of his projects.[15]

Nevertheless, even those who reject the existence of a managerial revolution and underline the continuing significance of family management accept that there has been a slow evolutionary change toward the professionalization of management.[16] As is the tendency to counter this trend, the trend itself is one which is present in different societies. Yet, the accounts of this process in different countries suggest that both the pace and the pattern of the change are determined by institutional and political factors as much as market-generated ones. In some cases—as in the Japanese zaibatsu—direct political action was taken to break the family control over the big business enterprise.[17] Also, in the absence of such direct intervention, sociopolitical factors—such as the characteristics of banking systems and financial markets, possibility of access to subsidized credit, tax legislation, and general characteristics of the policy process—all play a role in determining, not only the possibility of holding on to the structures of family management, but also the strength of the desire to do so.

In this regard, cultural factors reflected in the nature of the family as a social institution also undoubtedly play a role. For example, Japanese family codes, which prevailed well into the twentieth century, appear to be more strict than those found in any other society in limiting the private ownership of property by family members. Yet, with the aid of the Japanese adoption laws, they also allowed the introduction of new managerial talent into the family enterprise. Hence, although the house leadership was to be inherited by the eldest son in each generation, adopted sons, often chosen among the employees of the enterprise, could sometimes assume the leadership role when blood children were judged to be inadequate.[18] Contrasting with the Japanese situation is the Korean case in which inheritance rules do not allow for primogeniture nor the choice of a qualified heir, but require the division of property among family members. Moreover, the Korean family appears to be strictly patrilineal, with adoption rules allowing only for the adoption of a blood relative of the father who cannot become the legal heir as long as there is a living son. In fact, the character of the Korean family is sometimes contrasted with that of the Japanese family in comparative analyses of enterprise structure in these countries.[19]

The impact of such cultural factors might be offset, however, by forces emanating from the economic and political context of business activity as suggested, for example, by the contrast between David Landes's account of the French family firm and Ezra Suleiman's analysis of the professionally managed big enterprises in the same country at a later stage.[20] The extent to which the multiactivity firms could—and would—remain under the control of the founding family is determined, therefore, by different societal factors with divers effects on the enterprise management structure. In the following discussion of the Turkish holding company, it is also argued that the implications of this form of industrial organization for the success of the firm, and also its contribution to economic and social development are likely to be determined by the societal environment in which it functions. It is in this sense that the multiactivity firm appears, not as a universal economic category, but as a social institution.

This approach to the enterprise group as a social institution contrasts with certain analyses of the same phenomenon from a perspective marked by a methodological individualism based on the economic rationality postulate of the standard microeconomic theory. The latter is, for example, the perspective adopted by Nathaniel H. Leff's analysis of economic groups in developing countries.[21] Leff's study of group activity is largely an extension of the standard theory of entrepreneurship, and draws from Leibenstein's classical article on entrepreneurship in developing countries.[22] Factor market imperfections and the significance of risk and uncertainty appear here to be the key obstacles that the entrepreneur should overcome. In this analysis, the absence of organized capital markets which would distribute risk and uncertainty over a large number of individuals, and the shortage of entrepreneurial talent form the main constraints that should be dealt with. In this framework, Leff studies the group "as a pattern of industrial organization which permits structure rather than gifted individuals to perform the key interactivity function of entrepreneurship."[23] According to him, in developing countries, "this institution has permitted 'pure' Schumpeterian entrepreneurship to become effective."[24] He also believes that "the coordination of investment and production decisions by the group has both reduced the need and lessened the burden on government planning of the modern sector in developing countries."[25]

In a recent article on Japanese multiactivity firms, the keiretsu, Richard Jankowski also highlights the implications of group activity for macroeconomic planning. The starting point of Jankowski's analysis is Mancur Olson's much debated work on the role of interest groups in the "rise and decline of nations." Olson's distinction between the social implications of small organizations representing narrow interest groups and those of broad-based encompassing organizations forms the basis of Jankowski's analysis.[26] In this framework, the analysis is shaped around the idea that encompassing organizations, which represent a variety of interests spread over several sectors, are more likely to exert political pressure for growth-oriented policies than are small organizations that represent the interests of the producers of a single commodity. Economic growth on a national scale appears as a more meaningful objective to the former because they are more likely to have a broader perspective, given the size and scope of their constituency that would see their incomes increasing with the growth of the national product. In a parallel fashion, Jankowski argues that, unlike the activities of firms operating in a single branch, the pursuit of interests by horizontally integrated multiactivity firms involves a global management of interests over a wide variety of sectors. These multiactivity firms, therefore, tend to support "public good" policies rather than narrow self-interest. In other words, according to Jankowski, "the public good becomes the self-interest of the diversified conglomerate."[27]

Both these studies approach the implications of enterprise growth and diversification through a logical deduction process starting with the pursuit of private interest as the key explanatory factor of economic behavior. Their conclusions are logically derived from the individual pursuit of interest as the basic premise of microeconomic theory. In fact, Leff makes this particular methodological choice explicit as he writes that his study "has also provided an example of the now well-documented point that economic theory can be relevant beyond the more advanced countries where it was first developed. Thus, standard microeconomic concepts help explain the emergence of the group institutional pattern, a phenomenon which might easily be attributed exclusively to sociocultural or political conditions."[28]

Without attemping to explain the group phenomenon solely on the basis of sociocultural or political factors, I will, nevertheless, argue, in the following section, that such extraeconomic factors are crucial for the adequate analysis of the phenomenon in question. The Turkish holding company will, therefore, be presented as a social institution which both reflects and serves to maintain the particular characteristics of the business environment in the country. In this context, the nature of the role the state plays in the economy will be revisited as a significant factor which directs the strategy of activity diversification adopted by big Turkish enterprises. The political context of business activity will again be evoked in the discussion of the desire and the ability of Turkish businessmen to run their holding companies as family-managed organizations. The impact of this particular form of business organization on business outlook and behavior, as it appears in Turkey, will be discussed in the final section of this chapter, which is on the social and economic impact of holding activity in Turkey.

## THE PLACE OF HOLDING COMPANIES IN TURKISH ECONOMY

Reliable numerical estimations of the significance of holding companies in Turkish national production and income are rather difficult to provide because statistical data at the holding level of business is extremely scarce. Governmental agencies responsible for data collection and research as well as business associations of different types provide data on enterprises rather than on business at the holding company level. As to the annual reports of holding companies themselves, they are neither easy to obtain nor is the statistical information which they present of great reliability. As a result, it proves difficult to find even a complete list of holding companies presently active in the country. An incomplete list compiled by the Union of Chambers in 1988 names eighty companies. Although this list does not represent even half of the holdings in existence at this date, it is useful, perhaps, to give a rough estimate of their regional distribution. It shows that sixty-two of the eighty companies listed are situated in Istanbul. Seven are in Ankara, three in Izmir, two in Adana, two in Trabzon, and one each in Bursa, Gaziantep, Elazığ, and Erzurum. Some of these holding companies whose head offices are not in Istanbul have large economic significance at a national level. For example, Özsaruhan, Özakat and Raks Holding of Izmir, Okan Holding of Gaziantep, and Sönmez Holding of Bursa are among the important multiactivity enterprises in terms of the number of companies they control in industry, finance, and services as well as the economic significance of their operations.[29] Nevertheless, the numerical significance of these regional holdings remains quite limited, and the large majority of Turkish holding companies are based in Istanbul. A complete list of 210 holding companies based in Istanbul as of April 1990 compiled by the Istanbul Chamber of Commerce can thus be taken as representing most of the multiactivity groups in Turkey.

The information given by the Istanbul Chamber of Commerce indicates that thirteen of these enterprise groups became holding companies in the 1960s, ninety-six in the 1970s, eighty-seven in the 1980s, and six during the first quarter of 1990. These companies are not, quite naturally, of equal size and significance. Along with companies such as Sabancı, which has more than sixty enterprises in many different sectors of industry, finance, and services, there are holding companies, such as the Vakko group in clothing, with only two or three firms situated in the same sector. Unlike the Vakko group, some of these holding companies of limited activity diversification exist only on paper. They were baptized as "slum holdings" by the owner/manager of a well established holding company in textiles whome I interviewed. The motives behind the formation of these slum holdings will be discussed later, along with factors that led to the increasing importance of holding companies in Turkey. Before entering into this discussion, it would be useful, however, to refer to several indicators which reveal the economic significance of multiactivity groups in the country.

It is possible, for example, to get a fairly accurate idea about the place of these groups in Turkish economy by looking at their position among the 500 largest companies in Turkey. According to the 1988 annual survey of the Istanbul Chamber of Industry, the largest 500 companies consisted of 95 public and 405 private firms. Of these 405 firms listed as private enterprises, 9 belong to producers' cooperatives. Only 70 of the remaining ones appear as independent firms, with the shares of 314 of the largest 500 enterprises held by either one or more groups. Five large holding companies— Koç, Sabancı, Yasar, Anadolu Endüstri, and Çukurova Holding— appear as the shareholders of 85 companies among the 500 largest. It is also significant that in the ranking of these 500 companies, none of the independent enterprises appear among the first 250. In fact, most of the independents are ranked among the last 100.[30]

Another indication of the economic significance of large multi-activity firms is the nature of their relationship with Foreign Trade Companies which played such an important role in the export sector in the 1980s, as well as the extent of their involvement in the financial sector. In the second half of the 1980s, the share of Foreign Trade Companies in total exports reached around 50 percent. As shown in Table 4.1, overwhelming majority of the Foreign Trade

Companies operating in this period were set up as the exporting subsidiaries of large holding companies and were controlled by the central management of the group.

The role of multiactivity firms in the financial sector is equally important. As of September 1988, of the ten Turkish banks that held about 80 percent of the assets of deposit banks, four were state banks, and four were group-owned by Sabancı, Çukurova, and Doğuş. There is one bank owned and managed by its employee pension fund—Türk Ticaret Bankası. The tenth one, İş Bankası, has a rather peculiar legal structure and constitutes, in itself, a quasi-private group. After the post–1980 changes in banking regulations, the groups also began to play an important role in the newly flourishing trade/investment banking sector by forming joint ventures with foreign banks.[31]

Holding companies have also played an important role in the recent increase in foreign direct investment through the formation of joint ventures with foreign firms investing in Turkey. In 1989, we find—among the five hundred largest companies operating in Turkey—seventy-two that have a foreign firm as one of the investors. In thirteen of these seventy-two firms, there is either no Turkish partner or one with limited percentage of shares—usually less than 2 percent. Of the remaining firms, five have a public company as its Turkish partner while, in forty-seven businesses, the Turkish partner is an affiliate of a holding company. Among these partly foreign-owned firms, there is only one that is not group affiliated.[32]

As it would be noticed, I have been using the terms *multiactivity group* and *holding company* interchangeably. There are two reasons for this particular use of terminology. First, as the following discussion will indicate, there is little difference between the ownership and management structures of holding companies and other multiactivity enterprises. Both involve diversified activities under the centralized control of the family of owners. Second, the multiactivity groups of significance that have not organized themselves as holding companies are quite rare. Until recently, there were two prominent exceptions to this rule—The famous Altınyıldız Group in textiles and the Koçtuğ group in maritime transportation. The first group eventually established itself as a holding company in 1991. In the course of my interviews conducted in 1990 with the owner/managers of both groups, I was told that it would be reasonable to establish a holding company, but that it was just too complicated to go through all the accounts and do the necessary paper work at that stage. One of them has obviously thought, since then, that the advantages were worth the necessary work. The management of the second group would also perhaps come to the same conclusion at some point.

What, then, are the advantages of adopting the holding-company form of business in Turkey? In fact, three possible motives might well be of different significance for enterprise groups of dissimilar activity diversification patterns.

The most widely accepted motive behind the proliferation of holding companies in Turkey has to do with tax advantages associated with this type of industrial organization. Changes that were made in the corporate taxation system in the first half of the 1960s, indeed, rendered the holding form of business to be quite attractive for private sector firms. The most important change in this regard was the elimination of double taxation by making the revenues that the central holding company earned from its participations in affiliated firms tax exempt. While this exemption was abolished with changes made in 1986, certain other tax advantages still remain. For example, while the holding company is required to pay taxes on revenues from its participations, these taxes are payable only in the following year. In an environment of high inflation, this obviously constitutes an important advantage.[33]

An indirect—albeit very significant—tax advantage still enjoyed by holding companies is the ability to allocate costs and benefits among affiliated enterprises and, thus, to minimize the tax burden. This possibility is, in fact, exploited to its very limits in a way as to make all the operations within the group subservient to the requirements of financial management. Another important advantage enjoyed by holding companies in this process of financial management has to do with their abilities to realize capital increases through the revaluation of the shares of affiliated companies which are then transferred to the central holding firm.[34]

These financial advantages have been undoubtedly important in the increasing pace of the formation of holding companies in Turkey beginning with the mid–1960s. It is, nevertheless, significant to note that there was an interest among certain Turkish businessmen in the adoption of the holding form prior to changes made in the corporate tax law. In fact, it was clearly the business community itself that initiated legal changes which fostered formation of holding companies. The context in which original private sector demands concerning the legal basis of holding companies naturally highlights another reason for making this form of industrial organization so attractive to Turkish businessmen. One of the first examples in which private sector demands for elimination of double corporate taxation to render the adoption of holding companies feasible were formally pronounced was in a report prepared and presented to the government by the Union of Chambers on legal provisions for the establishment of family foundations. In this document, it is stated that Turkish businessmen would like to establish foundations on the basis of revenues generated within a holding-type structure, had the double taxation of corporate income not made the latter so unattractive as a form of industrial organization. It is mentioned, in the document in question, that the Union of Chambers was preparing another report to present its suggestions on the amendment of existing tax legislation concerning holding companies.[35]

It is not accidental that the demands for legal amendments concerning these two issues—family foundations and holding companies—were brought onto the agenda at about the same time. Both were presented as measures to assure the continuity of the family name and family business, and arguments to this effect were substantiated with reference to many wealthy individuals whose fortunes were dissipated after their deaths. "We do not have, in this country, one single business organization which is a hundred years old" is a statement that often accompanied these arguments.[36]

As was revealed in the course of my interviews with businessmen, this concern about the survival of family business was, and is still is, one of the most important factors leading to the recognition of the need to restructure enterprise management. As it has emerged after 1963—with the first step in this area undertaken by Koç—the holding company was clearly a response to this need. As with holding companies in general, Turkish holding companies were established to purchase the shares of other firms. In Turkey, however, they have operated from the very beginning as management units that maintain an active entrepreneurial participation in their manifold activities. The latter are controlled—as they were controlled before the advent of the holding firm—by the members of the founding family. The professionalization in this context does not imply the ebbing of family control. On the contrary, as they have prevailed in Turkey, attempts to professionalize management through adoption of the holding form of business organization were mainly directed at enabling family members to maintain a centralized control over activities covering a large number of sectors.[37]

Thus, interest in holding companies emerged first as a response to managerial needs of multiactivity family firms and then to business pressures for legislative changes that have later enhanced the attractiveness of this particular organizational form of business. In the 1960s and 1970s, owner/managers of many big multiactivity firms established themselves as holding companies because Koç had done so. In his autobiography, Sakıp Sabancı explicitly refers to the importance of the example provided by Koç in their managerial restructuring as a holding company. In fact, he writes that, as a family group, they have always very closely followed developments in the Koç group and tried to adapt them to their own establishment.[38] That this attitude is not peculiar to the Sabancı group was confirmed many times in the course of my interviews when several businessmen told me that, in many areas, the Koç group often presents an example to be emulated by the business community.

While several well-established multiactivity firms have adopted the holding company format by following the example provided by Koç, in later stages—especially in the 1980s—many aspiring entrepreneurs have emulated these groups in general by establishing themselves as holding companies from the outset. In the case of these new businessmen, a third and prestige-related motive seems to have played a more important role than did financial or managerial concerns. In fact, some of the managers of old and well-established companies seem to be quite sarcastic about the term *holding company*. "It is now fashionable to call your enterprise a holding," one of them told me. "To establish a holding company, all you need is TL 500,000 [less than $250 then, less than $100 today]. Then you appear to be more important than an ordinary businessman." When I asked him how this prestige associated with having a holding company was used, I was told that it was expected to be useful especially in relations with the state. Access to different types of state privileges, such as state-leased real estate for touristic establishments, is thought to be facilitated by the favorable impression created by the holding company label. When the prestige factor appears as the dominant motive for a company establishing itself as a holding firm, the extent of diversification can be very limited. For the purposes of this study, holding companies are of interest, not as legal structures, but as multiactivity groups with highly diversified activity bases. Nevertheless, those holding firms whose establishment has to do with the prestige factor are interesting to the extent that the attitude of their founders reveals a particular conception of the relations between big multiactivity holding companies and the state in Turkey.

In fact, this particular relationship appears to be important in two respects. It emerges, first, as an important factor shaping the diversification strategy of big Turkish companies. Second, it is shaped, in its turn, by the nature of the role which these multiactivity firms play in the economy. The first aspect of the relationship between the Turkish state and multiactivity firms tends to modify the Chandler thesis concerning the analysis of the enterprise strategy mainly as a response to market-emanated factors, and it highlights the market-shaping role of the state in Turkey. As was discussed in the second and especially the third chapters of this book, the state has often played a crucial role in the development of business enterprises by delegating willing entepreneurs to enter into ventures in designated areas. Transfers to Muslim businessmen of industrial property previously belonging to minorities have played a nonnegligible role in this process. As was mentioned in the discussion of the autobiographical material in the second chapter and in references to the developments of the 1980s in the third one, the decision to enter into a new area of activity is often taken via suggestions and recommendations of government authorities rather than through an evaluation of market signals. My interviews with businessmen also suggest that, especially in the case of construction companies, the turning point in development of the enterprise is associated with an important government contract.

In an environment of scarce entrepreneurial resources and limited capital, it is not surprising that the few individuals with previous entrepreneurial expertise would be encouraged to invest in those fields of economic activity which government authorities chose to leave to the private sector. The historical legacy of state-business relations in Turkey is also of a nature to foster this tendency. The much-emphasised distrust of state authorities toward private business and toward alternative sources of power emanating from the market might well have been instrumental in forming the preference that government authorities have had for encouraging a few large enterprises headed by trusted individuals to undertake economic functions in different fields. Under these circumstances, political connections of a particularist nature have inevitably played a role in shaping the historical development of big business enterprises and the current structure of large holding companies in Turkey.

There is, nevertheless, another important factor which must be evoked in an attempt to explain big business strategy and structure in Turkey. This factor has to do with the nature rather than the extent of state intervention in Turkish economy, and it consists in state-induced uncertainty in the economic arena. As was discussed in detail in the chapter 3 of this book, state intervention through frequent policy changes and highly discretionary forms of meddling with major economic parameters appears both as a significant source of opportunity in rent-seeking activity and as a risk-generating factor. Consequently, the activity diversification strategy of big business firm responds to this particular characteristic of the policy process and constitutes an attempt both in rent-seeking and risk-aversion.

The tendency to operate in many and often unrelated areas is, in fact, explained by many private sector representatives whom I interviewed in portfolio management terms. "You don't put all your eggs in the same basket" was an expression that was frequently used in this context. The concern for risk, in turn, is related to the erratic character of the policy process which was depicted, by the overwhelming majority of my interviewees, as the most significant characteristic of the Turkish business environment. As was also mentioned in the chapter three of this book, policy-induced business risks also form one of the dominant themes of Sakıp Sabancı's autobiography. Along with numerous examples of instability generated by the role which government plays in business life, Sabancı mentions the cases of some once very rich businessmen—Sapmaz and Süren, in particular—to show what might happen to those who do not appreciate the seriousness of the political risk factor as a dominant feature of business life in Turkey.[39]

However, as the previous discussion suggests, the state also appears as a major source of business opportunity for Turkish businessmen. It is, in other words, central to business life as the main determinant of both risks and profits. The strategy adopted by big business firms is, therefore, based on the acknowledgement of both facets of the state presence in business life as manifested in their pattern of activity diversification. Therefore, for a Turkish entrepreneur, it is important to quickly respond to opportunities stemming from policy changes, regardless of existing lines of specialization and expertise acquired in a given area. This type of unrelated diversification does not lead to exit from previous fields of activity following entry into a new field. Former activities are not abandoned, and the firm continues to grow by branching out in different directions. This particular structure of activity diversification appears to be advantageous because it helps the enterprise to spread risks over a large number of sectors and enhances the flexibility of movement between sectors which receive periodically changing degrees of preferential treatment.

As policy changes are especially frequent and unpredictable in the areas of foreign exchange and the trade regime, it appears to be particularly important to have the flexibility to move easily between import and export activities. The holding companies which have become important in the export sector through the establishment of Foreign Trade Companies in the 1970s and 1980s, for example, have never relied primarily on foreign export markets as a source of profits but have continued to remain well-rooted in production and import activities for the domestic market. Hence, toward the end of the 1980s when export activity lost its appeal as a result of changes in the incentives system and in the foreign exchange rate policy—companies began to restrict their investments in this area and retreated to other activities geared toward the domestic market.[40] A similar strategic move might be expected in the case of tourism-related activities that many holding companies undertook in the 1980s. In fact, tourism constitutes a typical sector in which the importance of government policy in the structure of activity diversification is clearly manifested. The number of companies entering in this field greatly increased in the 1980s, when this sector benefitted from a large variety of incentives. For example, of the twenty-six multiactivity companies for which I have detailed activity diversification charts, twelve have tourism-related activities. Eight of these companies entered the sector in the 1980s.[41] And, given the decline in the importance of the incentives provided to this sector, some of these companies might be expected to gradually leave the sector, and to do so without much difficulty because of the flexibility provided by their strategy of unrelated diversification.

Given this particular activity pattern of big enterprises in the country, it becomes highly difficult to approach business behavior with the aid of political economy approaches in which distinctions among sectoral localization of business interests is highlighted. It becomes largely irrelevant, for example, to refer to political choices of the business community among state policies geared toward export promotion or import substitution. Similarly, attempts to classify large multiactivity firms according to their main fields of specialization have a limited usefulness from an analytical point of view, and given the tendency to branch out in different directions which is present even in the case of the seemingly most specialized companies. In this regard, it would be interesting to compare the classification provided by the Turkish Foreign Trade Association as reproduced in table 4.1 with the activity diversification charts of eight companies presented in tables 4.2 to 4.9.

In the classification from the Turkish Foreign Trade Association, Sabancı, Yaşar, and Anadolu Endüstri Holding appear as "industrial complexes." Yet, they all have activities also in the financial sector and in services. The appropriateness of classifying Borusan as an iron and steel company is also questionable. Although the diversification strategy of this company does not appear to be as unrelated as in the case of Sabancı, Yaşar, or Anadolu Endüstri Holding, it also has highly diversified activities in machinery, automotive, construction, transportation, and marketing, as well as in iron and steel. Tekfen, which appears as a constructor [sic.] company in the Turkish Foreign Trade Association classification, has indeed started business through state contracts in construction projects. Nevertheless, it has, at present, many companies operating in sectors ranging from agriculture and food processing to tourism and banking. Altınyıldız and Akkök appear among the least diversified of the twenty-six holding companies for which I have activity diversification charts. Yet, one can see that, even in their cases, activities which have nothing to do with the main line of specialization are undertaken. Altınyıldız, an established corporation in textiles, is also involved in petroleum distribution and data processing, while Akkök, another established textile producer, is active in tourism and construction industries. It is only in the case of Tamek that

TABLE 4.1
Turkish Foreign-Trade Companies and Their Group Affiliations

| Name of Company | Year of Establishment | Source of Affiliation |
|---|---|---|
| *Industrial Complexes* | | |
| Ram | 1970 | Koç |
| Exsa | 1973 | Sabancı |
| Cam | 1976 | İş Bank |
| Mepa | 1976 | İş Bank |
| Çukurova | 1979 | Çukurova |
| Yaşar | 1971 | Yaşar |
| Erpeks | 1976 | Ercan |
| Anex | 1981 | Anadolu Endüstri |
| *Construction Companies* | | |
| Enka | 1972 | Enka |
| Tekfen | 1981 | Tekfen |
| Temel | 1982 | STFA |
| Imeks | 1974 | Doğu. |
| *Textile Companies* | | |
| Akpa | 1977 | Dinçkök |
| Edpa | 1980 | Akın |
| GDS | 1986 | Giyim San. Derneği |
| *Iron and Steel Companies* | | |
| Çukurova | 1979 | Çukurova Çelik |
| Çolakoğlu | 1982 | Çolakoğlu Metalurji |
| Meptaş | 1983 | Metaş D-C |
| Ekinciler | 1978 | Ekinciler D-C |
| İzdaş | 1981 | Izmir D-C |
| Borusan | 1975 | Borusan |
| Fepaş | 1983 | Feniş Aluminyum |
| *General Industrial and Commercial Companies* | | |
| Menteşoğlu | 1975 | Menteşoğlu |
| Penta | 1976 | Unaffiliated |
| Süzer | 1979 | Süzer |
| Okan | 1983 | Okan |
| Yavuzlar | 1982 | Yavuzlar |
| Sodimpek | 1986 | Renault Sodechanges Co. |
| Marmara | — | — |
| Taha | | |
| Bilkont | — | — |
| Batı | 1978 | Bilge |
| Eksel | 1975 | ECA |

Source: Prof. Dr. Sübidey Togan, Prof. Dr. Hasan Olgun, Assoc. Prof. Dr. Halis Akder, *Report on Developments in External Economic Relations of Turkey* (Turktrade Research Center, 1988).

TABLE 4.2
Sabancı Holding

| YEARS | TEXTILE | FOOD PROCESSING AND AGRICULTURE | TOURISM | FINANCE/ INSURANCE | CONSTRUCTION MATERIALS | PETRO-CHEMICAL INDUSTRY | PAPER AND PAPER PRODUCTS | AUTOMOTIVE AND MACHINERY | FOREIGN TRADE | DATA PROCESSING | DRUGS | ELECTRONICS/ OTHER |
|---|---|---|---|---|---|---|---|---|---|---|---|---|
| 1932 | CARDING FACTORY | | | | | | | | | | | |
| 1943 | | VEG. OIL | | | | | | | | | | |
| 1946 | | VEG. OIL | | | | | | | | | | |
| 1948 | | | HOTEL RES-TAURANT | BANK | | | | | | | | |
| 1949 | | FARM | | | | | | | | | | |
| 1951 | COTTON FABRIC | | | | | | | | | | | |
| 1953 | | FARM | | | ASBESTOS CEMENT PANELS | | | | | | | |
| 1957 | | FARM | | | | | | | | | | |
| 1958 | | CHEMICALS AND SEED | | | | | | | | | | |
| 1960 | | | | INSURANCE COMPANY | | | | | | | | |
| 1961 | | FARM | | | | | | | | | | |
| 1967 | | | | | CEMENT | NYLON THREAD | | | | | | |
| 1968 | | | | | | SYNTHETIC FIBER PLASTIC BOTTLES | | INDUSTRIAL MOTOR VEHICLES REPRESENTATION AND MARKETING | | | | |
| 1969 | | VEG. OIL | | | | PLASTIC PACKAGE | PAPER/ CARD BOARD | MARKETING | | | | |

|  |  |
|------|-----------|
| 1971 | VELVET, COTTON, SYNTHETIC THREAD |
| 1972 | CEMENT; FOREIGN TRADE |
| 1973 | WOOL THREAD AND CARPET; CORD FABRIC; DRUGS* |
| 1974 | TIRES; TWO INSURANCE COMPANIES |
| 1975 | TIRE MARKETING; DATA PROCESS |
| 1976 | CEMENT |
| 1977 | ELECTRONICS* |
| 1978 | FOREIGN TRADE/ WEST GERMANY |
| 1980 | DISTRIBUTION; FOREIGN TRADE/NEW YORK |
| 1981 | BOTTLED WATER; BANK/LONDON |
| 1984 | FOREIGN TRADE/ LONDON |
| 1985 | HOTEL; BNP-AKBANK; LIGHTING SYSTEMS |
| 1986 | WEAVING; ELECTRONICS |
| 1987 | THREAD PRODUCTION; HOTEL; STEEL CORD; R AND D |
| 1988 | HOTEL LEISURE CENTER |

Source: Company reports and interviews.
*Joint ventures

TABLE 4.3
Yaşar Holding

| YEARS | PAINT | HUSBANDRY AND FOOD PROCESSING | ALCOHOLIC BEVERAGES | TOURISM | FERTILIZERS AND AGRICULTURAL INPUTS | TOBACCO PROCESSING | PAPER AND PAPER PRODUCTS | CLOTHING | LEATHER AND LEATHER PRODUCTS | FOREIGN TRADE | TRANSPORTATION | CONSTRUCTION | MACHINERY | DATA PROCESSING |
|---|---|---|---|---|---|---|---|---|---|---|---|---|---|---|
| 1946 | IMPORTS | | | | | | | | | | | | | |
| 1954 | PAINT PRODUCTS | | | | | | | | | | | | | |
| 1963 | PAINT PRODUCTS | MILK PRODUCTS | | | | | | | | | | | | |
| 1967 | | | BEER PRODUCTION | | | | | | | | | | | |
| 1968 | PACKAGING | | | | | | | | | | | | | |
| 1970 | | | | RESTAURANT/CAFE | | | | | | | | | BOILER, MACHINERY | |
| 1971 | | | | | | | | | | FOREIGN TRADE | | | | |
| 1973 | | | | HOLIDAY VILLAGE | FERTILIZER PRODUCTS | | | | | | TRANSPORTATION CORPORATION | CONSTRUCTION CORPORATION | | |
| 1974 | CHEMICAL PRODUCTS | | | TOURISM AGENCY | | | | | | | | | | |
| 1977 | CHEMICAL PRODUCTS | | | | FERTILIZER AND SEED DISTRIBUTION | | | | | | | | | |

|  | | | | | | | | | | | |
|---|---|---|---|---|---|---|---|---|---|---|---|
| 1978 | PAINT RAW MATERIALS | | | | | | | | | | |
| 1979 | MARKETING | | | | | | | | | | |
| 1980 | | | | | | | FOREIGN TRADE | | | | |
| 1981 | PAINT AND DERIVATIVES | FLOUR AND MEAT PRODUCTS | | | | | | | | | |
| 1982 | PAINT AND DERIVATIVES | | | | PAPER PRODUCTS | | | | | | |
| 1983 | | MARKETING AND DISTRIBUTING | | | | | | TRANSPORTATION CORPORATION | | | DATA PROCESSING |
| 1984 | PAINT AND DERIVATIVES | WATER AND SEA PRODUCTS | | TOBACCO PROCESS. | | | | | | | |
| 1985 | | | AVIATION | | | | | | | | |
| 1986 | | REGIONAL DISTRIBUTION | REGIONAL DISTRIBUTION | | | CLOTHING | | | | | |
| 1987 | | HUSBANDRY | | | PAPER MARKETING | | | | | | |
| 1988 | | SUPERMARKET | HOLIDAY VILLAGE | | | | LEATHER BUSINESS | | | | |

*Source:* Company reports and interviews.

## TABLE 4.4
## Anadolu Endustri Holding

| YEARS | AUTOMOTIVE | MACHINERY PRODUCTION | FOOD PROCESSING/ AGRICULTURE | STATIONARY | PACKAGING | FOREIGN TRADE | FINANCE | TOURISM | CONSTRUCTION | TRANSPORTATION | ELECTRONICS | MARKETING |
|---|---|---|---|---|---|---|---|---|---|---|---|---|
| 1960 | IMPORTS | | | | | | | | | | | |
| 1965 | MOTOR PRODUCTION | | | | | | | | | | | |
| 1966 | MOTORBIKE, BUS PRODUCTION | | BEER PRODUCTION | | | | | | | | | |
| 1967 | | | BEER PRODUCTION REGIONAL DISTRIBUTION | | | | | | | | | |
| 1970 | | STEEL TANKS COOLING SYSTEMS | | | | | | | | | | |
| 1971 | | | PROVISIONING RAW MATERIALS | | | | | | | | | |
| 1973 | | | PROVISIONING RAW MATERIALS | | | | | | | | | |
| 1976 | | | | | CARDBOARD | | | | | | | |

| | MOTOR, AGRICULTURAL MACHINERY MARKETING | RAW MATERIAL PRODUCTION AND EXPORTS | | | | | | DATA PROCESSING, REPRESENTATIVES | |
|---|---|---|---|---|---|---|---|---|---|
| 1978 | MOTOR, AGRICULTURAL MACHINERY MARKETING | | | | | | | | |
| 1980 | | CHOCOLATE | | | | | | | |
| 1981 | VEHICLE PRODUCTION AND REPRESENTATION | PENCIL PRODUCTION | | FOREIGN TRADE | INVESTMENT/WEST GERMANY | CONSTRUCTION CORPORATIONS | | | MARKETING/CYPRUS |
| 1982 | MARKETING IMPORTS REPRESENTATION | | | | | | | | |
| 1983 | MARKETING REPRESENTATION | | | | | | | | |
| 1984 | | CIGARETTE REPRESENTATION | | | | | | | |
| 1985 | QA | PRODUCTION, EXPORTS | | | TOURISM AGENCY | | | | |
| 1986 | | BEER, WATER REGIONAL DISTRIBUTION | | | | | MARITIME TRANSPORTATION | ELECTRONIC CASHIER | |
| 1989 | | | | | | | MARITIME TRANSPORTATION | | |

*Source:* Company reports and interviews.

TABLE 4.5
Borusan Holding

| YEARS | IRON AND STEEL | MACHINERY | AUTOMOTIVE | CONSTRUCTION AND CONTRACTING | MARKETING AND TRANSPORTATION |
|---|---|---|---|---|---|
| 1953 | MARKETING OF PRODUCTS | | | | |
| 1958 | PIPE PRODUCTION | | | | |
| 1960 | STEEL PRODUCTION AND SALE | | | | |
| 1969 | | MACHINERY PRODUCTION | | | |
| 1970 | | | ENGINE PRODUCTION | | |
| 1975 | | | | | MARKETING ABROAD |
| 1976 | IRON PRODUCTION | | GALVANIZED IRON PLATE | | |
| 1984 | | | AUTOMOBILE REPRESENTATIVE | | |
| 1988 | | | COORDINATION OF AUTOMOTIVE GROUP | HOUSING, INDUSTRIAL AND TOURISTIC ESTABLISHMENTS CONSTRUCTION AND CONTRACTING | |
| INDETERMINATE | | | SHOCK ABSORBER PRODUCTION | | WAREHOUSE AND TRANSPORTATION DOMESTIC TRADE CORPORATIONS INTERNATIONAL TRADE CORPORATIONS |

Source: Company reports and interviews.

activities largely remain in nonalcoholic beverages and food processing, but the number of enterprises in this area is fairly large.

Activities of Turkish holding companies in the area of banking
and finance are particularly important as a determinant of the
society-specific characteristics of these companies. Given the underdeveloped state of Turkish capital markets and the essentially
family-firm character of big business enterprises, access to credit
has always been an important concern for the latter. The state, as
previously discussed, has remained the most important source of
credit for these enterprises. Even so, having one foot in the banking
sector has always been regarded as an attractive possibility. Hence,
as previously mentioned, a few of the major holding companies have
entered into this sector at a relatively early stage of their development and have established an extensive control over the private
banking sector. It is, nevertheless, important not to overlook two
aspects of holding company/bank relations in Turkey. First, unlike
the Japanese keiretsu, for example, Turkish holding companies do
not appear as tightly knit organizational forms centered around a
well-established, strong group bank. As table 4.10 shows, at least
until the 1980s, only a few of the major holding companies had their
group banks. During the last decade, multiactivity firms have
shown a greater interest in acquisition of shares in banking operations, sometimes through joint ventures with foreign investors.
However, today, as in the past, the significance of group banks for
the overall performance of the enterprise differs widely among
different companies. They are established at different stages of enterprise development, and their acquisition or sale do not seem to
constitute turning points in this development process. Sabancı,
Çukurova, and Doğuş, in fact, appear to be the only major conglomerates that manifested an active interest in the banking sector
prior to the 1980s. Other major holding companies have survived
well without a group bank. The purchase and subsequent sale of
shares of Garanti—an important private sector bank—have not, for
example, made a significant change in the success and status of the
Koç group as the most important business enterprise in Turkey. As
have several other groups of significance, Koç has remained without
any activities in the banking sector until the 1980s.

Second, the ownership of a group bank does not—or at least did
not, until quite recently—reduce the financial dependence of Turkish holding companies on the state. Somewhat paradoxically, inde-

## TABLE 4.6
## Tekfen Holding

| YEARS | CONSTRUCTION AND CONTRACTING | AGRICULTURE AND FOOD PROCESSING | TRANSPORTATION | FOREIGN TRADE | TOURISM | ELECTRICAL GOODS | MARKETING | FINANCE AND BANKING |
|---|---|---|---|---|---|---|---|---|
| 1956 | CONTRACTING FOR INDUSTRIAL AND PETROCHEMICAL INSTALLATIONS | | | | | | | |
| 1963 | | | | | | LIGHT BULBS | | |
| 1966 | | | | | | LIGHT BULBS | | |
| 1970 | CONTRACTING FOR INDUSTRIAL AND PETROCHEMICAL INSTALLATIONS | | | | | | | |
| 1971 | | | | | | | | HOLDING |
| 1974 | | FERTILIZERS | | | | | | |
| 1976 | | MILK PRODUCTION | | | | | MARKETING OF CONSUMPTION GOODS | |

|  | | | | | |
|---|---|---|---|---|---|
| 1979 | | | | | |
| 1980 | AGRICULTURAL INVESTMENTS | | | | |
| 1981 | EXPORTS AND IMPORTS OF AGRICULTURAL MACHINERY | | | MISCELLANEOUS TRADING | |
| 1982 | TRANSPORTATION OF RAW MATERIALS | | | | |
| 1983 | | FOREIGN TRADE | | | |
| 1984 | RESEARCH, ENGINEERING, PLANNING | | | | |
| 1985 | MAINTENANCE OF FOREIGN MILITARY INSTALLATIONS | | TOUR COMPANY | | |
| 1986 | FERTILIZERS: MARKETING AND TRANSPORTATION | | | | |
| AFTER 1980 | | | | | FOUR BANKS |
| AFTER 1980 | | | | | INVESTMENT COMPANY |

Source: Company reports and interviews.

TABLE 4.7
Altınyıldız Holding

| YEARS | TEXTILES, CLOTHING, AND FOOTWEAR | PETROLEUM | DATA PROCESSING |
|---|---|---|---|
| 1952 | FABRIC PRODUCTION | | |
| 1970 | CLOTHING PRODUCTION CLOTHING STORE | | |
| 1976 | THREAD EXPORT IMPORT | | |
| 1978 | FOOTWEAR | | |
| 1979 | | DISTRIBUTION AND SERVICE | |
| 1981 | CLOTHING EXPORT IMPORT/MARKETING | | |
| 1982 | CLOTHING STORE | | |
| 1983 | | | DATA PROCESSING |
| 1985 | CLOTHING STORE | | |
| 1986 | CLOTHING STORE | | |
| 1987 | FOOTWEAR STORE FOOTWEAR STORE | | |
| 1988 | CLOTHING STORE | | |
| INDETERMINATE | THREAD PRODUCTION | | |

Source: Company reports and interviews.

pendence might have even enhanced it because having one's own bank does not usually reduce the use of state subsidized credit, but facilitates its use by eliminating the discretion of commercial banks in the allocation of such credits.[42] Company banks in Turkey, therefore, do not play the same role that they do in Japan by alleviating the need for external borrowing without, nevertheless, undermining the strength of the bank itself. The financial position of big Turkish enterprises is, in fact, extremely fragile, and they have very high debt-to-equity ratios, which tend to increase with company size.[43]

TABLE 4.8
Akkök Holding

| YEARS | TEXTILES AND WEAVING | CONSTRUCTION MATERIALS | TOURISM | CONSTRUCTION |
|---|---|---|---|---|
| 1952 | THREAD PRODUCTION CARPET PRODUCTION | | | |
| 1968 | THREAD PRODUCTION | | | |
| 1973 | | FORMICA PRODUCTION | | |
| 1975 | THREAD PRODUCTION | | | |
| 1976 | EXPORT OF TEXTILES, WALLPAPER, FOAM | | | |
| 1977 | CHEMICAL PRODUCTS | | | |
| 1979 | THREAD PRODUCTION | | | |
| 1985 | THREAD AND DYE THREAD PRODUCTION | | | |
| 1988 | DISTRIBUTION, REPRESENTATION, EXPORTS | | | |
| INDETERMINATE | DISTRIBUTION MARKETING DISTRIBUTION/CARPET DISTRIBUTION/CARPET MARKETING | | YACHTING TOURISM COMPLEX TWO HOLIDAY VILLAGES | CONSTRUCTION CORPORATION |

Source: Company reports and interviews.

TABLE 4.9
Tamek Holding

| YEARS | NONALCOHOLIC BEVERAGES AND FOOD PROCESSING | ADVERTISING |
|---|---|---|
| 1955 | FRUIT JUICE AND CANNED VEGETABLES | |
| 1961 | DISTRIBUTION | |
| 1962 | FRUIT JUICE PRODUCTION | |
| 1969 | | ADVERTISING CORPORATION |
| 1974 | MARKETING, DISTRIBUTION | |
| 1977 | BOTTLING | |
| 1981 | FRUIT JUICE PRODUCTION IN CYPRUS | |
| 1983 | FRUIT AND VEGETABLE PROCESSING | |
| JOINT VENTURES | FOUR FRUIT JUICE ENTERPRISES EAU-DE-COLOGNE ENTERPRISE METAL CAP ENTERPRISE | |

*Source:* Company reports and interviews.

In the course of my interviews, I was told by several private sector representatives, especially professional managers, that, until the late 1980s, there was no such thing as an investment which does not benefit from some type of incentive, especially in the form of subsidized credit. Toward the end of the decade, however, the increasingly acute financial crisis of the Turkish state made it quite clear that things would have to change. The growing shortage of public funds used to support the private sector has thus been instrumental in leading big private enterprises to reconsider their financial strategies. These developments coincided with changes in banking regulations which enabled banks to deal with foreign currency operations and greatly liberalized the activities of foreign banks operating in Turkey. In this new environment, it became more attractive for banks to engage in merchant/investment banking rather than remaining in their traditional general commercial banking activities, often through the formation of joint ventures with foreign partners. This new orientation was especially attractive for holding companies because investment banks are not limited by the same regulations which restrict the amount of credit that a group bank can extend to any one single enterprise on the one hand and to affiliated enterprises within the group on the other.[44] Moreover, through joint ventures with foreign banks, group banks could raise much-needed capital resources in an environment in which subsidized credit was becoming scarce. In the second half of the 1980s, big Turkish enterprises have thus begun to consider joint ventures with foreign banks as a way of dealing with financial bottlenecks.

Hence, we find in this period several important holding companies which were not previously involved in the financial sector either acquiring shares in already existing banks or establishing new ones. As shown in table 4.10, important holding companies such as Tekfen, Akın, Enka, Net, Kavala, and Alarko present examples of this movement toward the financial sector in the 1980s. Koç Holding also entered the sector in the same period after its unsuccessful experience with Garanti Bankası.

Some of these new banks were formed without a foreign partner. Yet, joint ventures with foreign interests—not only in banking but also in other sectors—form an important characteristic of the 1980s which has the potential to modify the nature of state-business relations in he country. The foreign firm appears, in other words, as a new actor which might alter the relations of dependency between big business firms and the state. However, while they appear as a potential agent of change in this regard, it is also possible that foreign enterprises contribute to the continuity of certain other elements of the business environment. They could do so, for example, by presenting an alternative to the issuing of shares in the stock market to raise capital. By providing an alternative source of capital, they could thus support Turkish enterprises in their efforts to remain as family firms and to resist the loss of control that public offering of shares would imply. As will be discussed in the following section, the significance attached to the intergenerational continuity of family control over business operations also has a crucial role in shaping the organizational structure of Turkish holding companies.

TABLE 4.10
Group-Affiliated Banks in Turkey

| Bank Name | Date of Establishment | Share Holding Group |
|---|---|---|
| Esbank | 1927 | Zeytinoğlu |
| Türkiye Ekonomi Bankası | 1927 | Çolakoğlu |
| Türkiye İmar Bankası | 1928 | Uzan |
| Egebank | 1928 | Özakat |
| Tütüncüler Bankası | 1928 | Yaşar |
| Yapı ve Kredi Bankası | 1944 | Çukurova |
| Garanti Bankası | 1946 | Doğuş |
| Akbank | 1948 | Sabancı |
| Demirbank | 1953 | Cıngıllıoğlu |
| Pamukbank | 1955 | Çukurova |
| İnterbank | 1988 | Çukurova |
| Adabank | 1984 | Uzan |
| Türkiye Turizm Yatırım ve Dış Ticaret Bankası | 1988 | Lapis |
| Netbank | 1988 | Net Holding (recently sold to an individual investor) |
| Tekstilbank | 1986 | Akın Group |
| İmpexbank | 1984 | Eliyeşil |
| Tekfenbank* | 1989 | Tekfen |
| *Joint Ventures* | | |
| Koç-Amerikan Bank | 1986 | Koç with American Express |
| BNP-AK-Dresdner | 1986 | Sabancı with BNP and Dresdner |
| Birleşik Türk Körfez Bankası | 1988 | Doğuş with Qatari investors |
| Chemical Mitsui | 1985 | Enka with Chemical Mitsui |
| Birleşik Yatırım Bankası | 1989 | Kavala with shareholders from Jordan, Kuwait and Saudi Arabia |
| The First National Bank of Boston | 1990 | Alarko and Cerrahoğulları with OYAK** and the Bank of Boston Co. |

Source: Banks and Banking System (Istanbul: IBAR Co., Inc., 1991) seventh edition.
*Merchant Bank.
**Ordu Yardımlaşma Kurumu (Army Mutual Aid Society) constitutes one of the largest multiactivity enterprises in Turkey.

## TURKISH HOLDING COMPANY AS A FAMILY RUN ENTERPRISE

Presently, no matter how diversified their activities are, Turkish holding companies remain as enterprises owned and managed by the family of the founder or of the founding partners. This is clearly reflected in the organizational structures of multiactivity firms in which the mother company was often referred to by my interviwees as "the brain" and the affiliates as "the limbs" of the enterprise. The board of directors of the central holding company is controlled, sometimes exclusively, by family members of owners. Some members of this central board also appear on the board of directors of individual companies. Table 4.11 shows this particular organizational structure as it appears in board composition of some affiliates of three major multiactivity enterprises—Koç, Akkök, and Santral Holding. The most useful data source on this subject is the *Yearbook of Companies* published by Istanbul Stock Exchange which includes only companies whose shares are exchanged on the stock market. Because public companies are still exceptional in Turkey, these companies might not be perfect representatives of the general organizational structure which is likely to be more family-based than the table indicates. Statements by some of my interviewees— including those of two individuals from the Capital Market Board— suggest that individual firms whose shares the holding companies chose to market to the public are often unprofitable firms with financial difficulties. Furthermore, these are often firms in the manufacturing sector as opposed to service or financial sector firms. As these interviewees indicated, in the general body of a holding company, enterprises now left to professional management are frequently unprofitable firms in the manufacturing sector. Hence, table 4.11 might underestimate the extent of family control in holding companies, even though it clearly shows the significance of family domination, especially in the case of Santral Holding.

Other than family members, one finds, among these board members, two other types of individuals. First, there are those who are invited to sit on the board mainly for public relations purposes. It looks good to have a famous professor as a board member, and it sometimes proves to be politically useful to have a former politician or military officer. There are also certain professionals who appear on the boards of a large number of companies, and who, almost by force of custom, are made board members of one or several of the affiliates of different groups. Şahap Kocatopcu, who appears as a board member of three of the Koç affiliates presented in table 4.11, is a typical example of this latter category. Individuals, such as Kocatopcu as well as board members from the academia, might fulfill highly useful consultancy functions, but it is highly unlikely that they play managerial roles of any significance, especially given the large number of enterprises with which they are often involved within the same capacity. There are, however, other nonfamily members who have different positions on company boards. These are close associates of the family, who often appear also on the central board. Yüksel Pulat, who appears among the board members of every Koç affiliate and the central holding company, is one of these individuals who remains in the company for a long time and acquire the confidence of the owners. "They are more like the steward of a rural estate than the professional manager of an industrial corporation," as one of my interviewees put it.

The interviewees from the Capital Market Board, as well as several professional managers of some prominent holding companies, have told me that individual company boards do not function as boards of directors in the real sense of the term. I was told that they fulfill, at most, a consultancy role and act as an advisory board which can rarely affect decisions made by the central board of directors. However, this lack of autonomy of individual company boards—and hence the dependent status of affiliated companies themselves—was revealed more clearly by those interviewees, who insisted that, in their companies, affiliated enterprises and their managers enjoyed full autonomy. A professional manager active at the level of central holding company told me that there are *only* three areas in which individual companies can not make independent decisions. First, autonomy in investment decision is excluded because, as he explained, investment funds are provided by the holding company whose general coordinators naturally reserve the right to control allocation of these funds. Relatedly, financial coordination is the main prerogative of the central holding management which has infinite power to shuffle funds among different firms, both for the purposes of minimizing tax payments and for the requirements of a centrally determined investment strategy. Third, the personnel policy regarding both employment decisions and

TABLE 4.11
The Composition of Boards of Directors
of Some Group-Affiliated Enterprises

| Name of Company | General Manager | Board of Directors |
|---|---|---|
| *Companies in which the Koç Group is the main shareholder:* | | |
| Arçelik | Hasan Subaşı | Vehbi Koç (family) |
| | | Rahmi Koç (family) |
| | | Suna Kıraç (family) |
| | | Fahir İlkel (family) |
| | | Can Kıraç (family) |
| | | Fred Burla |
| | | Yüksel Pulat |
| | | Uğur Ekşioğlu |
| | | Demir Erman |
| Döktaş | M. Ali Berkmen | Rahmi Koç (family) |
| | | Suna Kıraç (family) |
| | | İnan Kıraç (family) |
| | | Can Kıraç (family) |
| | | Rafet Tanyıldız |
| | | Ali Yalman |
| | | Şahap Kocatopçu |
| | | Cüneyt Zapsu |
| İzocam | Ünal Çilingir | Rahmi Koç (family) |
| | | Şahap Kocatopçu |
| | | Yüksel Pulat |
| | | M. Kolay |
| | | T. Yaramancı |
| | | N. Arıkan |
| | | N. Alpen |
| Kav | Cem Önen | V. Koç (family) |
| | | S. Arsel (family) |
| | | Y. Pulat |
| | | T. Ulup |
| | | E. Karakoyunlu |
| | | Z. Baloğlu |

(continued)

TABLE 4.11 continued

| Name of Company | General Manager | Board of Directors |
|---|---|---|
| Koç Holding | Can Kıraç (family) | Rahmi Koç (family)<br>Suna Kıraç (family)<br>Fahir İlkel (family)<br>Can Kıraç (family)<br>Semahat Arsel (family)<br>Sevgi Gönül (family)<br>Yüksel Pulat<br>Şahap Kocatopçu<br>Zekeriya Yıldırım<br>Kemal Oğuzman |
| Koç Pazarlama | Erdoğan Kanber | Can Kıraç (family)<br>Yüksel Pulat<br>Haluk Cillov<br>Ömer Apa<br>Sebati Ataman<br>Mustafa Aysan<br>E. Karakoyunlu<br>Tevfik Altınok<br>Ali Arslan |
| Maret | Atıl Öncü | Rahmi Koç (family)<br>Suna Kıraç (family)<br>Nusret Arsel (family)<br>Yüksel Pulat<br>Tunç Uluğ<br>Alpay Bağrıaçık |
| Otosan | A. İhsan İlkbahar | Rahmi Koç (family)<br>Erdoğan Gönül (family)<br>Suna Kıraç (family)<br>Can Kıraç (family)<br>İnan Kıraç (family)<br>Fahir İlkel (family)<br>Ahmet Binbir<br>A. C. Lindgren<br>R. P. Sparvero<br>Reşit Egeli |

(continued)

TABLE 4.11 continued

| Name of Company | General Manager | Board of Directors |
|---|---|---|
| Türk Demirdöküm | Mete Nakipoğlu | Rahmi Koç (family)<br>Suna Kıraç (family)<br>Can Kıraç (family)<br>Yüksel Pulat<br>Tezcan Yaramancı<br>Necati Arıkan<br>Tamer Erkin<br>Kemal Oğuzman |
| Türk Siemens | Arnold Hornfeld | Arnold Hornfeld<br>J. Hammerschmidt<br>N. Ersel (family)<br>R. Koç (family)<br>R. Bertsch<br>W. Bucholz<br>D. Buschmann |
| Aygaz | Çelik Arsel | V. Koç (family)<br>F. İlkel (family)<br>S. Kıraç (family)<br>Y. Pulat<br>H. S. Picciotto<br>D. C. Dunn<br>S. Picciotto |

*Companies in which Santral Holding (Bezmen family)
is the main shareholder:*

| | | |
|---|---|---|
| Mensucat Santral | Halil Bezmen (family) | Fuad Bezmen (family)<br>Halil Bezmen (family)<br>N. K. Bezmen (family)<br>Turgud Bezmen (family)<br>Necdet Bezmen (family)<br>Selma Bezmen (family)<br>Necdet Aktay |
| Koruma Tarım İlaçları | Necdet Bezmen<br>(family) | F. Bezmen (family)<br>H. Bezmen (family)<br>T. Bezmen (family)<br>N. Aktay<br>A. Bilgen<br>R. Ş. Egeli |

(continued)

TABLE 4.11 continued

| Name of Company | General Manager | Board of Directors |
|---|---|---|
| Rabak | Bahri Ersöz | F. Bezmen (family) |
| | | H. Bezmen (family) |
| | | N. Bezmen (family) |
| | | S. Bingöl |
| | | B. Ersöz |
| | | İ. Karaoğlu |
| | | H. Uzel |
| Santral Holding | Halil Bezmen (family) | F. Bezmen (family) |
| | | H. Bezmen (family) |
| | | N. Bezmen (family) |
| | | T. Bezmen (family) |
| | | S. Bezmen (family) |
| | | N. Bezmen (family) |
| | | A. Yenisey |
| | | A. Gökęk |

*Companies in which the Akkök Group (Dinçkök family)
is the main shareholder:*

| | | |
|---|---|---|
| Aksa | Mete Tansel | R. Dinçkök (family) |
| | | Ö. Dinçkök (family) |
| | | A. Dinçkök (family) |
| | | O. Boyner (shareholder) |
| | | İ. Lodrik (shareholder) |
| | | A. Çeki, |
| | | C. Ayaz |
| Ak-Al | Engin Sayımer | R. Dinçkök (family) |
| | | A. Dinçkök (family) |
| | | A. B. Kafaoğlu |
| | | K. Satır |
| | | M. Çopuroğlu |
| | | İ. Lodrik |

Source: Istanbul Stock Eschange, Yearbook of Companies (I and II), 1990

determination of employee compensation is determined centrally with individual companies having little discretion in these matters.

According to those owner/managers who also thought that management of their firms was largely professionalized, these were, in general, the limitations of decision-making autonomy of professional managers. A young chairman from the second generation of the family of owners told me that their company is now a professionally run one. When I asked him whether the managers of affiliated firms could make independent investment decisions, he appeared to be surprised. "Of course they cannot," he said. "No investment decisions are taken without my approval." Especially for the older generation of founding families, the role of professional management is reduced to that of consultant. "My father never used to consult with anyone. I always ask my managers what they think of a particular project" a middle-aged interviewee, who is also a firm believer of professional management, explicitly told me. My interview with a partner in a company which is generally known as a highly professionalized one was especially interesting. After having explained to me the management structure, he said sadly, "As you know, we are three partners and we all have daughters who are not interested in business. I don't know whether it would have been the same if we had sons instead of daughters."

Sons have no choice but to assume a management role in the family firm. What is interesting here is the absence of significant cases of resistance to this family determined career path. I have asked, for example, the young chairman of the central board of an important holding company what his father's reaction would have been had he refused to assume the role assigned to him. He said, "Do you mean if I had decided to become a street painter in a resort town, drinking all day long? He would have been disappointed of course . . . " Most of the answers to this question—both by fathers and sons—were more or less along these lines. The refusal of a business career was interpreted as marginalization. My interviewees seemed to be genuinely unable to visualize a situation in which a person might refuse to become a businessman in order to chose another respectable career. This attitude might reflect the ideological atmosphere of Turkish society in the 1980s when money-making was considered to be the most rational—if not the only rational—objective of all human endeavor. In this atmosphere, which also dominated most Western societies in the same period, the businessman was the most popular of all popular heroes. Consequently, it would be quite out of place to expect, from a young man, a refusal to accept such a glamorous destiny. One must remember, moreover, that the younger generation of founding families get, in general, a first-class management education. Most of them have business administration degrees, often from leading American universities. Their whole upbringing, in other words, is of a nature to largely exclude the possibility of a strong resentment against a predetermined business career path.

The upbringing of the younger generation indicates that the continuity of family control does not necessarily exclude the professional management of the enterprise. The professionalization of the family, in other words, appears as an alternative to the professionalization of management. Training of the young is not the only way of achieving this. Integrating managers into the founding family could also be a means of reconciling family control with an efficient management structure. A typical example of this is provided by Koç Holding in which the founder's daughters are all married to relatives of prominent managers active in the company. In other companies—or with reference to them—expressions such as "he is like a son to me" or "he is almost an adopted son of the owner" are used quite often. As underlined by several professional managers whom I interviewed, the element of trust engendered by a close personal relationship is much more important than professional competence as a determinant of success in a managerial career.

This, however, has little to do with success in entrepreneurship in the classical sense. Among my interviewees, even those executives who held positions at the top of the administrative ladder had no illusions about their status. Several professional managers whom I interviewed told me that their role had little to do with the role of an entrepreneur in a Western country. One of them said, "No matter how you look at it, you cannot call us entrepreneurs. The functions that we fulfill, our position in the enterprise, and our status in society are all different from those of an entrepreneur." This is manifested, quite clearly, in the totally unambigious distinction that exists in Turkey between owners and managers. Both "the entrepreneur" and "the businessman" appear as terms designating the individuals in the first category. Any attempt to extend them to the second category would obscure the fact that innovation, risk-taking, and uncertainty management, as well as the relations with the state remain as the prerogative of the owner, areas in which managers are neither expected nor allowed to enter.

Although a couple of my interviewees expressed some resentment against this limited role, their attitude in general can best be described as a cynical acceptance. One interviewee, who deeply resented the centralized control of the family of owners, was the director of a profitable industrial enterprise within the body of a large conglomerate. Although his personal compensation was not in the least affected by it, he did not like to see the profits of his enterprise constantly drained to finance less successful ventures, especially since these profits did not even appear on formal accounts prepared for the purposes of tax payment minimization. Nevertheless, this particular interviewee, as did the other professional executives interviewed, claimed to understand the reluctance of the owners to extend managerial autonomy within the group. In the numerous examples he gave to document resistance to the separation of ownership from control, the major theme was invariably the lack of confidence in salaried managerial personel which, according to my interviewee, was a well-founded one. "Stealing from the boss is very common," he said, "and there are some legendary cases where a salaried manager makes a fortune by abusing his position in the enterprise. Owners know these cases, and they draw a lesson from them."

It was not, however, the owner managers whom I interviewed who brought up such examples of unreliability of professional executives.[45] It was rather the salaried managers who referred to them in their accounts of mutual lack of confidence between owners and managers. In the relationship that was described, both parties seem to be caught in a vicious cycle in which lack of confidence from the boss prevents the employee from developing a sense of belonging to or identifying with the enterprise. He develops, instead a sense of insecurity concerning his career and, thus, seeks to maximize whatever pecuniary advantages he could derive from his present status within the firm. This attitude, in its turn, reinforces the owners' reluctance to share information with and delegate responsibility to their salaried managers. This leads to the emergence of an atmosphere of mutual distrust which characterizes the organizational structure of Turkish holding companies and constitutes a significant barrier against the professionalization of management.

This "vicious cycle of mutual distrust," however, is not the only factor to which my interviewees referred in their attempts to depict obstacles against professionalization in Turkey. Another interesting point was made by a very well-known executive. The latter had experienced a rather painful relationship with his former boss who, although claiming to favor an organizational structure with full decision-making autonomy of hired executives, made it impossible, by his constant interference at all levels of business activity, for the executive to implement any decisions concerning the rational management of the enterprise. According to my interviewee—who could not continue to work under these circumstances—his former boss, as did most of his contemporaries who are now older than sixty years, had developed his business in an environment in which internal and external competition was practically nil. When government support was there, any venture that businessmen chose to undertake could easily become successful, and the possibility of any serious loss was extremely limited. Under these circumstances, rational calculation before decision-making, let alone detailed feasibility studies, was not a part of their business world. As my interviewee put it, these older businessmen were used to doing what seemed to be interesting. Today, they simply could not understand their younger executives when they mention priorities and constraints. Under these circumstances, no matter how good the intentions are, the hired executive soon begins to look like an unpleasant intruder preventing an individual from using his money in whatever way he wants to use it.

What is important to underline here is that the money, in fact, belongs to the boss and not to the company. The absence of a clear-cut distinction between private wealth of the founding family and capital of the enterprise formed a recurrent theme in my interviews with salaried executives. A former executive told me that "Salaried managers cannot make investment decisions because they do not know the source of investment funds. The boss might decide to sell a personal property to finance a project for which there is no alternative source of funding. The professional manager simply does not have the necessary information to play any role in this decision." This suggests, naturally, that the professional cannot control the use of available funds either, because the owner might well decide to put them to some personal use. This particular interviewee seemed to find this state of affairs perfectly natural, just as he found to be equally natural certain attitudes of government authorities which tend to undermine the position of hired managers.

Given the importance of the role which the state plays in Turkish business life, it is natural that contacts with politicians or bureaucrats constitute an important aspect of enterprise management. Yet, it is particularly in this area that salaried executives have little responsibility and power. What I have heard from owners and professional executives on this subject suggests that the exclusion of the latter from the arena of negotiations with state authorities has two different sources. First, politicians and bureaucrats—at least in the 1980s—seem to be reluctant to discuss matters of significance with salaried personnel, no matter what their status in the managerial structure of the enterprise is.

The inconfidence factor, which poisons the relationship between the boss and the hired executive at the enterprise level, also appears at this level of state-business relations in which it is considered unsafe to entrust professional managers with information or discretionary decision-making power. While the members of founding families have argued that it is "Ankara" that would insist on concluding any negotiation only with them, several professional managers have mentioned a major factor which might be instrumental in the reluctance of both the owners and the state authorities to include a third party in the area of state-business relations. This factor mainly pertains to the ambiguities which govern the policy-implementation process. When the rules—especially those which define the boundaries of legality and illegality or of legitimate and illegitimate behavior—are unclear it becomes difficult to delegate responsibility. As it was discussed in the previous chapter of this book, the legal basis of business activity is also far from being solid in Turkey. Given the ambiguities in this area, businessmen are preoccupied with questions concerning the legal aspects of their activities. As one executive told me, the bulk of the correspondence with Ankara consists of letters written to different ministries to demand clarification concerning the practical application of certain laws. He said, "Businessmen present their own interpretation of a certain clause, and they ask whether it is the right interpretation. They are constantly writing these letters to avoid doing anything which could compromise their reputation. This indicates the significance they attach to their public image. Hence, it is only natural that they take all the precautions to prevent a salaried manager's intentional or unintentional mistake in presenting their position to state authorities, or in interpreting the views of the latter concerning a particular activity of the enterprise." Although my interviewees did not comment on the issue, it seems quite plausible that the ambiguities characterizing the policy environment also foster a similar cautious attitude in bureaucrats and politicians who do not want to appear to be involved in illegitimate negotiations with the business community. If this is the case, then they would want to minimize the number of individuals involved in negotiations, believing that the possibility of misinterpretation or intentional circumventing of decisions would be the least when the message is directly given to the boss.

There is of course a less complicated explanation which would be based on the illegitimate deals between businessmen on the one hand, and bureaucrats and politicians on the other. When such deals exist, the parties involved would naturally want to exclude third parties from their negotiations. Similarly, business activities of a dubious legality would enhance the significance of the trust factor in the enterprise, and it would limit access to managerial positions of professionals who are not related to the owner through kinship or other personal ties. The preceding discussion suggests, however, that, even in the absence of such illicit behavior, the uncertainty of the policy environment fostered by the unstable nature of the legal system would be sufficient to create an atmosphere of lack of confidence which would strengthen the desire to maintain the family control over the enterprise. It would render the delegation of responsibility quite difficult, and would thus hinder the professionalization of management.

## SOCIAL IMPLICATIONS OF HOLDING ACTIVITY IN TURKEY

In general, my interviewees thought that these factors which determine the family-dominated character of Turkish holding companies could not continue to be effective in the long run. They believed that the professionalization of management was inevitable in third-generation enterprises, if not earlier. Nevertheless, some of them argued that trends toward professionalization would be preceeded by the collapse of many holding firms that would not be able to make the necessary adjustment in time. A professional manager even said that he would bet on the inevitable disintegration of the

Sabancı Group in the first quarter of the year 2000. Whether time would prove him right is yet to be seen. However, regardless of future developments in this area, the point that he made suggests that, in contradiction with previously discussed theoretical arguments in which groups are presented as highly efficient production and planning units, the holding company might not really be the most efficient form of allocating entrepreneurial resources. In a society in which access to high-quality education is largely dependent on the level of family income, the children of business families might be better positioned than are others to acquire entrepreneurial skills. Nevertheless, it is still a problem that the chances of talented people, who remain outside the circuit of owner families, using their entrepreneurial abilities effectively is limited by the family-controlled character of holding companies. It is, at least, a phenomenon which is contradictory to wide-spread beliefs concerning the extent of social mobility in capitalist societies in which status by birth is thought to be of limited significance in determining the economic success of an individual. Second, as my interviewee's prediction about the future of Sabancı Holding implies, the family domination of entrepreneurial functions endangers the very survival of the enterprise whose continuity becomes, within the given organizational structure, contingent upon the presence of competent family members. The absence of efforts to develop an organizational form in which a professional management team can successfully operate is likely to be detrimental to the enterprise, given the possibility of a rupture in the supply of managerial talent coming from within the family.

It is indeed difficult to regard Turkish holding companies as institutions which "have permitted 'pure' Schumpeterian entrepreneurship to become effective." Unlike the Schumpeterian entrepreneur whose role is defined by technological innovation, entrepreneurial function in a Turkish holding company has more to do with financial management and manipulation of the policy process. In fact, the managerial organization of a typical multiactivity firm in Turkey constitutes an environment which is hardly compatible with the development of an industrial outlook. It appears, rather, as a factor which serves to enhance the absence of such an outlook which, as was discussed in the second chapter of this book, reflects both the social background of the business community and the societal conditions in which the industrial development of the country has taken place. Turkish holding companies are clearly an institutional form in which commercial rather than industrial instincts are likely to dominate business behavior.

Lack of committment to a particular line of activity and dominance of financial concerns over industrial ones appear as attitudes accentuated by the extent of centralized control over the activities of the group. As previously discussed, general managers of individual companies who, by virtue of their functions, are more involved in the actual production process have very limited decision-making powers. Moreover, given the nature of the relationship between owners and salaried managers, the degree of committment of the latter to the enterprise is often quite low. Under these circumstances, matters specifically pertaining to production tend to be dominated by financial concerns, with central management yielding to a traditional traders' mentality instead of concentrating on the profitability of industrial operations. Although it would be difficult to document, speculative activity also probably constitutes an important source of revenue for big businessmen. Real estate speculation, in particular, appears to be a common precaution against business failure, as well as a highly lucrative activity. In an interview, I asked one owner/manager, who had voiced many complaints about the difficulties he has as a contractor of state infrastructure projects, why he has chosen to remain in the field. He said, "I remain in business because I love the work. But the profits are not important. I have made a lot of money because I have always bought land wherever we went to build a dam or a road. These properties have greatly appreciated in value." The significance of real estate speculation by holding companies is, in fact, reflected in the extremely frequent use of real estate transfers among the portfolios of affiliated companies to enable desired capital increases.[46] It is interesting in this regard that in Turkey, the instances of conflict between businessmen and politicians frequently turn into mutual accusations in which the latter publicly state that businessmen, instead of complaining about government policy, should sell their real estate property to deal with financial difficulties. Although this might not have much weight as a political statement, it is probably based on the recognition of an important aspect of business life in Turkey.

It should be mentioned, nevertheless, that, in the 1980s the state indirectly contributed to the diversion of private sector funds from productive investments through increased use of internal borrowing as a source of government revenue. In this period, the failure—or the reluctance—to finance government spending by raising taxes led the MP government to sell government bonds and treasury bills to the public as extremely attractive options for portfolio investment. Toward the end of the decade, the extent of private sector investment funds used for purchase of government bonds and treasury bills became a widely discussed issue. It was argued that, especially in the case of banks, government debt had become a major source of revenue for the private sector.[47]

These observations concerning entrepreneurial activity in Turkish holding companies are of a nature to challenge the idea that the intersectoral character of group activities carries a potential for the identification of private interest with public interest. In light of the preceeding discussion, it seems doubtful that the multiactivity character of the Turkish holding company necessarily provides an incentive to take into account more than sectoral interests. It is, of course, true that these companies have interests located in more than one sector of the economy. It is, therefore, difficult to explain their behavior in terms of narrow sectoral interests. This does not mean, however, that, at any given moment in time and in relation to any given policy change, the company would invariably try to protect the totality of its interests spread through all the sectors in which it is active. In other words, company interests are not necessarily identical with the interests of all these sectors. The intersectoral character of the holding company does not imply that all these sectors are equally important for central management. There are priorities which could, at times, lead to a less-than-favorable treatment of certain activities. These activities could, thus, be neglected or even abandoned. This is especially true given the organizational structure of Turkish holding companies in which the individual enterprises, with their practically unoperational boards of governments, have little autonomy apart from central management. Hence, affiliates located in different sectors have little power to stand for their specific interests and, in their powerlessness, can do little against unfavorable treatment of the activities in their sector when global interests of the holding company necessitates it.

The convergence of private and public interest requires, therefore, more than an activity diversification structure which covers a large number of sectors. The social implications of this multisectoral structure seem to be determined, rather, by the characteristics of the sociopolitical environment in which business activity takes place—by societal characteristics, it should be underlined, that could be shaped by appropriate policy measures. This is clearly manifested, for example, in the differences between the performances of South Korean and Turkish industries, both dominated by large multiactivity firms. Although, as mentioned in the beginning of this chapter, they are at the present under state pressure to limit their activities to a few chosen areas of specialization, the Korean chaebol, like Turkish holding companies, have, so far, appeared as diversified producers of items as unrelated as noodles and computers. They have, however, contributed to a rapid industrial growth and an impressive export performance. Their performance in introducing technological change and in improving the competitive position of South Korean products in international markets have also been impressive, while the Turkish apertura has resulted more in innovations in rent-seeking activity than in improved standards in industrial production.[48]

The differences between the roles that state plays in these two economies could largely explain the convergence of private and public interests in the Korean case and its absence in the Turkish one. One major source of the differences in business outlook and behavior could easily be depicted by comparing the South Korean state as a mechanism of stability with the Turkish state as the major risk factor in business life. There is, however, another yet related factor of significance that should be taken into account in a comparison of the implications of group activity in these two countries. The contributions of the chaebol to South Korean economy should be explained, at least in part, with reference to the ability of the Korean state to discipline big business—a role which the Turkish state has not been able to play although political intentions in this regard have not been absent. This difference between the two societies could perhaps be explained by arguing that the extent of state autonomy is greater in South Korea than in Turkey. The nature of the financial system in Turkey could, in fact, be regarded as a factor limiting the autonomy of the state. The absence of a comprehensive control over the financial system—as seen in South Korea—could have, indeed, limited the ability of the Turkish state to channel investments in socially desirable directions. Similarly, the absence of controls over the credit mechanism, which has enabled the Korean state to prohibit speculative activity and even conspicuous consumption, could have been instrumental in the powerlessness of the Turkish state to take effective action in these areas. Nevertheless, it should not be overlooked that the Turkish state also had a considerable scope of action that it could have used through the allocation of incentives, subsidized investment credits in particular. Given the extent of dependence of Turkish businessmen on the state for subsidized credit, for input supply and output demand, and given the place of unexpected economic policy changes at the center of the daily business concerns, it would be difficult to suggest that it is the business control over the policy process which has prevented the state from taking effective action in reshaping business behavior.

This suggests that the differences in question can be better explained with reference to determinants of limited state capacity in Turkey as they were analyzed in the preceeding chapter on the nature of the policy process in the country. It seems, in other words, that the inability of the Turkish state to discipline big business in a way to assure the convergence of private and social benefits has to do, more than anything else, with the failure to implement the right policy mix at the right time as well as with determination and consistency.

I have so far emphasized the social implications of holding activities with reference to their contribution to economic growth, industrial development, and international trade performance. However, the social impact of this type of business organization is hardly limited to the role which it plays in the economy. It is also instrumental in redefining the role of business associations in state-business relations and, at a more general level, in determining the character of associational life in the country. Currently, the size and multisectoral character of holding companies enable them to enjoy important advantages in their relations with state authorities. These companies have, in particular, highly significant channels of presenting their demands to the government. In this regard, they seem to render redundant, in many ways, the organized channels of interest representation. In a society, such as Turkey's in which associational life is quite underdeveloped, this state of affairs creates important asymmetries in interest representation and in the organized participation of different social groups in the policy process. This problem will be discussed in the next chapter of this book which presents a general picture of the evolution of business associations in Republican Turkey.

# 5. BUSINESS ASSOCIATIONS IN TURKEY

## INTEREST ASSOCIATIONS AND PUBLIC POLICY: A GENERAL OVERVIEW OF CURRENT TRENDS

The place of business associations in a given society appears as an area in which the nature of the business environment in general—and the basic characteristics of state-business relations in particular—are clearly reflected. It is, therefore, natural that this chapter on Turkish business associations will present, to a large extent, a field of application for the arguments presented in the previous discussions of the societal context of business activity in Turkey. It will build on these arguments, and will also try to further clarify and substantiate them.

Analytical work on Turkish business associations is quite scanty. The works of R. Bianchi and M. Heper, with their differences on certain conceptual issues, present a notable exception in this regard.[1] The differences of opinion of these writers—or rather the criticism of Bianchi's approach by Heper—refer to the concepts of pluralism, corporatism, and neo-corporatism and, as such, they address some of the issues raised in the neo-corporatist literature. Consequently, the introduction to this chapter also refers to these issues in the discussion of the Bianci-Heper debate. The questions raised in neo-corporatist literature are, in general, quite relevant for the present study because they highlight the intermingling of the realms of private interest and public policy. My analysis of Turkish business organizations which emphasizes the political determinants of interest group activity therefore draws on some of the ideas brought forth by the neo-corporatist literature.

On the basis of a survey of interest group activity through the political development of modern Turkey, Bianchi concludes that the Turkish experience in this area was of an oscillation between pluralism and corporatism, with the current tendency (at the end of the 1970s) being predominantly toward the expansion of state corporatism.

As opposed to this approach, we find the arguments of Heper, who affirms that the Turkish state tradition is incompatible either with pluralism or corporatism, both categories of limited usefulness in the analyses of interest group activity in Turkey. In Heper's approach, the key concept is the degree of "stateness," which appears as the main factor which shapes the political development process and the place of interest group activity in this process.

> Any study of interest group politics must be carried out with systematic reference to the type of the state, or the degrees and the kind of the "stateness" encountered in the polity. . . . It is . . . proper to argue that depending upon the state or governmental tradition a polity has had in the past, interest group politics would tend to evince, during the later historical periods, not a *mix* of different patterns of interest group politics but one *dominant* pattern. That dominant pattern of interest group politics, I would like to suggest, would depend upon the particular configuration of the state-civil society relationship that has been established in the past, and which still lingers on. This is because each pattern of interest group politics has a particular logic behind it which closely fits one type of state, or government, and not others. Pluralism requires a government basically responsive to civil society; neo-corporatism necessitates a harmonious relationship between the state and civil society. Neither pattern of interest group politics would be encountered in a polity dominated by a strong state.[2]

Any debate around this issue, in order to avoid presenting an exaggerated picture of the divergences between these two views, requires a clarification of the term *corporatism*. In this regard, the distinction between "state corporatism" and "societal corporatism" should be made explicit once and for all. Schmmiter presents state corporatism as a form which emerges as a result of the demise of nascent pluralism in societal contexts of dependent development and nonhegemonic class relations, while societal corporatism appears in a process of gradual decay of advanced pluralism in developed Western countries.[3] W. Grant takes up the same distinction in an argument which seeks to highlight the difference between corporatism and etatism. In his formulation, state corporatism is associated with etatism, and it involves involuntary organizations created by and kept as auxilary and dependent organs of the state. Societal corporatism on the other hand involves "hierarchical, noncompetitive, singular organizations which are autonomous in their origins." Gradually, these organizations develop a symbiotic relationship of mutual dependence and responsibility with the state. Consequently, interest associations are assigned a public function to secure the compliance of their members in the implementation of policy agreements, while the legitimacy of the state becomes partly reliant on the active consent of interest organizations.[4] What Bianchi unambigiously has in mind when referring to corporatist trends in Turkey is state corporatism that he finds compatible with the etatist tradition of this country where there have been strong cultural inhibitions to private interest articulation and representation.

For the purposes of this study, the difference between the general line of Bianchi's analysis and Heper's emphasis of the state tradition does not seem to be too significant. It is, indeed, quite difficult not to agree with Heper's statement that, in any given country, the pattern of interest group politics would be shaped by the historically established configuration of state-civil society relationship, unless the statement is to be interpreted as assigning an entirely passive role to civil society in its interaction with the state. Although the literature on neo-corporatism, from which Bianchi amply draws, places the emphasis on the relative historical significance of pluralist and corporatist traditions in the explanation of political developments in a given country, this emphasis hardly appears in the form of a counterargument against the idea that state structures would be important in influencing the nature of interest representation. In fact, in tracing the origins of the theories on ("neo-," "quasi-," "liberal," or "societal") corporatism, Grant writes that they have stemmed from a discontent with the explanations of the relations between the state and interest groups given by pluralist theories which assign too passive a role to the state in this relationship.[5]

I nevertheless share Heper's view that there is not a mix, as Bianchi argues, but one dominant pattern of interest group politics in Turkey. As I will discuss in detail, the oscillations between pluralism and corporatism which Bianchi highlights seem to reflect, quite clearly, the nature of the policy process in Turkey which is characterized by the absence of a clear strategy in which the legitimate domain of state intervention and the private pursuit of interest could be clearly defined. As to the examples that he gives in this regard, many of them appear as perfect manifestations of the characteristics of the Turkish legal system as a mechanism of intermediation in state-business relations and its failure to contribute to the emergence of a stable policy network.

This suggests that the dominant pattern of interest group politics is, indeed, shaped by the Turkish state tradition. However, while Heper explores the extent of state intervention as the major factor which shapes the character of interest group activity, in the discussion presented in this chapter the emphasis is shifted toward the form of intervention as the main determinant of societal differences in interest group politics and its social implications. This constitutes an approach which tries not to overlook the differences between forms and implications of business interest articulation and representation in countries with similar degrees of interventionism and state strength.

The form of state intervention in the realm of private interest constitutes, therefore, a major explanatory variable in the following discussion of interest group activity. The structure of social classes in general and the social position of the business class in particular, too, is undoubtedly a significant factor affecting the nature of the interest group activity in a given society. The weakness of social differentiation along class lines appears as a dominant historical characteristic of Turkish society depicted both by Bianchi and Heper. Both writers suggest that this historical characteristic is instrumental in the emergence of a political culture, which reflects a value system in which hierarchy consciousness is weak, and equality is a major social value. This particular value system also appears as a manifestation of the dominant society-shaping role of state. In this type of interaction between the state and society, the weakness of the economic position of the private business is likely to hamper the development of voluntary business associations, but the effectiveness of the latter would also be limited by the egalitarian values of a society with a very underdeveloped hierarchy consciousness.

While class structure and state policy mutually interact in shaping the social environment of interest group activity within a given political culture, the state-class interaction and, consequently, the nature of interest representation also take place under given domestic and international economic constraints. In societies in which the consciousness of these constraints leads both state authorities and business leaders to act in cooperation, business associations acquire a quasi-public role which extends beyond the simple pursuit of material gain, often with a positive impact on the economic performance of the country.

In certain discussions of neo-corporatism, for example, the emergence of neo-corporatism is traced to the post–World War II era, when the task of reconstruction of war-ravaged Europe imposed the need for the development of effective forms of cooperation among labor, capital, and the state. It is thus argued that the imperative of reconstruction and development led to a situation in which interest representation was attributed a sociopolitical character, and the gap between the pursuit of class interest and its social implications was largely bridged.[6] As was mentioned in the introduction of this study, Claus Offe refers to a similar development in European patterns of interest representation in relation to the transition that occured, according to him, from conjuctural to structural political strategies in the 1960s. While conjuctural policies attempt to respond to problems as they emerge, given the existing economic parameters of production and institutional parameters of interest representation, structural policies emerge as a response to economic and institutional crisis situations. They also involve redesigning the parameters in question. Hence, Offe argues, as a response to changing circumstances, both in domestic political situation and in international markets, it has become necessary to eradicate new types of institutional structures to alleviate the conflict between distibutional demands of interest associations on the one hand, and socioeconomic requirements and potentialities on the other. It is in this context that interest representation has become a matter of political design—in part, a dependent rather than an independent variable of policy making.[7] The same idea is undertaken by T. Skocpol in her emphasis of the increasingly clear "society-shaping" role of the state "not only in developing countries, but also in developed, Western countries in today's world of more intense and uncertain international competition."[8]

The problems of social stability and economic development to which these writers refer are naturally more pressing in the context of late industrialization. One could surmise, therefore, that the necessity of reconciliating distributional demands and socioeconomic objectives defined at a national level would be more important than it appears to be in developed Western nations. Whether this necessity would lead to a state-interest group cooperation of the type observed in the West is, however, a totally different matter. In relation to the forms of interaction between state and business interest associations in late-industrializing countries, it seems plausible to assume that the significance of this interaction for the national economy would be different in countries adopting inward- and outward-looking development strategies. State-business cooperation in the pursuit of national objectives, which involves a certain interpendence between interest representation and public policy, largely appears as a phenomenon peculiar to those countries where a highly impressive export performance forms an important component of a very successful economic development performance. As such, it presents a role model to other late-industrializing countries, such as Turkey, that attempt to enhance the international competitiveness of their exports and to follow an outward-looking development strategy.

Both Japan and South Korea present much-discussed examples of impressive export performance based on the successful management of state-business relations. In these countries, it is observed that the significance of the mutually determining relationship between interest representation and economic policy is enhanced with the increasing importance of international economic relations. Relatedly, a certain modification of interest group activity is observed in Japan starting with the 1950s, and in South Korea beginning with the Park era in the 1960s. Although the character of this transformation is naturally affected by the historical legacy of interest representation and state-business relations, what seems to be common to both cases is the trend toward strengthening of the social position of big business which has developed increasingly close ties with the state.[9] Certain writers suggest that, in South Korea, certain rather important changes have taken place in business interest representation with the transition from the First Republic (1948–1960) characterized by a weak state to the Park era (1961–1972) in which a strong state control over the economy was established. It is argued that in the first period, certain factions of the business class in the Korean Chamber of Industry and Commerce had begun to ask for more state-business cooperation within a strategy of "planned capitalism." This faction of the Korean bourgeoisie, which was mainly comprised of big businessmen representing chaebol interests, have gradually disassociated themselves from the Chamber and formed, in 1961, The Federation of Korean Industries with active support of the government. This federation, controlled by a small minority of the largest chaebol leaders, seems to have a quasi-governmental function with its executives acting under close guidance and surveillance of the Korean state. However, this quasi-public role that the Federation performs in a close relationship with the state is not accompanied by mandatory membership or state funding. In this regard—as well as with regard to its membership structure dominated by big businessmen—it does not resemble the associational forms that emerge under a standard corporatist system, in spite of the political responsibilities it assumes.[10]

As was mentioned in the introduction of this study the partnership between the Japanese business community and the state seems to be a more equal one than South Korean state-business relations. The post–World War II alliance between these groups was formed on the basis of already existing voluntary associations controlled by big business interests.[11] Peak business associations have played an active and significant role in the formation of the Liberal Democratic Party in 1955, which has had, since then, an uninterrupted tenure of office. Funds channelled to the business association constituted the bulk of the Party's income, and, consequently, big business has had a considerable say in political matters. Yet, state guidance of business activity also remains important, and, in this regard, association-mediated relations seem to be less important than direct contact between state authorities and business executives which form a policy community educated in similar institutions effectively disseminating elite values.[12] There are, in fact, some parallels among certain descriptions of Japanese and French

policy communities comprising graduates of elite schools that occupy executive poitions in the public or the private sector quite
indiscriminately. In both societies, with effective elite forming institutions, the common cultural and educational background of
business executives and state authorities contribute to the formation of a stable policy network without necessarily calling for the
intermediation of associations.[13] Although the distinction between
association-mediated and particularist relations becomes blurred in
environments in which associations are controlled by a handful of
group interests, it is still possible to suggest that, in Japan, close ties
of the big business community with the state are even more direct
than in South Korea where associations probably play a more important role in the state guidance of industrial activity.[14]

As far as the nature of interest representation by big business is
concerned, the examples of South Korea and Japan share one important characteristic. One observes, in both cases, a certain disassocia-
tion of a faction of the big business community from the rest of the
business class in an attempt to take an active public role in a
particular system of economic organization which little ressembles
the standard model of a liberal economy. In this process, which
takes place in an economic system under heavy state guidance, big
business gives up a standard type of interest group activity directed
at the pursuit of private economic interest to acquire a solid social
position with a quasi-governmental status. This trade-off implies
that Japanese and South Korean big business give up the struggle for
a larger share of a given cake to contribute to the national objective
of expanding the size of the cake in which it has a significant share.
Moreover, any social resentment generated by the significance of
this share becomes easier to manage, given the consolidated social
status of the big business community by virtue of its positive contribution to the policy process.

The trade-off between the pursuit of private interest and the
consolidation of social status through the acceptance of a public
responsibility does not take place only in late-industrializing countries such as Japan and South Korea, where improvement of the
country's economic performance has a crucial significance for private as well as public interest. A similar choice can be made by big
business groups elsewhere, in contexts in which the economic role
of the state is more limited and economic development does not
appear as such a dominant parameter in state-big business relation-

ships. M. Useem's *Inner Circle*, in fact, traces a similar process in the United Kingdom and the United States, where a small fraction of the big corporate businessmen have begun to play a very significant sociopolitical role which has served to consolidate the social status of businessmen as a class, albeit through the sacrifice of some short-term interests of class members. Useem explains the emergence of this "inner circle" consisting of class—as opposed to private interest—conscious big businessmen with reference to certain social developments that have taken place in the 1970s in England and in the United States. In the former, it was Labour-Party-led movements for "industrial democracy" which triggered a reaction from top corporate executives who feared the consequences of increasing union power over enterprise management. In the United States, it was increasing government regulation which generated questions concerning the boundaries of legitimate domain of intervention and created an initiative for a fraction of the big business leaders to take an active part in the policy process for a reconciliation of their class interests with wider social objectives. The main point of emphasis in Useem's account of these developments is the distinct character of inner circle members from the majority of the business community who do not have the same vision with regard to the necessary relationship between class interest and public good, and who generally act in a way so as to compromise the broader class interest in a short-term pursuit of immediate gain. Inner circle members internalize, therefore, the elements of an ideology in which both the notion of civic responsibility and the recognition of the need for government guidance of economic activity figure in a significant way. Given their differences from the rest of the business community who are largely driven by a system of thought still dominated by notions of private interest and free enterprise, they often find themselves in positions of conflict with the rest of their class and, by virtue of their economic power and social status, force the rest of the business community to yield to the requirements of social obligation and public good.

One of the important requirements for becoming an inner circle member is, according to Useem, the holding of important administrative posts in business associations. It is not, however, leadership in any association that would be an asset on the road to the inner circle. It is the activities undertaken in peak associations of the big business community and not sectoral or local associa-

tions that confer a big businessman the potential influence on matters pertaining to economic policy or social life. The formation of
the Business Roundtable in the United States reflects, for example, a
lack of faith in the ability of broader associations with wide
memberships—such as the Chamber of Commerce or the National
Association of Manufacturers—to effectively promote the position
of the business class in the formation and implementation of public
policy.[15] In fact, it is, at times, possible to observe rather significant
divergences of opinion and differences of attitude on economic and
social issues between peak associations from which inner circle
members are recruited and the rest of the business community and
their associations. Useem refers, for example, to the reconciliatory
role played by the Confederation of British Industry to assuage the
hostile reaction of the rest of the business community and their
associations against union activity. According to him, it was the
ideological position of the British inner cicle which was manifested
in the CBIs move to restrain business demands in favor of more
antilabor legislation in 1980.[16] In Useem's account, therefore, those
peak associations—which either have an exclusive membership of a
small fraction of the big business community or larger ones which
are nevertheless controlled by such a small elite group—contribute
to the increasingly important sociopolitical role played by the big
business community in the orientation of social and economic policy. The broad-based organizations with a wide membership, or
sectoral associations of the standard type of interest group activity
do not figure dominantly in these current trends whereby interest
representation acquires a new dimension with significant implications for the business class and for the rest of the society.

These trends depicted in different countries by different currents of analysis seem to capture a widely shared tendency toward
domination of associational activity by a small group of big businessmen who, by virtue of the ideas and beliefs that they internalize, give interest group activity a political character of crucial social
significance. Those individuals who control peak associations,
which are generally of an exclusive character, work in close collaboration with the state in the formation of public policy. Notwithstanding these widely shared characteristics, there are significant
differences in the manner in which the trend manifests itself in
different societies. Most significantly, the circumstances which give
rise to the tendency in question differ among countries. In some

societies the consciousness of economic constraints imposed by domestic and international factors result in the attribution of a political status to interest group activity. In others, a small fraction of the big business elite aspires to a socially significant role beyond private interest-oriented action because it feels, rightly or wrongly, that there are certain forces emanating from society or the state which threaten its social position as a class. Second, there are differences with regard to the effectiveness of the state-business cooperation in influencing the direction of the policy process. There are also societal differences, as opposed to direct and informal ties, pertaining to the role of associations in mediating the relationship between the two parties in question. Regardless of the forms of intermediation in state-business relations, through these develop-ments the big business community acquires a quasi-public role. The implications of this role for the economic development of the coun-try on the one hand, and for other social groups such as labor or small business on the other, largely depends on the historical legacy of associational life and the dominant political culture.

Even at a general level, the quasi-public role assigned to inter-est groups is likely to have different implications for business and labor. Offe, for example, mentions two reasons why it would be difficult for labor to participate in such a social arrangement on equal terms with capital.[17] First, in a situation in which both groups agree to act in conformity with certain national objectives, business representatives would have little chance to assure that their constit-uency would, indeed, comply with decisions reached in a tripartite agreement. Hence, while labor representatives would normally keep their promises in preventing, for example, a major strike for the increase of wages above the socially accepted levels, business repre-sentatives could not be expected to deliver their promises for the prevention of investment cut backs. Second, the means that the business community has to influence the orientation of economic and social policy are simply not available to labor. The latter has, as its major tool of pressuring the public authority, economic obstruc-tion via strikes. A tripartite deal, in which labor representatives give assurances that this weapon would not be used, deprives, therefore, their constituency of their major means of improving their econom-ic situation while businessmen maintain the control of divers re-sources to manipulate the policy process, thanks to the continuing significance of private investment decisions.

These concerns appear in a social setting in which there is a tradition of interest group activity with labor and capital organizations of comparable strength. In fact, certain writers argue that the success of neo-corporatist arrangements would be more likely in an environment in which the strength of the business community is undermined for some reason.[18] The argument suggests that, in a context in which it is economically strong and socially secure, private business would see little reason to enter into a social deal in which it would be asked to compromise its unhampered pursuit of pecuniary gain.

The only reason why the relative weakness of business appears as a factor contributing to a redefinition of the pursuit of interest in social terms might not be the balance of power between labor and business stemming from the weakness of the latter. The extent of dependence of the business community on the state might also be significant in the former's acceptance of certain social constraints in the pursuit of interest. In a situation in which the business community is in a position to need the support of the state to consolidate its economic and social position, businessmen would be willing to assume a quasi-public role, along with the social responsibilities it implies, in a partnership with the state. Such are, for example, the state-business partnerships that one finds in South Korea or Japan. In these countries labor and other third parties do not figure in the process whereby big business activity is attributed a public status. While the masses are excluded from this type of corporatist arrangements in which labor is absent, the arrangements—or rather the partnerships in question—seem to have been quite successful in assuring a certain trickle-down of economic progress to them. As C. Johnson writes in his analysis of the industrialization experience of Japan, Taiwan, and South Korea, "All three nations compensate labor for its decreased political role through policies of comparatively equal distribution and automatic wage increases tied to increases in productivity."[19] Although this is, of course, an arrangement which appears in a totally different social setting than the one in which West European neo-corporatism has developed, it still manifests the already mentioned trends whereby the associational activity is dominated by a small group of big businessmen who assume—or seek to assume—a public role in the policy process. It is the manifestation of these trends in Turkey that

I will next explore through a discussion of the social role of business associations in Republican period.

## BUSINESS ASSOCIATIONS IN MODERN TURKEY

A survey of the activities of business associations in Republican Turkey suggests that, until the late 1960s, business association activity was limited to Chambers with compulsory membership and was under close government control. Perhaps with the exception of a brief period during the preparation and implementation of the First Development Plan between 1962–1968, the Chambers had little influence on the policy process, and their cooperation with the government in economic policy related matters was extremely limited. Neither were they very effective in channelling the demands of their membership to government authorities, as the discussion presented in chapter three shows. The formation of voluntary associations began in the 1960s, but they became significant mainly in the late 1970s and, especially, in the 1980s. The increasing significance of voluntary associations in Turkey largely conforms to the already mentioned international trends. These voluntary associations are formed by and operate under the initiative of a small group of big businessmen who attempt to play a socially significant role by accepting to forego the pursuit of material gain as their main objective. In this regard, their leadership is distinguished from the rest of the business community on which they attempt to impose certain socially responsible and ethically correct norms of behavior. The emergence of such a distinct group of big businessmen and their associations could be explained, in the Turkish context, with reference to two factors of significance. First, the development of the private sector in the 1950s and 1960s has brought along a group of big businessmen whose social power was enhanced by the significance of their activities for the national economy. There were, in other words, certain changes taking place in the economic power held by the business class. Second, social developments of the 1960s and 1970s led certain factions of the big business community to reconsider their position as a class vis-à-vis the totality of the Turkish society and its future. While social movements with an antibusiness outlook which emerged in the 1960s, in the political environment provided by the liberal 1961 constitution were probably instrumental in leading a small group of businessmen to seek ways of consolidating the social position of their class, it was mainly the politically turbulant atmosphere of the 1970s,[20] which fostered the development of class organizations geared towards the achievement of political and economic stability in a society in which the business class would not feel threatened.

The activities of such voluntary associations in the 1980s were strongly marked by the rememberance of the terror and anarchy of the previous decade. They were guided not by the economic fear of union activity, but by the political fear of social instability. There was also a fair amount of criticism of economic policies in implementation, but the critical stand of voluntary big business associations was far from being guided by short-term economic interests. These associations demanded, rather, a planned approach to economic policy in a way to alleviate both business uncertainty and social discontentment at a national level. Moreover, at least in some cases, they were successful in imposing a similar public-good-oriented approach on other types of business organizations by convincing them of the inseparability of private-class-social interests. The response of the government to these developments was strongly marked by the legacy of state-business relations in the country. Adhering to a strictly probusiness attitude conforming to the political fashion of the decade, the MP government encouraged the pursuit of private interest, as the DP government had done in the 1950s. As did the DP government, however, the MP government remained hostile to group action for the pursuit of class interest. The hostility toward business aspirations to take part in the formation of public policy was even stronger, especially as these aspirations were often formulated with a critical attitude toward existing policy orientation. Hence, the government encouraged unintermediated, particularist relations in interest representation, and its generally tolerant attitude toward business associations has, at times, left its place to public threats and insults. This has, naturally, compromisd the support that business leaders could expect from their constituencies. Especially by accepting demands for nonassociation-mediated presentation of particular problems by individual businessmen, government has undermined the associations' strength.

The reluctance to cooperate with business associations was somewhat less in the area of international relations. The government, in fact, showed some willingness to assign a quasi-public role to certain business organizations active in the realm of foreign economic relations. However, as will be discussed in the following section, even in these cases, the effective role that the organization could play in the foreign policy process was largely determined by the personalities of a few individuals who have maintained good relations with the government. In this regard, they hardly constitute a real exception to the general particularist character of state-business relations in the country.

### Chambers As Governmental Bodies and Interest Associations

The few studies that exist on Turkish Chambers of industry and trade all emphasize the extent of government control as well as political patronage involved in the activities of these organizations.[21] Nevertheless, these studies also document the lack of a clear-cut pattern of interaction between the state and the Chambers through the Republican period. Rather, they indirectly point at the existence of a pattern characterized by the ambiguity of acquired rights and social responsibilities.

In Turkey, several different organizations are included under the general category of chambers. Having a similar legal status to that of the Chambers of Industry, Trade, and Commercial Exchanges, there are organizations of professional groups such as medical doctors, engineers, and lawyers. The establishment of the Union of Chambers, which is the umbrella organization of involuntary business associations, dates to 1950. This 1950 legislation which established the Union also covers the Chambers of Trade and Industry, Chambers of Trade, the Chambers of Industry, and Commercial Exchanges. Chambers of Industry are found only in cities, and they cannot be established in smaller units of municipal administration. With the foundation of a Chamber of Industry in a given city with a previously existing Chamber of Trade and Industry, the latter automatically becomes a Chamber of Trade. Currently, most of the big cities have a Chamber of Industry while, in smaller cities, Chambers of Trade and Industry remain active.[22]

Although legislation concerning the rights and responsibilities of the Chambers has undergone many changes in the Republican era, one permanent characteristic which they have displayed throughout this period appears as geographical as opposed to sectorial characteristics of their organizational basis. In spite of the

existence of Industry Committees designed to deal with sector specific problems, the Chambers largely remain as undifferentiated
groupings of mixed interests. A similar lack of differentiation exists
in relation to the size distribution of the member firms. This particular structure, which attempts to simultaneously represent a wide
variety of heterogeneous interests, has naturally constituted an
obstacle to the effective functioning of the Chambers as interest
associations. Hence, in the Republican period, the latter have been
important largely by virtue of public functions which they fulfilled,
and the advantages which they could confer to their members have
mostly been based on the extension of the relations of patronage
that the leadership had with government authorities to their constituency. Nevertheless, Chambers have not been merely public
bodies. They have also had an interest representation function
which has been instrumental in the efforts of different governments
to keep them under close surveillance through many changes in
legislation, as well as through several changes in relevant clauses of
the constitution.

In Turkey, the first Chambers were instituted as voluntary
organizations during the Ottoman Empire. The foundation of the
Istanbul Chamber of Industry and the Istanbul Chamber of Trade
dates to 1887. This was followed by the establishment of similar
organizations in many other cities. In that period, they were largely
regarded as consulting organs to the government in matters pertaining to the economy. During the CUP rule, the government attempted to regulate the activities of these Chambers through a law
enacted in 1910. Also under this legislation, the Chambers remained as voluntary associations with the possibility of membership for non-Turkish citizens.

Involuntary membership and the exclusion of non-Turkish
citizens from the Chambers were the two new principles brought
along by the first Republican legislation enacted in 1924. While
there was no fundamental change in the way in which the functions
of the Chambers were defined in this new piece of legislation, the
latter, with the many detailed and intricate clauses it incorporated,
marked the beginning of a series of laws designed to control Chamber activity not only through restrictions, but also through the
ambiguities of their text.[23] The next revision of the legal basis of
Chamber activity was, however, unambigiously more restrictive in
its letter and spirit. The nature of this revision of 1943 is quite

similar to that of the Law of Associations of 1938. They both reflect the atmosphere of the etatist period marked by a strong suspicion of any social initiative undertaken independently of the state. The 1938 Code, indeed, made virtually impossible the formation of any associations other than those whose activities were limited to charity or beautification. In a similar spirit, the 1943 Law of the Chambers of Trade and Industry and Commercial Exchanges largely extended the state regulation of the activities of these organizations, and the extension of state control was mainly justified with reference to the lack of moral integrity manifested in the behavior of the business community. The 1943 Code thus stated that the Chambers "were established to maintain and to develop professional ethics and discipline in conformity with the needs and interests of the people." To assure the functioning of these organizations in a way such as to contribute to this objective, the Chambers would be established by the Ministry of Commerce, and their activities could be suspended by the Ministry whenever it was deemed to be necessary for economic or social reasons.

The next legal code of Chamber activity regulation was accepted in 1950, and it followed the more liberal 1946 Law of Associations which had replaced the 1938 Law. Albeit several changes in rights and responsibilities of the Chambers that have taken place since then, the 1950 Law still forms, to a large extent, the legal basis of Chamber activity. The modifications in question, however, are by no means insignificant, especially to the extent that they reflect the character of state-business relations.

The 1950 Law has largely eliminated the tutellage of the Ministry of Trade over the Chambers. Throughout the decade, the Chambers have flourished, both in number and in social significance. While their relations with the government was very amicable in the early stages of the DP rule, in the second part of the decade—as was discussed in chapter three—they were increasingly critical of the economic policies in implementation. Toward the end of the decade, as the criticism became stronger and the DP government politically weaker, the latter made certain attempts at reconciliation by increasing the powers of the Chambers. Consequently, in 1958, the Chambers were given two very significant public functions. They were assigned, first, the responsibility of allocation of import quotas to individual importers, and, second, they were held responsible for the registration and control of imported goods. These responsibilities naturally enhanced the significance of the Chambers for their members. Furthermore, they constituted an important source of revenue complementing membership fees on which these associations had hitherto relied. It was in the same year that a new law giving the government extensive powers over the administration of the Chambers was enacted. This law gave the government the authority to postpone the elections of governing bodies of the Union of Chambers. The DP government in power soon used the powers conferred to it by this new statute and interfered in the Union's electoral process in the same year.[24]

These developments of the late 1950s are especially significant because they took place at the end of a brief period when the Chambers had just started to engage, albeit cautiously, in interest group activities benefitting from the probusiness atmosphere of the DP rule. With the new definition of the functions and administrative regulation of the Chambers, however, the latter were given a very clear message about the legitimate boundaries of interest group activity in Turkey. Businessmen were made to understand, in other words, that their associations would have government support to the extent that their leadership shared the same outlook as the government and behaved in conformity with government policy. An independent orientation in interest articulation and representation simply would not be allowed.

Leadership of the Union, as well as of most of the individual Chambers seem to have gotten the message as, until the very end of the DP rule, they carefully avoided any manifestation of sympathy or even interest in the views of other parties. As was discussed in the third chapter of this book, this was part of the reason why the Istanbul Chamber of Commerce refused to accept the visit of a RPP delegation in 1960. It was also the reason why, in the same year, the Ankara Chamber of Commerce and Industry expressed its solidarity with the government after a major student demonstration against the latter. After the military take-over in 1960, all governing bodies of the Union and local chambers were abolished because the military authorities made no distinction between Chambers and displaced DP government. Given the fact that the overwhelming majority of delegates to the Union's General Assembly, which was held shortly before the coup, were DP members, the attitude of the junta was not totally unfounded.[25]

Concerning associational liberties, the 1961 constitution pre-pared after the military take-over was, however, by far more liberal than was the previous one. While it did not neglect to take necessary precautions against socially disruptive effects of interest group ac-tivity by allowing for the possibility of limiting associational free-dom by statute when such a limitation seemed to be necessary, the new constitution also reflected a clear understanding that these associations form an integral part of modern democracy. Although there was a considerable uncertainty within the business com-munity anout the attitude of the new regime vis-à-vis the private sector, the Chambers have probably never been as effective as they were in the early 1960s as far as their involvement in the policy process was concerned.[26] The public functions that the Chambers were assigned in this period were beyond simple bureaucratic duties. They participated in the establishent and the functioning of the State Planning Organization and, given the distance between the new government and the business community, they could fulfill their representational function free of particularist tendencies which had hitherto undermined this role.

Nevertheless, with the right wing, probusiness JP in power, the Chambers again gradually reverted to their standard position, in which their social strength is contingent upon their degree of identi-fication with the government in power. This dependency on the goodwill of the government did not necessarily affect the business community in a negative way as there was no conflict between the two parties. Hence, as is indicated in a study on Turkish Chambers, the latter felt that they could safely assume a passive role in the second half of the 1960s, because the government in power was clearly sympathetic to business interests.[27] The fact that, in the Turkish context, the probusiness stand of a government does not necessarily imply its respect for business associations became, how-ever, quite clear at the end of the decade when Necmeddin Er-bakan[28] won the Union elections in 1969 through a campaign against JP candidates. He had successfully mobilized the small and medium businesses who felt alienated by the Chambers' leadership which was largely controlled by big business interests. The govern-ment retailiated by a series of attacks on the Chambers which included the transfer of the Chambers' authority in import licensing and registration to the Ministry of Trade. This decision, which deprived the Chambers from a significant source of revenue, was soon reversed after the replacement of Erbakan's group by a JP-supported team in the Union leadership.

The reversal of the decision in question was, however, a short-lived one because after the military intervention of 1971, the import quota allocation privilege of the Chambers was withdrawn. While military intervention had, thus, significantly limited public functions of the Chambers, their role in the realm of interest representation was also curbed by the 1971 constitutional revisions which were designed to keep under close surveillance those liberties accorded by the 1961 constitution. This constitutional restriction was clearly directed more at curbing labor union activity than at business associations. It was also a reflection, nevertheless, of the political authorities' attitude toward interest group activity which was not at all seen with a favorable eye. Given this attitude toward association activity, it was quite natural for the business community to rely on particularist ties of goodwill with the ruling government, and to entrust the leadership of their associations to individuals close to government circles. Under these circumstances, the rule of a party which was distant or cold to business interests implied further limitations of privileges accorded to business associations. Hence, the coalition government formed by the social democratic RPP of Ecevit and the Islamic NSP of Erbakan—in an atmosphere of hostility fostered both by politicians and the business community itself—has withdrawn the two remaining privileges of the Chambers. The latter first saw their import price registration function abolished and, second, the Union's right to print the official daily *Ticaret Sicili Dergisi* (The Commercial Register) was withdrawn by the Ministry of Commerce.

The 1982 constitution, which is still in effect, is much more radical than the 1971 revision in its determination to keep interest group activity under political control. Largely aimed at a comprehensive depoliticization of the society, it involves extensive measures which would amount to a total strangling of associational life when fully implemented. During this decade, the activities of certain associations, including those of labor unions, were indeed strangled.[29] Business associations did not share this fate. In fact, they became extremely vocal organs of interest representation with an important public opinion-forming role. Successive MP governments in power did not seriously challenge that role. However, they have not made any serious effort to build formal channels of cooperation with business organizations, either. The Chambers were not at the forefront of this new associational vivacity. They could not develop as strong interest associations and, as the previous discussion suggests, their public functions had been gradualy abolished. One of my interviewees said that, with the declining importance of their bureaucratic functions, the Chambers would probably be more successful as interest organizations. This possibility seems to be somewhat limited, however, by the size and the heterogeneity of different interets represented by these associations. Furthermore, the traditional Turkish distrust against interest associations, even though it is gradually becomirg weaker, still creates a reluctance to present interest group activity as the main function of an organization. Business associations thus chose to appear as social organizations whose activities are mainly directed at the pursuit of social objectives defined at a national level. In this area, the Chambers are also overshadowed by certain voluntary associations that made their appearance on the public scene starting in the 1960s. As was mentioned in the beginning of this chapter, this type of development in the representation of business interests as an integral part of national well-being is, in fact, an international one common to a large number of different societies. The way in which this development manifests itself in different societies is naturally shaped by a historically given character of associational environment.

*Voluntary Business Associations in Turkey*

In Turkey, the emergence of voluntary business associations can be traced to social developments of the 1960s. They have largely emerged, in other words, in response to social developments of the liberal environment created by the 1961 constitution. Although the right to unionize was accepted in 1947, labor union activity became significant in Turkey only in the 1960s. The Turkish Labor Union Confederation (Türk-İş) founded in 1951 was very passive in defending workers' rights. It began to raise its voice in behalf of its constituency in an effective manner only after the foundation of the militant Turkish Revolutionary Labor Unions' Confederation (DİSK) in 1967, which, until it was closed by the military in 1980, presented a serious challenge to Türk-İş's position as the largest representative of the labor community. The virtual absence of union activity until the 1960s was due to restrictions which the 1947 Law imposed on labor unions, according to which unions could exist only as organizations contributing to the national interest and not as bodies defending the interests of workers as a social class. In 1963, a new labor law was enacted on the basis of the 1961 constitution.[30]

It was particularly the subsequent strengthening of labor union activity and the increasing popularity of socialist ideas among the intellectual community which convinced the business community of the need to assume a more active social role. At a very general level, it is possible to depict two attitudes characterizing the political position of the business community vis-à-vis the new social developments. The overwhelming majority, especially small and medium businesses, were inclined to enter into a downright confrontation with the labor movement and its left wing supporters. There was, however, a very small fraction of the big business community with a broader vision of a social orientation in which the business community could have a stronger social position without necessarily trying to eliminate union activism and left-wing politics.

In the 1960s, Turkish Confederation of Employers' Unions (TİSK) has emerged as the main representative of the first position. Its increasing strength and social importance was largely contingent upon the alarm over the labor militancy that it succeeded to generate among the business community. Well into the 1980s, even in periods when the labor movement was reduced to practical nonexistence through antilabor legislation and economic crisis, the Confederation has, at times, taken a public stand against union pleas and demands.[31]

Such an alarmist attitude was not shared by a small number of big businessmen who opted for a moderate stand vis-à-vis the labor movement and the spread of antibusiness sentiments. The cleavage between these two groups is discussed in the autobiography of Nejat Eczacıbaşı who led the second group in the establishment of a forum in which social, economic, and political problems would be discussed with a view to find moderate solutions within a private enterprise system. This forum, which was mentioned in the discussion of Eczacıbaşı's autobiography in chapter 2 of this book, is the Conference Board on Economic and Social Issues, designed as a tripartite organization bringing together bureaucrats and politicians, certain prominent academics, and members of the business community.

Structurally, the administration of the Conference Board consists of a group of fifteen individuals among which members of the three social groups in question are equally represented. The main objective of the organization is to eliminate mutual distrust that has existed between the business community and public sector representatives and intellectuals. It has been effective in organizing a series of conferences in which the most important issues of the day are discussed in the presence of experts invited regardless of their political views and their positions toward the business community. Hence, beginning with the 1960s, at least a fraction of the business community has had an acquaintance with moderate socialist views, and some moderate socialists have met with the business community in a rather amicable atmosphere. For Eczacıbaşı, this was a rather successful attempt to prove the social existence of the business community to both friend and foe, and, at the same time, to calm down the political fears of businessmen which could lead to tactless acts of a nature to generate public hostility against the community.[32]

Conference Board meetings still take place, and they bring together different elite groups of the society at dinner-time conferences in which expert opinions are heard on topical issues. Nevertheless, the Board seems to have fulfilled its social function today and plays a very limited role compared to that assumed by new business associations. Even those businessmen who are still involved in the activities of the Board tend to think that it is now largely rendered obsolete both by changes in the sociopolitical atmosphere of Turkey and by the presence of other channels of contact among the social groups involved. These businessmen seemed to share the opinion that there are other business organizations that now play a socially more relevant role.

Among these other organizations, the Turkish Industrialists' and Businessmen's Association (TÜSİAD) appears to be one whose establishment reflects concerns which are quite similar to those that have given birth to the Conference Board. As is the Conference Board, TÜSİAD is the organization of a small group of big businessmen who believe in the necessity of social consensus generating approaches for the creation of a political and economic environment in which the business community would have a solid, noncontested status.

The twelve businessmen who signed the TÜSİAD Founders' Memorandum were owner/managers of big groups of companies.[33] Other than the similarity in their sociopolitical approach, this was the only common characteristic that they shared. In spite of attempts which different social scientists have, at times, made to explain the role of TÜSİAD with reference to the diverging interests of industrialists from those of merchants, or of exporters as opposed to those of importers, it seems far-fetched to seek any such communality of economic interest among the association's leaders .[34] The founding members of TÜSİAD, as well as successive TÜSİAD presidents, included representatives of highly diversified companies active in many fields of commerce and industry such as Koç, Sabancı, and Yaşar, and less diversified companies mainly active in textiles (such as Altınyıldız), in metallurgy and automotive (Özsaruhan and Özakat), or in ceramics (Bodur). It seems quite clear that it is a communality of sociopolitical outlook concerning the best means of assuring a solid status for the business community in a stable environment which has brought these individuals together in this new organization. As Nejat Eczacıbaşı writes in his autobiography, they had a political vision which could not be realized within heterogeneous mass of interests represented in the involuntary business associations which are frequently subjected to political manipulation because of their official status.[35] As suggested by many of my interviewees who acted as president of this association at some point—and as explicitly stated by an interviewee who was not even a member—"TÜSİAD was founded, not to pursue specific interests of businessmen, but to *prove* [sic.] the social existence of the private sector." As such, its main prerogative appears as the consolidation of the status of the business community as a social class. It is a class organization par excellence, which nevertheless sometimes finds itself confronting the members of the business community in which the private pursuit of interest by the latter conflicts with wider class interest.

Several cases of such confrontation is indeed characteristic of the early 1970s and of the years immediately before and after the foundation of TÜSİAD. The divergences of outlook in matters pertaining to social policy were especially clear in relation to attitudes toward labor movement. The antilabor militancy of TİSK, for example, was overtly condemned by some of the prominant members of TÜSİAD who thought that the uncompromising stand of the Confederation was fostering class conflict and was clearly detrimental to social peace and democratic development of the country.[36]

It was quite clear from the outset that the societal model that the leadership of TÜSİAD had in mind was deeply inspired by the social structure of developed Western countries in the era of late capitalism. As such, there is no contradiction between this model and a particular form of "private sector friendly" interventionism, not only through indicative planning or standard fiscal and monetary policy channels, but even through state investment in certain areas of the industrial sector. In fact, it was explicitly stated in the Founding Members' Memorandum that the association stood for the principles of a mixed economy model. Although the idea of mixed economy has been gradually eliminated from the agenda in the liberal atmosphere of the 1980s, TÜSİAD has remained faithful to the principle of strategic planning, not only to realize rapid growth of the economy, but also to bring about a better distribution of income to prevent the rise of socially disruptive movements detrimental to the business community more than to any other social group. In fact, it was a couple of months before the foundation of TÜSİAD that one of the prominent founding members, Vehbi Koç, publicly criticized the right wing JP government in power and pointed at the urgent need for economic reform and rational planning.[37] The same need was emphasized again and again throughout the 1980s, too, sometimes generating important frictions with the MP government.

In the second half of the 1980s, especially beginning with the presidency of Ömer Dinçkök, the young second-generation owner/ manager of the well-established Akkök Group, the frictions between government and the association have become important. As the tone of the criticism the association directed against the unplanned, instability-generating interventionism of the government has become harsher, the government authorities have, also, at times, made public declarations to the effect that TÜSİAD was surpassing the limits of legitimate associational activity. Particularly anti-TÜSİAD were the reactions of Yusuf Özal, the Minister of State responsible for the economy and the brother of the then Prime Minister Turgut Özal. In 1988, for example, he stated that the association should be dealing with specific problems of the private sector rather than occupying itself with economic policy issues by relying on the documents of the State Planning Organization.[38] The idea that "the association was not minding its own business" was indeed such a wide-spread one among the MP government circles that it even led to an incident in which Cem Boyner, another very young businessmen who replaced Dinçkök as the president of TÜSİAD, was called to the prosecutor's office for interrogation because of his so-called illegal political speeches in early 1990.[39] The idea that TÜSİAD adheres to an old-fashioned idea of planning was also a very popular one among MP government authorities. Very recently, after the electoral defeat of the party in 1991, President Turgut Özal, who has always remained, before anything else, the founder of the MP, left a conference by the current president of TÜSİAD, Bülent Eczacıbaşı, in undissimulated anger, telling the journalists that young Eczacıbaşı, just as was his father Nejat Eczacıbaşı, is unable to leave the old interventionist ideas and accept the principles of a liberal economy.[40]

It is quite clear that the three young businessmen—Ömer Dinçkök, Cem Boyner, and Bülent Eczacıbaşı—who have successively acted as president of the association, had uncompromisingly critical attitudes toward MP government policies which were, in many ways, typical of the economic policy process in Republican Turkey. It is less clear, however, whether this attitude of the leadership is fully shared or, rather, fully understood, by the overwhelming majority of the leadership. Although there is an unambigious continuity between the spirit of the founders' memorandum and the critical stand of the last three presidents, the firmness of the tone of this criticism appears to be something quite unusual given historical characteristics of business outlook and behavior in the country. The unscrupulousness of the reaction against government policy in this period was not, probably, unrelated to the age group of the association's leaders. These were second-generation young businessmen who did not have the experience of their fathers in the area of state-business relations. There was, therefore, at least at an initial stage, a difference between their bold attitudes and their elders' more prudent stand. In the second half of the 1980s, there were, in fact, several incidents in which this difference of attitude was clearly manifested. During the presidency of Dinçkök, for example, a questionnaire was sent to TÜSİAD members with a view to assess their evaluation of the economic policies then being implimented. The answers reflected a highly critical, even hostile, attitude toward the ruling government's approach to economic policy. These results appeared in the press, and a meeting was organized to discuss them in the presence of government authorities. In this meeting, Dinçkök was almost totally isolated by his constituency which declined to confront the politicians in a critical manner. The whole thing was obviously quite embarrassing for the leadership, and it is even possible that it was partly instrumental in Dinçkök's resignation shortly after the incident.

In the course of my interviews, I asked several businessmen to comment on this particular event. There were, in general, two types of answers. One group of businessmen said that the questionnaire was very inefficiently distributed and, at the time of the meeting with the politicians, very few businessmen had actually any idea about either the questions or the answers. There were others, however, who thought that the whole incident closely reflected the nature of state-business relations and the usual lack of courage characterizing the business community. "What do you expect?" one of my interviewees asked. "Everybody had some business in Ankara the next day."

"Everybody's business in Ankara" is probably part of the reason why some older businessmen have periodically reacted to the critical speeches by Dinçkök and his successor Boyner by demanding them to speak for themselves and not for the association.[41] Older members of the business community were, in general, more prudent than younger ones because their experiences in the area of state-business relations had taught them what the government can give to, but also take away from, businessmen through discretionary methods. Their prudence, however, probably reflected more than an element of fear. There was also an element of gratitude to the ruling MP government that had significantly contributed to the establishment of a probusiness ideology. As one of my interviewees explicitly stated, "One has to be careful when criticizing a government which is not against private enterprise." This particular mixture of fear and gratitude is an obvious sign of weakness, which the businessmen openly admitted in the course of our private interviews in which, nevertheless, a genuine admiration for the young presidents of TÜSİAD was also expressed.

These divergences of opinion concerning the tone of the criticism directed at government policy largely remain as divergences within the leadership of the association, with the rest of the members hardly expressing any opinion on the subject. It would, indeed, be misleading to suggest that the attitudes of the leadership of TÜSİAD closely reflect the outlook and mentality of the majority of the association's members. It is, in fact, quite important not to overlook the fact that the organizational structure of the association is a highly undemocratic one in which the decisions are mostly taken either in the Board of Directors or the Advisory Council, with at least as much input from outside experts as from members of the association. As a recent study on TÜSİAD has shown, in this particular structure of decision-making, the opinions of ordinary members carry little weight, and a small number of prominent businessmen representing major enterprise groups run the association. The study in question documents this particular characteristic of the association, not only by the analysis of the responses given to a questionnaire sent to all the members, but also through the disribution of the members who have returned the questionnaire and those who have not. The response rate to the questionnaire was, in general, very low, something surprising in itself for such a vocal association attempting to secure itself an important position in the social scene. The distribution of the respondents show, however, that the majority of them were members of the Executive Committee, the Board of Directors, or the Advisory Council. As it would be expected, therefore, the vocal leadership had not failed to express its opinion on the issues pertaining to the position of the association in Turkish society. It was the response rate of the ordinary membership which was very low. Comments offered by the latter, indeed, revealed that the questions were found to be either "politically sensitive" or "beyond an ordinary member's concern or knowledge."[42]

This suggests that the views or attitudes generally attributed to TÜSİAD are hardly representative of the Turkish business community or even of the particular fraction of the big businessmen who belong to the association. These views and attitudes appear to be those of a handful of big businessmen representing a class mission rather than a given category of interests. It is quite natural, therefore, that there is no one-to-one correspondance between their outlook and the outlook of their constituency, let alone that of the business community represented in other business associations. In fact, until quite recently, the latter had seen TÜSİAD as a threat to their own social position, and, at times, they have regarded its critical stand as a dangerous one which could provoke government hostility against all the members of the business community.[43]

The coldness—or, at times, even animosity—between representatives of involuntary associations and TÜSİAD continued until the late 1980s. In the middle of the decade, there were even rumors about some attempts to end the separate existence of the association through its unification with the Union of Chambers. It is interesting that a founding member of TÜSİAD, Sakıp Sabancı, was involved in these attempts, which most probably enjoyed the full support of a government discontented with mounting criticisms of the association's leadership.[44] In 1988, the president of the board of directors of the Istanbul Chamber of Industry, Nurullah Gezgin, was quoted as saying that TÜSİAD "has become harmful for the Turkish economy. This association should be closed without wasting any time."[45] The next year, however, Gezgin lost the leadership of the Istanbul Chamber of Industry to Memduh Hacıoğlu whose list of members in the Chamber assembly included Ömer Dinçkök, then the president of TÜSİAD, as well as several representatives of big holding companies. Some of the supporters of Gezgin interpreted the leadership change as marking the beginning of a process of "Tüsiadization" of the Chamber.[46]

It seems easy, indeed, to interpret the victory of the Hacıoğlu team as a victory of big business interests over the interests of small and medium businessmen. Nevertheless, after the leadership change, there was more emphasis than ever before on the problems of small businessmen. This concern of the Chamber leadership for small business interests was clearly reflected, for example, in a heated debate between Hacıoğlu and the TİSK leadership over a particular legal issue concerning the collective bargaining process. According to a hitherto unapplied clause of the relevant legislation, wage increases negotiated in a given enterprise would automatically apply to other enterprises operating in the same industrial branch. The president of TİSK, Refik Baydur, recently took steps to make this clause operative in wage negotiations. The leadership of the Istanbul Chamber immediately reacted against this move on the grounds that implementation of the piece of legislation in question would be detrimental for small industry. As Hacıoğlu also stated, the clause reflected a total disregard for differences in costs of living in big cities and smaller towns, which enabled the industries in the latter to survive thanks to their lower wage costs.[47] It is quite obvious that the big industrialists who maintained control of the Chamber since the 1989 elections have little to lose with implementation of the clause because they often pay the highest prevailing wages. Elimination of small and medium enterprises would only imply a gain through reduced competition for most of them. The attitude of the leadership on this matter suggests, therefore, that it would be misleading to analyze associational activity solely on the basis of material interest.

To say the least, there is no indication that the so-called Tüsiadization of the Istanbul Chamber of Industry has led to the predominance of big business interests in overall interest representation activity. In other ways, however, the Tüsiadization process is a very real one, of which the change in the leadership of the Istanbul Chamber of Industry is probably a reflection rather than a cause. It is a process in which the leaders of the business community representing different involuntary and voluntary associations have begun to make public statements in which the concern for public interest dominates the concern for the specific problems of the business community. In 1988, we heard, for example, the president of the Union of Chambers stating at a Union meeting that "we must first express the interests of our country and then the interests of the private sector and the problems we are faced with."[48]

In a way, this attitude is in full conformity with the traditional characteristics of the Turkish business environment in which the social legitimacy of the pursuit of private interest has been quite precarious. What is new about the current situation is the bold expression of critical views by the representatives of most business associations that have found themselves in an open confrontation with the government by the end of the decade. It was not only TÜSİAD and the Istanbul Chamber of Industry, but other associations such as the Istanbul Chamber of Commerce,[49] or the Eskişehir Chamber of Industry,[50] as well as many other local chambers that joined in an increasingly strong criticism of the economic policy process. In fact, in 1990, several businessmen representing local chambers or associations such as TİSK responded to TÜSİAD's call for pressuring the ruling MP government to hold early elections.[51] In the Union of Chambers, even during the rule of a progovernment leadership, critical opinions were increasingly heard and, in the elections held in 1990, this leadership was replaced by one supporting the True Path Party,[52] then in opposition. Although this last election was not too different from the previous ones, given the dominance of party politics as a determinant of electoral behavior, it nevertheless constituted one of the rare instances in which change in the leadership of the Union anticipated rather than followed change in the ruling government.

Interestingly, even TİSK joined in the criticism of the MP government which was, by far, the boldest of the elected Turkish governments in its firm stand against wage increases and its resistance to the expansion of union rights. The president of the Confederation, Refik Baydur, was thus quoted as saying "Does the Turkish state not have any soldiers to send to the front other than the industrialists and industrial workers?"[53] The Federation— previously alienated, as was discussed earlier in this chapter, by certain members of the big business community in the 1960s and 1970s for its probusiness militancy—seemed to have a rather different position in the late 1980s when its leaders talked about "opening the doors of the federation to workers' representatives"[54] and even of following a common strategy with labor union federations against wage cuts,[55] or "expressed their sympathies for some social democrat leaders"[56]. This milder attitude of the Federation vis-à-vis labor issues is in conformity with the prevailing trends in business associations' attitude toward the level of wages in particular and income distribution in general. While unequal income distribution has always been underlined as a serious problem threatening the private enterprise economy and political democracy by TÜSİAD, in the late 1980s the leadership of the Istanbul Chamber of Industry also often commented on the low level of wages to contest the views about the inflationary impact of wage increases.[57] In the same period, the spokesmen for the business community have in general expressed similar views indicating that they do not regard workers and labor organizations as their opponents, and they do not regard social democratic movements as something to be feared and confronted.[58]

Could we, then, interpret these TÜSİAD-led developments in the social attitudes of Turkish business representatives as a sign of the community's becoming a well-established class with a sense of class ethics and social responsibility? This, I believe, is the intention and hope of certain business leaders who, nevertheless, are but a small minority. It is unlikely that the social project that they have in mind is fully understood and accepted even by all of the founding members of TÜSİAD. That they currently control the leadership of most of the important business associations does not necessarily mean that the possibility of a future change, whereby the business community would resume its usual indifference to issues not directly related to its specific interests, is totally excluded. It does not mean, either, that traditional particularism characterizing state-business relations would leave its place to association-mediated relations carried out with full consciousness of rights and respon-sibilities. Relatedly, while an increasingly stronger and well-established business community is likely to have an increasingly greater say in matters pertaining to public policy, it is not at all clear whether this trend would necessarily have positive implications for the economic and social development of the country. I believe that certain characteristics of associational life in Turkey are of a nature to justify a somewhat pessimistic attitude with regard to future developments in these areas.

These characteristics could be explained with reference to the continuity and change in the role of Turkish business associations. The change lies, as highlighted in the previous discusssion, in the increasingly articulate demands of a fraction of the business com-munity to take part in the social and economic policy process. There is a continuity even here because this has been a wish of the business community throughout the Republican era, which could be more forcefully expressed as part of a critical approach to govern-ment policy after a certain level of development of the private sector had been reached. There have always been, therefore, private sector demands to take part in policy formulation and implementation. On the other hand, what has been absent until recently is an effort to legitimize the pursuit of interests and the position of business or-ganizations as interest associations. The legitimization of interest group activity, in other words, has almost never appeared as one of the demands of the business community. In parallel to this particu-lar historical trend, one observes a situation in which those business organizations which appear as instruments for the promotion of specific business interests cannot easily develop and become influ-ential in Turkey. It is mainly those organizations whose stated objectives have to do with the promotion of national interest which can develop and subsequently become effective in consolidating the social status of the business community as a whole. Under these circumstances, the pursuit of specific business interests is largely carried out in a particularist manner. This is, in fact, a paradoxical situation because the strengthening of the business community and its associations is not accompanied by a parallel weakening of particularist ties of dependency that Turkish businessmen have traditionally had with the state. The state, in its turn, acts in a way to maintain these ties by refusing to grant the business associations the most important monopoly right that neo-corporatist states accord to associations to consolidate their public role: namely, the refusal to negotiate with private businessmen who wish to take their complaints and demands directly to state authorities without the intermediation of their associations. By allowing—or rather encouraging—nonassociation-mediated relations with individual businessmen, state authorities undermine the significance that associations have for their members and consequently hamper consolidation of their positions in society.

In this regard, two of the owner/managers whom I interviewed suggested that particularism was encouraged especially by right-wing, probusiness governments that tend to have a pragmatic approach and believe that the intermediation of associations complicate things. "They view this type of indirect contact as being too bureaucratic" one of these interviewees said. These two businessmen thought that other types of governments, on the other hand, are reluctant to discuss policy matters with representatives of business organizations because they fear appearing to be guided by business interests. Whether it is well-founded or not, this observation is interesting in that it reflects the views of businessmen on the effectiveness of organized channels of contact with the government. As most of my interviewees indicated, big businessmen in TÜSİAD are too big to need the organization to take their problems to the government. They do not have any difficulty in meeting with government authorities and presenting their cases. In fact, there seems to be an understanding among most of its prominent members that TÜSİAD should carefully avoid getting involved in pressure group politics, concentrating instead on questions pertaining to national objectives. The difficulties of interest representation by the Chambers, with their large and heterogeneous leadership, have already been discussed. Some of my interviewees thought that the Professional Committees of the Chambers of Industry[59] are quite effective in promoting the interests of small businessmen. The presidents of two sectoral associations whom I interviewed thought, however, that there is no way in which these committees could be effective, given the bureaucratic structure of the Chambers and the hetero-geneity of the enterprises brought together under the same profes-sional grouping. They believed that professional associations had a very important function to fulfill in spite of the reluctance of the Chambers to admit the significance of their role.[60]

However, there are certain problems which seem to limit the effectiveness of this role. First, these sectoral associations have financial difficulties because of the refusal of the government to accord them the status of socially useful associations which would enable them to benefit from tax-deductable contributions. Second, as one of my interviewees bitterly complained, the lack of interest and committment of businessmen to their sectoral associations prevent these associations from becoming really influential. "The big [ones] think that they do not need the association" he said, and "the smaller ones feel that the association is there anyway and would try to solve their problems without their contribution." This interviewee also thought that the government did not try to curb particularist tendencies and continued to receive individual pleas which are supposed to be channelled through the association.

The president of the second sectoral association whom I inter-viewed seemed to be happier with the attitude of the membership as well as with the association's relations with the government. Ac-cording to him, the solidarity between the members of his associa-tion is an exceptional one, owing largely to the strong guild tradition which is still dominant in the trade. As to their good relations with the government, he explained them by pointing out their compliant attitude and their carefulness in limiting their demands to strictly technical issues without any attempt to discuss broader policy mat-ters. He even explained how he had recently silenced a member of their board who wanted to make a public criticism of the the foreign trade policy in implementation. Because their sector was closely affected especially by the exchange rate policy, I asked him whether it was not too difficult to avoid the issue. As an answer, he endlessly complained about the seriousness of the harm inflicted on their sector by the overvalued exchange rate policy then in implementa-tion, but concluded that it was not their association's business to deal with it. "Let the Chambers do it" he said. "Let TÜSİAD do it."

The prerogative of the association, indeed, seemed to be a

rather limited one as some of the problems related to the relocation of production units in this sector—an issue which is also obviously a sector-specific one—were taken to government authorities by the Istanbul Chamber of Industry rather than the association itself. My interviewees have, in fact, confirmed that the Chambers often must interfere in relations between the state and sectoral associations to handle certain problems situated at a macro level and beyond the associations' reach. Under these circumstances, the amicability of the sectoral associations' relations with the state remains contingent upon the systematic avoidance of broad policy issues, and the defense of those sectional interests affected by the latter is left to those business organizations who emphasize the pursuit of public good, as opposed to the pursuit of narrow interest, as their main objective. Interest representation, as previously suggested, remains in its traditional marginal position in associational activity in spite of the increasingly dynamic appearance which the latter has recently assumed.

In the meanwhile, concerning the national policy-shaping orientation of their activities, the success of business associations appears to be limited by the reluctance of the government to establish formal channels of contact to discuss policy issues with businessmen. The MP government authorities have, in fact, made several references to the need to establish joint committees to assure the participation of business representatives in the policy process and, toward the end of the MP rule, a specific attempt was made in this direction. Nevertheless, the nature of this particular attempt itself is of a nature to reveal, in a strikingly clear fashion, the particularism that marks the state-business relations in Turkey. In this particular step, taken to improve the diologue between the two parties in question and to call forth a more significant business input to the policy process, one of the Ministers of State responsible for the economy called a meeting with fourteen big businessmen. While the meeting ended, according to the subsequent declarations of the participating businessmen, without a precise decision having been taken, the minister announced the next day that a business council—which would meet regularly to serve as a forum in which government authorities and businessmen would discuss and take decisions concerning major policy issues—was going to be formed.[61] Quite expectedly, such a council was never formed. More significantly, neither the presidents of the major Chambers nor the

president of TÜSİAD were among the fourteen businessmen invited
to the meeting, and the minister's announcement included no explanation about the criterion of choice adopted in the invitation. The
whole incident has, thus, presented a manifestation of the government's disregard for business associations.

It would not be justified to overlook, however, the potential
that a particular type of business organization has as an important
actor in the social policy arena. The organizations in this category
are those which are founded as quasi-governmental bodies, active in
specific areas of public policy. A particularly important one among
those—The Economic Development Foundation (İKV)—was established in the 1960s to be active in the area of Turkish-EEC relations.
It was founded by the Istanbul Chamber of Industry and the Istanbul
Chamber of Trade, and its members include several business associations, such as TÜSİAD and TİSK. The Foreign Economic Relations Organization (DEİK), on the other hand, was founded with the
initiative of the Union of Chambers and Stock Exchanges as an
umbrella organization bringing together the Regional Business
Councils and major private sector organizations. In 1990, eleven
Regional Councils under the umbrella of DEİK had a total membership of 527. These Councils are considered to be the most active
agents influencing the development of Turkey's foreign economic
relations.[62] While it is mainly active in the area of international
trade and investment, main objectives of DEIK also include the
establishment of a healthy dialogue between different private sector
organizations and to coordinate their activities.[63]

In spite of their wide organizational membership, both İKV and
DEİK appear as organizations whose effective role in public policy is
largely determined by the personalities of a few individuals who
maintain good relations with the state. As to their ability to remain
on good terms with government authorities, it is probably not unrelated to the fact that the activities of these organizations are geared
toward the international arena and are detached from the field of
domestic policy where divergences between government action and
private sector interests are more likely to emerge. It is possible to
state, therefore, that the nature of these organizations is in conformity with the traditional particularist character of state-business
relations in which harmony is contingent upon the careful tuning of
any criticism directed at government policy. Yet, they also reflect
some new trends whereby the increasing economic significance of

the big business community is accompanied by the special position it has acquired in policy formation and implementation.

It seems unlikely, however, that these trends would culminate in the emergence of a European type neo-corporatism in Turkey. In this regard, the differences between the Turkish history of associational activity and the European one are likely to be determining in two different ways. Concerning the role of business associations in shaping relations between the private sector and the state, perhaps the most striking characteristic of the Turkish experience is the reluctance of the political authority to accept associations as the legitimate medium of interest representation. This has to do, at least in part, with the lack of social legitimacy of any activity directed at the pursuit of private interest. Nevertheless, even those governments which are willing to accept private interest as the engine of economic growth and development appear to be hostile to the organized pursuit of interests structured along class lines. In other words, even when the notion of private interest loses its negative connotations, the pursuit of class interest is still regarded as being socially disruptive and politically dangerous. Under these circumstances, the Turkish business community finds itself in a situation in which it has to act as a class, ready to assume a social responsibility at a national level without having acquired a proper experience in interest articulation and representation. Moreover, with a small fraction of its members trying to make other businessmen understand and endorse a particular social project, the community faces a state which does not express much willingness to accord a social role to business associations structured along class lines. This defines a situation in which the tendency toward the successful management of state-business relations in a neo-corporatist framework would be dominated by particularist tendencies in rent-seeking activity.

Even the limited possibility of economic success that might be brought about by a nonorganized alliance between the state and individual big businessmen would not necessarily constitute a socially desirable outcome. This would be an economic success achieved without any input from third parties, such as small business or labor. In the overall underdeveloped state of associational life in Turkey, these groups find themselves in an incomparably less privileged position than is big business. The assymmetry between the organized representation of business interest and labor demands appears to be especially severe throughout most of the Republican period. If the activities of business organizations are not encouraged or supported by the state, labor union activity was, at times, actively and forcefully contained, controlled, and restricted by the political authority. In the 1980s in particular, the unprecedented dynamism of business associations was accompanied by a quasi-total silencing of labor unions. It was in this period that the country witnessed very unusual phenomena such as the defense of worker's rights by industrialists or the criticism of income inequalities by the wealthiest members of the society. The socially conscious rich could perhaps continue to raise their voices in behalf of the poor. Similarly, part of the economic benefits of the alliance between individual businessmen and the state could now be used to compensate the social groups who remain outside the policy process. The presence of a certain economic compensation would, however, be hardly sufficient to offset the politically undesirable nature of an arrangement in which the masses passively remain at the mercy of the partnership between the state and big business for any improvement of their economic position. Both socially and politically this would constitute a situation which little resembles the case of West European countries where neo-corporatist arrangements prevail. It would perhaps be closer to the case of East Asian countries such as Japan or South Korea where the partnership between the state and big conglomerates determine the course of economic life to the exclusion of third parties. Naturally, given the differences between the East Asian states and the Turkish ones, many questions also emerge concerning both the sustainability and possible economic implications of such a model in Turkey.

# 6. Concluding Remarks

In this overview of the evolution of business activity in Republican Turkey, the factors that define the sociopolitical context of entrepreneurship were investigated in four areas. First, sources of entrepreneurship and the politics of mobilizing entrepreneurial talent were explored by looking at the development of the private sector in the Republican period. Policy process under successive Republican governments constituted the second area in which the determinants of business outlook and behavior were studied. Socially defined features of the structure of the typical big business unit or the holding company were then analyzed for a further investigation of society-specific characteristics of business life. Finally, the nature of business associations was explored as an arena in which the social position of private businessmen as well as the relations with the latter and the public authority are revealed most clearly.

The elements depicted in these four areas do not, naturally, form a static framework which has remained unchanged over time. Change is observed, in particular, in the first and the third areas, in which both the development of the private sector and its institutional restructuring via the advent of the holding company appear as forces of transformation in the economic and sociopolitical coordinates of private business activity. Continuity appears, however, to overshadow change as far as the policy environment in the country is concerned. In this area, policy-induced uncertainty of business life remains a constant throughout the Republican era and contributes to the vulnerability of the private sector vis-à-vis the state, in spite of the economic and institutional developments which have led to a nonnegligible consolidation of the social status of the big business community. The nature of the policy process also constitutes a factor which serves to perpetuate the historically given characteristics of business behavior. Hence, we observe that, in Turkey, the private sector has grown without necessarily developing an industrial outlook, and big holding companies continue to function as commercial operations, with speculative concerns often dominating the concern for productive efficiency.

This emphasis on continuity appears to be particularly useful for an evaluation of post–1980 developments in Turkish economy. It is undeniable that post–1980 attempts for the establishment of a market economy have introduced certain major transformations, especially in the foreign exchange regime and foreign trade policy. In these areas, the structural adjustment initiated in the 1980s, indeed, represented a break with the import substitution strategy of the past decades. In this period, successive MP governments have also taken certain important steps to prepare the institutional basis of a self-regulating market system. Nevertheless, these attempts at the restructuring of the economy did not lead to the retreat of the state, an objective which was stressed as a major component of the official ideology of the decade. There was a reorganization of the state apparatus which brought about a centralization of decision-making by enlarging the powers of the executive branch in general and of the Prime Minister in particular. The legislative, as well as the legal and bureaucratic state institutions, were undermined in this process, but this did not imply, in any way, a decline in the significance of the state for business activity. The state remained—perhaps more significantly than in any other period in the Republican era—the central focus of the Turkish businessman's daily concerns.

The nature of state-business relations in the 1980s was also in conformity with the historical legacy of this relationship. Policy environment continued to influence business outlook and behavior in the same way as it had before. In this environment, rent-seeking activity flourished, and some Turkish businessmen found ample opportunity to put to use their talents in zero-sum entrepreneurship developed during the previous import-substitution regime. While this type of business behavior was encouraged by the incoherent character of the policy process, with the significance they now had in national economy, big business community contributed, in turn, to the arbitrariness of government policy by affecting or circumventing it in conformity with their individual interests. In other words, while state autonomy remained significant, state policy was marked by a strong element of particularism which enhanced the incoherence of the economic strategy in implementation.

This evaluation of the post–1980 structural adjustment experience of Turkey points at mutual interaction between the institutional and cultural environment of business activity and the policy process as a major determinant of policy outcome in a given society. As such, it contributes to the analysis of the economic process in its sociopolitical framework in different societies of varying historical experience, cultural fabric, and political tradition. One area in which this type of analysis can be applied is the study of economic organizations, and of business firms in particular. From this perspective, which challenges the overemphasis of the standard principles of economically rational behavior in the analysis of business organizations, the differences that the latter manifest in different societal contexts may be accounted for with reference to historically determined sociopolitical variables. The study of business organizations could, indeed, benefit from such a political economy perspective especially in the investigation of differences in structure, strategy, and contribution to macroeconomic performance of multiactivity enterprises which, today, play a significant role in the economies of many late-industrializing countries, and which are likely to assume a similar role in the economies of former socialist countries now undergoing major transformation processes.

At a more general level, the line of analysis developed in this study might contribute to the elaboration of models which could serve to predict the socially determined outcome of a given policy mix in different contexts. One could, for example, build a model in which business environment would be defined both by institutional forms of business organization, and historically and culturally given forms of business behavior. The nature of the policy process would appear to be a crucial variable affecting the business environment, but the latter would, in turn, influence the ways in which a society tries to attain the policy objectives which it sets for itself. The pattern that would emerge as a result of this interaction between policy environment and business environment could be investigated by looking at the extent to which the policy mix in implementation *aims at* bringing about changes in and *actually affects* business behavior and the structure of business organizations, as well as the extent to which the latter *present an obstacle* or *contribute to* the implementation of the policy mix in question.

Application of such a model to the post–1980 economic restructuring attempt in Turkey was not an objective of this book. Nevertheless, through a discussion of the cultural and institutional framework of business activity in its interaction with the state in Republican Turkey, the study has naturally led to the conceptualization of such a model. The historical survey presented in this book, in fact, provides most of the elements of an analytical approach such as the one briefly outlined in the preceeding paragraphs. This could be of relevance, I believe, for studies of patterns of structural change in societies other than in Turkey.

The structural adjustment initiated in Turkey in the 1980s, in fact, had many parallels with initiatives taken by other late-industrializing countries earlier or at around the same time. The recent economic istories of late-industrializing countries have, indeed, been marked by the implementation of such structural adjustment programs, usually undertaken by conditional assistance from the International Monetary Fund. One could thus speak of a certain convergence in policy orientation, whereby the role of the state is redefined and a greater importance is assigned to the competitive discipline of the market. The empirical reality in late-industrializing countries in general reveals, however, significant divergences in the forms of implementation as well as the degree of socioeconomic success of the fairly standard guidelines of the IMF type programs. One observes, in other words, a global response to past policy failures and to the challenge of an increasingly competitive and increasingly small world economy, a response, which, nevertheless, takes different forms and leads to different results in different societal contexts.

This particular policy convergence—which is accompanied by marked divergences in policy implementation and outcome—presents an interesting challenge to development economics. More specifically, it constitutes a challenge which calls for the endogenization of certain political, cultural, and institutional variables hitherto regarded as exogenous to the analysis of economic development. In other words, it highlights the need to redefine the boundaries of the subdiscipline in the light of empirical reality in late-industrializing countries.

Furthermore, such a redefinition of the boundaries of development economics is in a position to take into account the empirical reality in developed Western countries where global forces of competition in an increasingly small world economy have led to the emergence of state society relations which hardly conform to standard market economy models. In these countries, too, similar economic challenges lead to similar responses that are, nevertheless, shaped differently by different societal factors. The experience of developed Western countries thus points at the limited usefulness of the pure market model even in those countries where it was originated. Consequently, the political economy of developed countries—which was hitherto considered to be in full conformity with the pure market model and hence of limited interest for the developing world—appears to be relevant for analyses of economic performance in late-industrializing countries.

The trends highlighted by these observations of policy choice and policy outcome are, in a somewhat paradoxical fashion, of convergence and divergence at the same time. Similar strategic choices adopted by different countries seem, on the one hand, to reassert the universality of "economic rationality" while, on the other hand, different patterns emerging in these countries suggest that economy is, indeed, embedded in society. The analysis of societal determinants of economic activity thus appears as a necessary component of all investigations of policy outcome in different societies. It is this observation pertaining to the contemporary international system which makes me believe that the type of analytical model emerging from this study on Turkey might also be useful for other countries.

In particular, I believe that the present study could provide some insights for evaluation of the current experience of former socialist countries exploring ways of introducing the market into their economic systems. There are certain intellectuals who seem to think that the market system forms a complete and coherent entity with given institutions and a given value system. They also seem to think that, once these institutions and values are properly established, private entrepreneurs would automatically emerge and provide the motor force of economic development. These intellectuals manifest, therefore, a certain impatience with continuing state involvement in the economy, and they are especially critical of the former political elite's appearing as the main source of entrepreneurship in these countries.[1] This type of reaction reflects the basic assumptions of standard economic models in which the embeddedness of the economy is largely ignored. It leaves out, therefore, both the political element in the creation of the market and sociopolitical factors that determine the forms of business behavior and types of business organization, as well as the social implications of business activity. A more realistic approach to the experience of former socialist countries must incorporate all of these elements—which are precisely the ones that this book explored across the experience of Republican Turkey.

# APPENDIX

## LIST OF INTERVIEWEES

İhsan Akköy, manager, private auditing company

İzak Alaton, owner-manager, Alarko Group

Evren Artam, professional manager, director of the foreign trade company of the Koç group

Aydın Aybay, specialist in property law

Semiha Baban, administrative secretary, YASED (Association for Foreign Capital Coordination)

Feyyaz Berker, owner/manager, Tekfen Group; founding member and former president of TÜSİAD; president of DEİK

Alber Bilen, owner/manager, Türk Henkel; president of the Association of the Producers in Chemical Industry

Cem Boyner, owner/manager, Altınyıldız Group; president of TÜSİAD at the time of interview

Lori Burla, owner/manager, Burla Group

Ömer Dinçkök, owner/manager, Akkök Group; former President of TÜSİAD

Nejat Eczacıbaşı, owner/manager, Eczacıbaşı Group; founding member and former president of TÜSİAD; founder of the Conference Board on Social and Economic Issues

Şinasi Ertan, professional manager, president of the board of directors of the Aegean Chamber of Industry

Ersin Faralyalı, owner/manager; former president of the board of directors of the Union of Chambers

Nurullah Gezgin, owner/manager, former president of the board of directors of the Istanbul Chamber of Industry

Deniz Gökçe, consultant to the private banking sector

Memduh Hacıoğlu, owner/manager, Balinler Co.; president of the board of directors of the Istanbul Chamber of Industry

Servet Harunoğlu, professional manager, Çukurova Group

Mehmet Kabasakal, professional manager, Kavala Group; active in the Association of the Exporters in Clothing Industry; also active in the Conference Board on Social and Economic Issues

Jak Kamhi, owner/manager, Profilo Group; President of İKV.

Erdoğan Karakoyunlu, professional manager, Koç group; former president of the Union of Employers in Mining and Metal Industry

Yılmaz Karakoyunlu, former professional manager, Sabancı group

Fikret Keskiner, professional manager, Enka Group

Numan Ketenci, Turkish Capital Market Board

Vehbi Koç (written interview), owner/manager, Koç Group; founding member and former president of TÜSİAD

Ali Koçman, owner/manager, Koçtuğ Group; founding member and former president of TÜSİAD

Turgut Koşar, owner/manager, Koşar Leather Co.; president of the Association of Leather Producers

Tavit Köletavitoğlu, share-holding professional manager, Net Group

Ali Naili Kubalı, former professional manager, Yaşar Group

Can Paker, professional manager, Türk Henkel

Atıl Öncü, professional manager, Koç Group

Cihangir Özer, professional manager, director of the foreign trade company of the Çukurova Group

Güler Sabancı, owner/manager, Sabancı Group

Ayhan Şahenk, owner/manager, Doğuş Group

Selami Şengül, Turkish Capital Market Board

Besim Tibuk, share-holding manager, Net Group; president of the Association of Investors in Tourism

Osman Nuri Torun, professional manager, Hür Holding; former bureaucrat active in the establishment of the State Planning Organization, also active in the preparation of the Turkish holding company legislation

Eser Tümen, professional manager, STFA Group

Aydın Ulusan, professional manager, Kavala Group

Güngör Uras, professional manager, Sabancı Group; former administrative secretary of TÜSİAD

Feyhan Yaşar-Kalpaklıoğlu, owner/manager, Yaşar Group

# NOTES

## CHAPTER 1

1. A. Buğra, "The Late Coming Tycoons of Turkey," *Journal of Economics and Administrative Studies*, 1:1 (Winter 1987).

2. The autobiographies in question were the following: Vehbi Koç, *Hayat Hikayem* (Istanbul: Apa Ofset Basımevi, 1979); Nejat F. Eczacıbası, *Kuşaktan Kuşağa* (Istanbul: Nejat Eczacıbası Vakfı Yayını, 1982; Sakıp Sabancı, *İşte Hayatım*, Istanbul: Aksoy Matbaacılık, 1985). Other autobiographies by leading Turkish businessmen include Alber Bilen, *Türk Sanayiinde Kırk Zorlu Yıl* (Istanbul: Final Ofset Matbaası, 1988); Bernar Nahum, *Koc'ta 44 Yılım* (Istanbul: Milliyet Yayınları, 1988); Fevzi Akkaya, *Ömrümüzün Kilometre Taşları: ST-FA'nın Hikayesi* (Istanbul: Fevzi Akkaya Temel Eğitim Vakfı, 1989); Süreyya İlmen, *Teşebbüslerim ve Reisliklerim* (Istanbul: Hilmi Kitabevi 1949) and Koray, Enver ed., *Selahattin Adil Pasa'nın Anıları* (Istanbul: Zafer Matbaası, 1982) are among the earlier autobiographies by big businessmen.

3. The instrumentalist approach is mainly associated with the name of Ralph Miliband and the functionalist approach with that of Nicos Poulantzas. See, in particular, R. Miliband, *The State in Capitalist Society* (London: Quartet Books, 1973); and N. Poulantzas, *Les Classes sociales dans le capitalism d'aujourd'hui* (Paris: Editions du Seuil, 1974).

4. J. M. Keynes, *Essays in Persuasion* (New York: W.W.Norton and Co., 1963) 319.

5. L. Dumont, *From Mandeville to Marx* (Chicago: University of Chicago Press, 1977) 106.

6. J. Schumpeter, *Capitalism, Socialism and Democracy* (New York: Harper Torchbooks, 1963) 121–130.

7. Keynes (1963) 306–7.

8. Takeshi Ishida, "The Development of Interest Groups and the Pattern of Political Modernization in Japan" in R. E. Ward, ed., *Political Development in Modern Japan* (Princeton, N.J.: Princeton University Press, 1968) 300.

9. S. A. Kochanek, "The Federation of Indian Chambers of Commerce and Industry and Indian Politics," *Asian Survey*, 1:9 (September 1971) 866.

10. G. G. Alpender, "Big Business and Big Business Leaders in Turkey," unpublished doctoral dissertation (Department of Management, East Lansing, Michigan: Michigan State University, 1966) 1.

11. For such an interpretation of the South East Asian success, see, for example, B. Balassa, "The Lessons of East Asian Development," *Economic Development and Cultural Change*, 16:4 (April 1988).

12. Among many recent analyses along these lines, see, for example, R. Wade "Industrial Policy in East Asia: Does It Lead or Follow the Market?" in G. Gereffi and D. L. Wyman, eds., *Manufacturing Miracles: Paths of Industrialization in Latin America and East Asia* (Princeton, N.J.: Princeton University Press, 1990).

13. A. Amsden, "The State and Taiwan's Economic Development" in P. B. Evans, D. Rueschemeyer, and T. Skocpol, *Bringing the State Back In* (Cambridge: Cambridge University Press, 1985) 87.

14. A. Amsden, "Third World Industrialization: Global Fordism or A New Model?," *New Left Review*, 182 (July/August 1990) 22.

15. See, for example, C. Offe, "The Attribution of Public Status to Interest Groups" in S.Berger, A. O. Hirschman, and C. Meier, eds., *Organizing Interests in Western Europe: Pluralism, Corporatism, and the Transformation of Politics* (Cambridge: Cambridge University Press, 1981).

16. See, for example, W. Grant's comments on German business associations. W. Grant, "Why Employer Organisation Matters: A Comparative Analysis of Business Association Activity in Britain and West Germany" (Coventry: University of Warwick, Politics Working Papers 42, June 1986).

17. See, for example, D. Coates, "Britain" in T.Bottomore and R.J.Brym, eds., *The Capitalist Class: An International Study* (New York: New York University Press, 1989).

18. C. Leys, "Thacherism and British Manufacturing: A Question of Hegemony," *New Left Review*, 151 (May/June 1985) 17.

19. See, in particular, S. J. McNamee, "Du Pont-State Relations," *Social Problems*, 34:1 (February 1987).

20. E. Mason quoted by D. Vogel, "Why Businessmen Distrust Their State? The Political Consciousness of American Corporate Executives," *British Journal of Political Science*, 8 (January 1978).

21. This idea is pursued, for example, in M. Useem, *The Inner Circle: Large Corporations and the Rise Of Business Political Activity in the U.S. and U.K.* (Oxford: Oxford University Press, 1984).

22. R. J. Brym, "Canada" in Bottomore and Brym, eds. (1989).

23. For an analysis of the rise of neo-liberalism following the widespread concern of the bourgeoisie for the State's trespassing of the boundaries of legitimate intervention, see, D. McEachen, *The Expanding State: Class and Economy in Europe since 1945* (New York: Harvester Wheatsheaf, 1990).

24. See P. F. Drucker, *The New Realities* (London: Heineman, 1989).

25. See, on these developments, Useem (1984), and R. Nader and W. Taylor, *The Big Boys: Power and Position in American Business* (New York: Pantheon Books, 1986).

26. We find an extensive analysis of this phenomenon in Useem (1984) ch. 4. The irrelevance of neo-liberal non-interventionist position for contemporary business life is forcefully expressed also by Lee Iacocca. L. Iacocca, *Iacocca: An Autobiography* (New York: Bantam Books, 1985).

27. See, especially, K. Polanyi, *The Great Transformation* (Boston: Beacon Press, 1957a), and K. Polanyi, "The Economy as Instituted Process" in K. Polanyi et al., eds., *Trade and Market in the Early Empires* (Chicago: Gateway, 1957b).

28. Against those writers who give an earlier date for the social transformation process culminating in the advent of the market society, Polanyi shows that the conscious effort to establish a self-regulating market society was a development of the period following the industrial revolution. All through the mercantilist era, he argues that "The economic system was submerged in general social relations; markets were merely an accessory feature of an institutional setting controlled and regulated more than ever by social authority" (Polanyi, 1957a, 67). For a different interpretation of the economic organization in the mercantilist era, see, J. Appleby, *Economic Thought and Ideology in the Seventeenth Century England* (Princeton, N.J.: Princeton University Press, 1979).

29. Polanyi (1957a), especially chapter 5. See, also, J. Attali, *Au propre et au figure* (Paris: Fayard, 1988) for many interesting examples of the

measures taken in different societies for the containment of the market activity.

30. For example, M. E. Tigar and M. R. Levy, *Law and the Rise of Capitalism* (New York: Monthly Review Press, 1977) describe the social status of the merchant class in feudal Europe in the following terms:

> For the modern reader in the West, the respectability of the merchant class is self-evident. The word has become commonplace, and we use it automatically, without considering the system of laws which over the centuries has put these people in the center of economic activity.
>
> But when he first appeared in Western Europe in about the year 1000 A.D., the merchant had a somewhat different image . . . In the halls of the feudal lords, the merchant was an object of derision, scorn, and even hatred . . . Profit taking was considered a form of usury, and the merchant's soul was thought to be in jeopardy . . . (T)o the extent that one can speak of law in the jungle of feudal life, it was either silent about trade or hostile to it. The merchant was therefore in these terms a social outcast, who saw the legal system—the system which issued orders backed up by institutional force—as hostile and alien. 3–5

31. 31. H. S. Maine's classical work, *The Ancient Law*, presents a real challenge to the modern idea that individual property is the normal state of things while commonal ownership is only an exception to the general rule. H. S. Maine, *The Ancient Law* (Gloucester, Mass.: Peter Smith, 1970).

32. Polanyi (1957a) 152.

33. Offe (1981).

34. See, for example, P. B. Evans, D. Rueschemeyer, and T. Skocpol, *Bringing the State Back In* (Cambridge: Cambridge University Press, 1985).

35. See, especially, P. Katzenstein, "Introduction and Conclusion: Domestic and International Structures and Strategies of Foreign Economic Policy," *International Organization*, 31:4 (Autumn 1977) 587–606 and 879–919.

36. Polanyi (1957a) 156

37. C. Lindblom, *Politics and Markets: The World's Political-Economic Systems* (New York: Basic Books, 1977).

38. I am therefore adopting the definition given by A. Amsden (1990).

39. F. H. Cardoso, "The Industrial Elite" in M. Lipset and A. Solari, eds., *Elites in Latin America* (New York: Oxford University Press, 1967). For

a general survey on the question of entrepreneurship in the context of underdevelopment, see W. Nafziger, *Entrepreneurship, Equity, and Development* (London: Jai Press, Inc., 1986).

40. It is possible to find, in A. Gerschenkron's pioneering work, many insights with regards to the characteristics of institutional structure in late-industrializing countries. A. Gerschenkron, *Economic Development in Historical Perspective* (Cambridge, Mass.: Harvard University Press, 1962).

41. M. Shimuzi et al., *Introductory Notes for the study of Pressure Groups in Egypt* (Cairo: Middle East Studies Series, 1988).

42. See, in particular, R. Jenkins, The Political Economy of Industrialization: A Comparison of Latin American and East Asian Newly Industrializing Countries," *Development and Change,* 22 (1991); P. Evans, "Class, State, and Dependence in East Asia: Lessons for Latin Americanists" in F. C. Deyo, ed., *The Political Economy of New Asian Industrialism* (Ithaca: Cornell University Press, 1987); and G. Gereffi, "Big Business and the State" in G. Gereffi and D. L. Wyman, eds., *Manufacturing Miracles: Paths of Industrialization in Latin America and East Asia* (Princeton, N.J.: Princeton University Press, 1990). See also G. Ranis and J. C. H. Fei, "Development Economics: What Next?" in Gustav Ranis and T. P. Schultz, *The State of Development Economics: Progress and Perspectives* (Oxford: Basil Blackwell, 1990).

43. Jenkins (1991). See, also L. P. Jones and I. Sakong, *Government, Business, and Entrepreneurship in Economic Development: The Korean Case* (Cambridge, Mass.: Harvard University, Council on East Asian Studies, 1980); and B. Cummings, "The Abortive Apertura: South Korea in the Light of Latin American Experience, *New Left Rewiew,* 173 (February 1989).

44. See, for example, L. P. Jones and I. Sakong (1980) 293.

45. In an analysis of this partnership between Japanese businessmen and their state, we read, for example, that "The armed revolt of Satsuma in 1877 was put down by a conscript army, transported by Mitsubishi's ships, supplied by Mitsui Bussan and paid by the Mitsui Bank." R.Boyd, "Government-Industry Relations in Japan: Access, Communication, and Competitive Collaboration" in S. Wilks and M. Wright, eds., *Comparative Government—Industry Relations* (Oxford: Clarendon Press, 1987).

46. Jenkins (1991).

47. Cummings (1989).

48. See, in particular, B. Stallings, "The Role of Foreign Capital in Economic Development" in G. Gereffi and D. L. Wyman, eds. (1990). Also Jenkins (1991).

49. See, for example, E. S. Mason et al., *The Economic and Social Modernization of the Republic of Korea* (Cambridge, Mass.: Harvard University Press, 1980); C. Johnson, "Political Institutions and Economic Performance: The Government-Business Relationship in Japan, South Korea and Taiwan" in F. C. Deyo, ed. (1987); Jenkins (1991), and Wade (1990).

50. See, for example, M. Heper, *The State Tradition in Turkey* (London: The Eothen Press, 1985).

51. B. Cummings, "The Origins and Development of the Northeast Asian Political Economy: Industrial Sectors, Product Cycles and Political Consequences," *International Organization*, 38:1 (1984); and C. Johnson (1987).

52. Jenkins (1991).

53. In Taiwan, for example, small firms make a much greater contribution to national product and total exports than in other East Asian countries. See Richard D. Whitley, "East Asian Enterprise Structures and the Comparative Analysis of Forms of Business Organization," *Organization Studies*, 11:1 (1990); and Garry G. Hamilton and Nicole W. Biggart, "Market, Culture and Authority: A Comparative Analysis of Management and Organization in East Asia," *American Journal of Sociology*, 94 (1988).

54. Jones and Sakong (1980) present a detailed discussion of the Korean chaebol. The Indian "managing agency firm" as a similar organizational structure is discussed by A. F. Brimmer, "The Setting of Entrepreneurship in India," *Quarterly Journal of Economics*, 69:4 (November 1955). For a general evaluation of the role of the multiactivity firm in developing countries, see N. Leff, "Industrial Organization and Entrepreneurship in Developing Countries: The Economic Groups," *Economic Development and Cultural Change*, (July 1978). See also R. Jankowski, "Preference Aggregation in Firms and Cellular Encompassing Organizations," *American Journal of Political Science*, 33:4 (November 1989).

55. For a discussion of such measures in the Italian context, see A. Martinelli and A. M. Chiesi, "Italy" in T. Bottomore and R. J. Brym, eds. (1989).

56. Hamilton and Biggart (1988).

57. Alfred D. Chandler, Jr., *Strategy and Structure: Chapters in the History of Industrial Enterprise* (Cambridge, Mass.: The M.I.T. Press, 1962).

58. Oliver E. Williamson, *Markets and Hierarchies* (New York: Free Press, 1975); and O. E. Williamson, "The Economics of Organization," *American Journal of Sociology*, 87 (1981).

59. See Nathaniel Leff, "Industrial Organization and Entrepreneurship in Developing Countries: The Economic Groups," *Economic Development and Cultural Change*, 28:4 (July 1978).

60. Hamilton and Biggart (1988) 53.

61. G. R. Carroll et al., "The Political Environment and Organizations: An Ecological View" in B. M. Staw and L. L. Cummings, eds., *The Evolution and Adaptation of Organizations* (Greenwich, Conn.: JAI Press, 1990).

62. See Richard D. Whitley, "The Social Construction of Business Systems in East Asia," *Organization Studies*, 12:1 (1991); and also Whitley (1990).

63. Geert Hofstede, "The Cultural Relativity of Organizational Theories and Practices," *Journal of International Business Studies*, 14:2 (Fall 1983).

64. Whitley (1990).

65. Gereffi (1990).

66. What D. Landes writes, for example, about the stubborn refusal of French entrepreneurial families to use easy credit resources which would alleviate the family control over business operations may not be a peculiarity of the French society. D. Landes, "French Entrepreneurship and Industrial Growth in the Nineteenth Century," *Journal of Economic History* 9 (May 1949). Many entrepreneurial families in different societies seem to have acted similarly, and have tried to maintain family control often by refusing to yield to economic necessity. For discussions of such attempts through the evolution of enterprise management structures through the process of industrialization in different societies, see, for example, L. Hannah, ed., *From Family Firms to Professional Management: Structure and Performance of Business Enterprise*, Proceedings of the Eighth International Economic History Congress (Budapest, 1982); and A. Okochi and S. Yasuoka, eds., *Family Business in the Era of Industrial Growth* (Tokyo: University of Tokyo, 1984).

67. See Cardoso (1967) for a discussion of the role that family firms play in an environment of uncertainty.

68. A decree issued in 1974, for example, was directly intended to professionalize management and to open enterprises to the public. There were also decrees prohibiting firms with financially weak structures from acquiring nonoperating real estate or facilitating the liquidation of firms' nonoperating land holdings. See Jones and Sakong (1980) 280–285.

69. S. Lall, "Industrial Success in the Developing World" in V. N. Balasubramanyan and S. Lall, eds., *Current Issues in Development Economics* (London: MacMillan, 1991).

70. See, for example, Cummings (1989) on this aspect of the Korean society and its implications.

71. See, especially, Ş. Mardin, "Power, Civil Society, and Culture in the Ottoman Empire," *Comparative Studies in Society and History,* 11 (June 1969); and Ş. Mardin, "The Transformation of an Economic Code" in A. Ulusan and E. Özbudun, *The Political Economy of Income Distribution in Turkey* (New York: Holmes and Meier Publishers, Inc., 1980). In his analysis of interest group activity in Turkey, R. Bianchi, too, presents a discussion of the same historical characteristic of the Turkish society: R. Bianchi, *Interest Groups and Political Development in Turkey* (Princeton: Princeton University Press, 1984).

72. A discussion of the lessons of an East Asian model of state-business relations is presented, for example, in J. D. Fleck, "The Business Council on National Issues and Canadian International Competitiveness" in V. V. Murray, ed., *Theories of Business-Government Relations* (Toronto: Trans-Canada Press, 1985).

## CHAPTER 2

1. C. Kafadar, "A Death in Venice (1575): Anatolian Muslim Merchants Trading in the Serenissima," *Journal of Turkish Studies,* 10 (1986) (Special issue of essays presented to Halil İnalcık on his seventieth birthday).

2. Kafadar (1986) 210.

3. The representative agency, in fact, continued to be an important element of the business life in Turkey until quite recently. As discussed in the third section of this chapter, the acquisition of such an agency constitutes a significant point in the business career development of many important non-Muslim and Muslim businessmen.

4. See, for example, Ç. Keyder, *State and Class in Turkey: A Study in Capitalist Development* (London: Verso, 1987) 20–23.

5. See, for example, Yusuf Kemal Tengirşenk, *Türk İnkılabı Dersleri: Ekonomik Değişmeler* (Istanbul: Resimli Ay, 1935) 47.

6. G. Ökçün, *Osmanlı Sanayii: 1913, 1915 Yılları Sanayi İstatistiki* (Ankara: Ankara Üniversitesi Siyasal Bilgiler Fakültesi Yayınları, 1971) 12.

7. The study estimating the ethnic and religious distribution of ownership was conducted by the owner of the journal *Sanayi* that represented the views of the Muslim-Turkish entrepreneurs. See Z. Toprak, *Türkiye'de "Milli İktisat" (1908–1918)* (Ankara: Yurt Yayınları, 1982) 191.

8. See Toprak (1982) 168–181.

9. For a discussion of the CUP attempts in these areas, see, F. Ahmad, "Vanguard of a Nascent Bourgeoisie: The Social and Economic Policy of The Young Turks 1908–1918" in O. Okyar and H. İnalcık, eds., *Social and Economic History of Turkey* (Ankara: Meteksan Ltd., 1980).

10. Toprak (1982) 168–171.

11. F. Ahmad (1980) 341–2 referring to an article published in *Revue de Turquie* (Lausanne) in 1918.

12. G. Ökçün, "1909–1930 Yılları Arasında A. Ş. Olarak Kurulan Bankalar" in O. Okyar, ed., *Türkiye İktisat Tarihi Semineri* (Ankara: Hacettepe Üniversitesi Yayınları, 1975).

13. See Toprak (1982) 202–205.

14. Ökçün (1975) 430–433.

15. See Toprak (1982) 312.

16. Toprak (1982) 301.

17. Ahmad (1980).

18. Ökçün (1975) 439–442.

19. This sensitivity is clearly manifested in the several legal cases of political power abuse for illicit wealth accumulation in which many prominant statesmen were involved in the 1930s. See, for these cases, C. Kutay, *Cumhuriyet Devrinde Suistimaller* (Istanbul: Ercan Matbaası, 1958).

20. E. Karakoyunlu, *Türkiye'de Yatırım ve İhracat Teşvikleri* (Istanbul: Yased, 1987) 22.

21. Toprak (1982) 207–9.

22. The table in question is formed on the basis of a survey of the Istanbul Chamber of Industry and Trade conducted in 1923–1924, in which the name of the owner of the enterprise is given. The ethnic distribution of ownership in table 2.3, is an estimation based on these names, and the information it gives is therefore subject to some error.

23. A. Payaslıoğlu, *Türkiye'de Özel Sanayi Alanında Müteşebbisler ve Teşebbüsler* (Ankara: Siyasal Bilgiler Fakültesi Maliye Enstitüsü, 1961) 36.

24. G. G. Alpender, *Big Business and Big Business Leaders in Turkey,* unpublished doctoral dissertation (Department of Management, East Lansing, Michigan: Michigan State University, 1966) 129. The big business firms included in the sample are chosen among those employing forty or more workers and having a present capital of $10,000 at the time of research. The sample includes enterprises operating in mining, commerce, and banking as well as in manufacturing.

25. E. Soral, *Özel Kesimde Türk Müteşebbisleri* (Ankara; Ankara Iktisadi ve Ticari Ilimler Akademisi Yayınları, 1974) 30.

26. Of the enterprises established before 1900, 80 percent are in agriculture, 19.17 percent in food processing, and 0.83 percent in textiles. While the sample includes no enterpises established in the period of 1901–1910, 92.31 percent of those established in 1911–1920 are in agriculture and 7.69 percent in food processing. (Soral 1974) 33.

27. S. İlmen, *Hatıralarım,* Book 2: *Teşebbüslerim ve Reisliklerim* (Istanbul: Hilmi Kitabevi, 1949).

28. The *Journal of the Istanbul Chamber of Industry,* Special Issue on Turkey's Five Hundred Largest Industrial Establishments, 1988.

29. D. La Vere Bates, "The Origins and Career Path Development of the Modern Turkish Business Elite," unpublished doctoral dissertation, (Department of Business Administration, University of Arkansas, 1973) 59–60.

30. Alpender (1966) 173.

31. See, especially, Ç. Keyder (1987) 126; and Ç. Keyder, "The Agrarian Sector and the Genesis of the Bourgeoisie in Turkey," paper presented at the conference on Socio-Economic Transformation, State and Political Regimes: Egypt and Turkey, May 24–25, 1991, Cairo.

32. See, for example, O. Silier, *Türkiye'de Tarımsal Yapının Gelişimi (1923–1938)* (Istanbul: Boğaziçi Üniversitesi, İdari Bilimler Fakültesi, 1981).

33. See, for example, F. Ahmad's reference to Necmettin Sadak's views on this subject. F. Ahmad, *Turkish Experiment with Democracy* (London: C. Hurst and Co., 1977) 11.

34. Soral (1974, 29), for example, refers to A. P. Alexander's study *Greek Industialists* which indicates that a significant percentage of Greek industrialists whose previous occupation is craftsmanship are either immigrants from Anatolia or sons of artisans who have immigrated from this region.

35. The significance of this esthetic concern is well documented in the literature on technology transfer policies in developing countries. See,

in particular, F. Stewart, *Technology and Underdevelopment* (Boulder, Colo.: Westview Press, 1977). Many developing-country governments also share a deep-rooted belief in the wastefulness of competition and encourage economic concentration through different types of measures. See, on this subject, Jones and Sakong (1980) ch. 8; and D. McNamara, "Origins of Concentration in Korean Private Enterprise," paper presented at the conference on the International Sociological Association Research Committee on Economy and Society, Milan, 1989. See, also, R. H. Silin, *Leadership and Values* (Cambridge, Mass.: Harvard East Asian Monographs, 62, 1976), 14 and 21. Silin mentions that the Taiwanese government actively encourages the combination of smaller firms, and the trade associations with compulsory membership play an active role in this process.

36. See, in particular, S. İlkin and İ. Tekeli, *Uygulamaya Geçerken Türkiye'de Devletçiliğin Oluşumu* (Ankara: Orta Doğu Teknik Üniversitesi Yayınları, 1982) 24–25.

37. Istanbul Ticaret Odası, *Türkiye'de Küçük ve Orta Ölçekli İşletmeler: Yapısal ve Finansal Sorunlar, Çözümler* (Istanbul, 1991) 102–103.

38. In stark contrast to this Turkish case is the case of Britain, where such insiders coming from the sectors of domestic industry which were identical with or closely linked to the branch in which they became factory masters, have played a crucial role in industrial development. This type of endogenesis characterizing the development of modern industry in England is highlighted by F. Crouzet, *The First Industialists: The Problem of Origins* (Cambridge: Cambridge University Press, 1988).

39. The information about the origins of Altınyıldız was provided by Cem Boyner, second generation owner/manager of the company, in the course of an interview. For Akın, see, M. Sönmez, *Kırk Haramiler: Türkiye'de Holdingler* (Ankara: Arkadaş Yayınevi, 1990) 191–2.

40. R. W. Kerwin, "Private Enterprise in Turkish Economic Development," *Middle East Journal*, 5:1 (Winter 1951).

41. Payaslıoğlu (1961) 64–65.

42. Payaslıoğlu (1961) 65–66.

43. Soral (1974) 98.

44. See Soral (1974) 71–72; Payaslıoğlu (1961) 27–28; Alpender (1966) 109 and 183–184.

45. Alpender (1966) 179.

46. D. La Vere Bates (1973) 22–24. Another study, also conducted in the 1970s, finds that 56 percent of the businessmen in the sample had

graduate and postgraduate university degrees and 35 percent had high school education: Soral (1974) 76.

47. Hakkı Nezihi, *50 Yıllık Oda Hayatı: 1882-1932* (Istanbul: Sanayii Nefise Matbaası, 1932).

48. Bates (1973) 42.

49. See, on this subject, E. W. Nafziger (1986) 137-138.

50. Joint venture agreements with Turkish partners were, in any event, often imposed on foreign investors by certain legal provisions of the foreign investment code. For a discussion of the legal rules and their modifications throughout the Republican period, see T. Berksoy, A. S. Doğruel & F. Doğruel, *Türkiye'de Yabancı Sermaye* (Istanbul: Türkiye Sosyal Ekonomik Siyasal Araştırmalar Vakfı, 1989).

51. S.İlmen (1949).

52. In fact, he has a book on the history of aviation in Turkey. S. İlmen, *Türkiye'de Tayyarecilik ve Balonculuk Tarihi* (Istanbul: Hilmi Kitabevi, 1947).

53. İlmen (1949) 209.

54. İlmen (1949) 138.

55. İlmen (1949) 138.

56. S.İlmen, *Zavallı Serbest Fırka* (Istanbul: Muallim Fuat Gücüyener Yayınevi, 1951) 24.

57. İlmen (1949) 82.

58. İlmen (1949) 203.

59. İlmen (1949) 116-119.

60. Koray (1982) 436.

61. V.Koç (1979).

62. Koç (1979) 58.

63. *The Koç Group Annual Report*, 1988.

64. Nahum (1988).

65. Nahum (1988) 48.

66. Nahum (1988) 52.

67. See, for example, Nahum (1988) 53.

68. Nahum (1988) 253.

69. Nahum (1988) 77–78.

70. There are two biographies of Hacı Ömer Sabancı written in the 1980s: Sadun Tanju, *Hacı Ömer* (Istanbul: Apa Ofset, 1983); and Nimet Arzık, *Ak Altının Ağası: Hacı Ömer Sabancı'nın Hayatı* (Istanbul: Faik Yolaç Ofset Basım, 1985). The autobiography of Hacı Ömer's son, Sakıp Sabancı, who currently heads the operations of the Sabancı Holding, also provides extensive information on the foundation of the enterprise. Sabancı (1985).

71. Sabancı (1985) 60–61.

72. Sabancı (1985) 31.

73. Sabancı (1985) 191.

74. The foundation of the Industrial Development Bank can be traced back to the 1940s when the Turkish governent began negotiating with the World Bank around the issue. The Bank was founded in 1950, with Vehbi Koç among the members of its board of directors. As he relates in his autobiography, however, Koç was soon pressured to resign, with the rest of the members of the board, by the DP government.

75. An activity diversification chart of the company is provided in chapter 4. See table 4.2.

76. Sabancı (1985) 146.

77. Sabancı (1985) 120.

78. Sabancı (1985) 117–121.

79. Sabancı (1985) 112–114.

80. Eczacıbaşı (1982) 17.

81. Eczacıbaşı (1982) 60.

82. See end note 38.

83. Bilen (1988).

84. Bilen (1988) 68.

85. Akkaya (1989).

86. The name of the company is composed of the initials of the two friends, Sezai Türkeş and Fevzi Akkaya.

87. In his autobiography, Fevzi Akkaya writes that his diploma number was 554, indicating that he was the 554th graduate of this only modern engineering school in the country. (1989) 32.

88. Akkaya (1989) 288–289.

## CHAPTER 3

1. See, for example, S. Sabancı, *İşte Hayatım* (Istanbul: Aksoy Matbaacılık, 1985) 108.

2. Sabancı (1985) 32–33, 309.

3. The full text of the principles adopted in the Congress is given by Afet İnan, *Izmir İktisat Kongresi: 17 Şubat-4 Mart 1923* (Ankara: Türk Tarih Kurumu, 1989.

4. See, especially, B. Kuruç, *Mustafa Kemal Döneminde Ekonomi* (Ankara: Bilgi Yayınevi, 1987); and B. Kuruç, *İktisat Politikasının Resmi Belgeleri: Söylev, Demeç ve Yazılar* (Ankara: Siyasal Bilgiler Fakültesi Maliye Enstitüsü, 1964).

5. Kuruç (1987) 34–37.

6. See, for example, S. İlkin and İ. Tekeli *Uygulamaya Geçerken Devletçiliğin Oluşumu* (Ankara: Orta Doğu Teknik Universitesi Yayınları, 1982) 290–291.

7. See, for example, Kuruç (1987); and D. Avcıoğlu, *Türkiye'nin Düzeni* (Istanbul: Cem Yayınevi, 1973) 1:458.

8. İlkin and Tekeli (1982) 215.

9. For a detailed discussion of the economic policies of the period see, especially, Selim İlkin and İ. Tekeli, *1929 Dünya Buhranında Türkiye'nin İktisadi Politika Arayışları* (Ankara: Orta Doğu Teknik Üniversitesi, 1977); Tekeli and İlkin (1982); Korkut Boratav, *Türkiye'de Devletçilik* (Istanbul: Gerçek Yayınevi, 1974); Kuruç (1987). For the analyses of the developments in question by the contemporaries see, in particular, Haldun Derin, *Türkiye'de Devletçilik* (Istanbul: Çituri Biraderler, 1940); and Yorgaki Effimianidis, *Cihan İktisad Buhranı Önünde Türkiye* (Istanbul: Kağıtcılık ve Matbaacılık A.Ş., 1935).

10. İlkin and Tekeli (1982) 219.

11. The quota system was abolished in 1937 to the satisfaction of importers.

12. İlkin and Tekeli (1982) present a classification of different definitions of etatism provided by political autorities and intellectuals close to government circles, and they document the confusion created by the sometimes conflicting views on this issue. For a general survey of different views on etatism, see also, Arif T. Payaslıoğlu, "Türkiye'de Siyasi Partilerin Ekonomik Görüşleri" in *Türkiye Ekonomisinin Elli Yılı Semineri* (Bursa: İktisadi ve Ticari İlimler Akademisi, 1973).

13. *Akşam*, 16 December 1945. Also quoted by F. Ahmad, *Turkish Experiment in Democracy: 1950–1975* (London: C.Hurst and Company, 1977) 123.

14. See, for example, Derin (1940) and Yusuf Kemal Tengirşenk (1935).

15. Effimianidis (1935) and İsmail Hüsrev Tökin, *Türkiye'de Köy İktisadiyatı* (Ankara: Kadro Mecmuası, 1934).

16. Falih Rıfkı Atay, *Moskova-Roma* (Istanbul, 1932.

17. Payaslıoğlu (1973).

18. Kuruç (1987) 137.

19. Ahmet Ağaoğlu, for example, was a liberal in this sense. The absence of liberal intellectuals in the strict sense of the term in Turkey of the 1930s is discussed in A. (Buğra) Trak, "Liberalizm-Devletcilik Tartışması: 1923–1939" in *Cumhuriyet Dönemi Türkiye Ansiklopedisi*, 4 (1984).

20. See, for example, İ. İnönü, "Fırkamızın Devletcilik Vasfı," *Kadro* 221 (1934); R. Peker, *İnkılap Dersleri Notları* (Ankara: Ülkü'nün Kitapları, 1936); A. Hamdi Başar, *İktisadi Devletcilik*, 6 vols. (Istanbul, privately printed, 1931–1943). For a general discussion of these views on state and economic development, see, A. (Buğra) Trak, "Development Literature and Writers from Underdeveloped Countries: The Case of Turkey," *Current Anthropology*, 6:1 (February 1985).

21. See, for example, V. Nedim Tör, "Bizde Hususi Teşebbüsün Zaferi," *Kadro* 131 (1933); and A. Hamdi Başar, "Sanayici Efendilerimiz Biraz Susar mısınız?," *Kooperatif*, 1:5 (1932).

22. İlkin and Tekeli (1982) 225–227.

23. This type of private sector attitude was remarked upon and criticized by some politicians of the era. For references to such remarks and criticisms, see, Ilkin and Tekeli (1982) 233–234.

24. See B. Kuruç (1987) 123.

25. Kuruç (1987) 205–206.

26. Kuruç (1987) 138–140.

27. Development economists, W. Arthur Lewis in particular, often depict the existence, in a given country, of an agricultural revolution preceeding industrial development as a significant factor determining the success of subsequent economic performance of that country. See, for example, W. A. Lewis, "Reflections on Development" in G. Ranis and T. P. Schultz, eds., *The State of Development Economics: Progress and Perspectives* (Oxford: Basil Blackwell, 1990). This factor could explain in part, for example, the South Korean economic success.

28. For a comparison of the First and the Second Plans, see, for example, Korel Göymen, "The Stages of Etatist Development in Turkey," *METU Studies in Development*, 10 (1979) 55–81.

29. Kuruç (1987) 206.

30. Kuruç (1964) 65.

31. Kuruç (1964) 68.

32. Kuruç (1964) 68.

33. See *Cumhuriyet*, 31 May 1945.

34. Faik Ökte, *Varlık Vergisi Faciası* (Istanbul: Nebioğlu Yayınevi, 1950).

35. It is not very clear whether the category "convert" (*dönme*) refers simply to former non-Muslims converted to Islam or to the followers of Szevi, who, in the seventeenth century Ottoman Empire, declared himself as the Messiah, and was expulsed from the Jewish community who asked the Sultan to execute the troublemaker. Sultan declared that he would pardon Szevi if he accepted to convert to Islam. The conversion was accepted, with the common knowledge that it was a false one. Thereafter, the followers of Szevi have called themselves "converts" and followed a semi-secret religion behind the facade of Muslim faith. There is almost no research on the community in Turkish, yet it is generally believed that its members have a strong bent for business, and several prominent business families are known as "converts." It is, therefore, more likely that the designers of the Wealth Levy had this particular group in mind when introducing this third cartegory of taxpayers whose rates were higher than those of Muslims but less than those of non-Muslims.

36. S.Sabancı(1985) 53, 76.

37. Akkaya (1989) 108–110.

38. Yılmaz Karakoyunlu, *Salkım Hanımın Taneleri* (Istanbul: Semavi Yayınları, 1990).

39. F. Ökte (1950).

40. See *Cumhuriyet*, 9 November 1945.

41. *Cumhuriyet*, 13 November 1945.

42. *Cumhuriyet*, 8 and 9 December, 1945.

43. See, on this subject, Ahmad (1975) 11. Also Kuruç (1964) 86–94.

44. *Cumhuriyet*, 2 March 1945. This is one of a series of articles that this daily published in the beginning of March to calm down the panic generated by the ungoing discussions of the land reform.

45. It was accepted, more specifically, on 11 June 1945, which was declared the "Land Holiday." See *Cumhuriyet*.

46. See, for example, Doğan Avcıoğlu (1973), 2:548.

47. See, on the 1946 plan, and on its successor prepared in 1947, Selim İlkin and İlhan Tekeli, *Savaş Sonrası Ortamında 1947 Türkiye İktisadi Kalkınma Planı* (Ankara: Orta Doğu Teknik Üniversitesi, 1974).

48. İlkin and Tekeli (1974).

49. The program of the prominent businessman Nuri Demirağ's National Development Party, indeed, resembles more the Beveridge Plan than anything else (see *Cumhuriyet*, 11 July 1945). It is interesting that the program included the establishment of a universal social insurance system which, after 45 years, has been recently brought on the political agenda again by the new program of Süleyman Demirel's Straight Path Party.

50. Kuruç (1964) 95.

51. Payaslıoğlu (1973) underlines the similarity between the economic programs of the two parties.

52. See *Cumhuriyet*, 9 July 1950.

53. Kuruç (1964) 115–116.

54. See Sabri Ülgener's analysis on this subject: "Value Patterns of Traditional Societies" in Conference Board on Economic and Social Issues, *Social Aspects of Economic Development* (Istanbul, 1964). Also quoted by F. Ahmad (1977) 137.

55. See Kuruç (1964) 154.

56. See Türkiye Ticaret Odaları, Sanayi Odaları ve Ticaret Borsaları Birliği, *Türkiye'de Özel Sektör ve Kalkınma* (Ankara, 1966).

57. *Forum*, 15 January 1955.

58. *Forum*, 15 July 1954.

59. See *Cumhuriyet*, 8 July 1950.

60. Kuruç (1964) 143.

61. Doğan Avcıoğlu presents several such cases of illicit wealth accumulation involving prominent businessmen still active today. See Avcıoğlu (1973) 2:727–757.

62. See Avcıoğlu (1973) 2:745–747 for a more detailed discussion of the common ways of circumventing and abusing foreign trade regulations.

63. See *Forum*, 1 September 1954.

64. Avcıoğlu (1973) 755.

65. See, for example, *Cumhuriyet*, 13 June 1954 and 6 July 1954.

66. *Cumhuriyet*, 2 June 1956.

67. See, for example, *Cumhuriyet*, 2 June 1957.

68. See *Cumhuriyet*, 21 June 1959.

69. See the news coverage of a speech by the president of the Aegean Chamber of Commerce. *Cumhuriyet*, 5 July 1959.

70. *Forum*, 15 June 1957.

71. *Forum*, 15 August 1958.

72. See the editorial of the *Forum*, 1 December 1957.

73. *Forum*, 15 August 1958.

74. *Forum*, 1 September 1959.

75. Osman Okyar, "İktisadi Sistemimiz üstüne Düşünceler," *Forum*, 1 January 1960.

76. Yet, it is important to note that, with this modification, the extent of government control over the Chambers was also extended, giving the government the power to interfere in the elections and thus to silence the dissenting voices in the organization. See Ayşe Öncü, "Chambers of Industry in Turkey: An Inquiry into State-Industry Relations as a Distribu-

tive Domain" in A. Ulusan and E. Özbudun, eds., *The Political Economy of Income Distribution in Turkey* (New York: Holmes and Meier Publishers, Inc., 1980).

77. *Cumhuriyet*, 15 March 1960.

78. See, "İş Adamları ve Demokrasi," *Forum*, 15 April 1960.

79. See *Cumhuriyet*, 22 March 1960.

80. *Cumhuriyet*, 23 June 1960.

81. See, for example, the declaration of the mayor of Istanbul at the end of September (*Cumhuriyet*, 1 October 1960) and, especially, the speech of President Gürsel to the representatives of the business community (*Cumhuriyet*, 7 Ekim 1960).

82. See, for example, Keyder, *State and Class in Turkey: A Study in Capitalist Development* (London: Verso, 1987) chapter 7.

83. *Cumhuriyet*, 1 February 1962.

84. See, especially, Türkiye Ticaret Odaları, Sanayi Odaları ve Ticaret Borsaları Birliği, *Kalkınma Planı Hakkında Özel Sektörün Görüş ve Dilekleri* (Ankara, 1962); and Türkiye Ticaret Odaları, Sanayi Odaları ve Ticaret Borsaları Birliği, (16 Nisan 1962 tarihli toplantıda ilgili bakanlara takdim olunan), *Özel Sektörü İlgilendiren Başlıca Konular Hakkında Rapor* (Ankara, 1962).

85. Given the Union of Chambers' repeated criticisms of the erratic, unplanned policy-making process of the DP era, such statements about the necessity of planning are likely to be more than a reflection of the necessity of getting adapted to circumstances that could not be changed. They rather seem to be genuine expressions of a desire to function in a stable, predictable environment.

86. Türkiye Ticaret Odaları, Sanayi Odaları ve Ticaret Borsaları Birliği (1962a).

87. Türkiye Ticaret Odaları, Sanayi Odaları ve Ticaret Borsaları Birliği (1962b).

88. *Cumhuriyet*, 2 January 1965.

89. Türkiye Ticaret Odaları, Sanayi Odaları ve Ticaret Borsaları Birliği, (10 mart 1964 tarihli toplantıda ilgili bakanlara takdim olunan) *Özel Sektörü İlgilendiren Başlıca Konular Hakkında Rapor* (Ankara, 1964).

90. See *Cumhuriyet*, 24 August 1967.

91. One such attempt consisted in the formation of a Committee for the Development of Turkish Industry with participation of representatives of the State Planning Organization, and the Ministries of Industry, Finance, and Commerce. The project was severely criticized by the Istanbul Chamber of Commerce with the chamber representatives raising questions about the way the ressponsibilities and powers of individual ministries would be defined and distinguished from those of the Committee. See *Cumhuriyet*, 13 January 1968.

92. For a comprehensive discussion of the problems with and changes in the system of incentives throughout the post–1960 period, see Rıza Aşıkoğlu, *Türkiye'de Yatırım Teşvik Tedbirleri* 278 (Eskişehir: Anadolu Üniversitesi Yayınları, 1988).

93. See Istanbul Istanbul Ticaret Odası, *Türk Sanayiinde Teşvik Tedbirleri Semineri* 25 December 1978.

94. See, for example, Besim Üstünel, "Devalüasyon ya da . . . ," *Cumhuriyet*, 19 September 1968.

95. See the reference to a Union of Chambers report dealing with this problem in *Cumhuriyet*, 22 May 1966.

96. For such a demand put forward by the Aegean Union of Chambers, see *Cumhuriyet*, 19 August 1967.

97. See Eczacıbaşı (1982) 149–158.

98. See the declaration of Vehbi Koç, *Cumhuriyet*, 10 April 1971.

99. *Cumhuriyet*, 9 December 1971.

100. See, for example, Y. Arat, "Politics and Big Business: Janus-Faced Link to the State" in M. Heper, ed. (1991).

101. Z. Öniş, "Anatomy of Unorthodox Liberalism: The Political Economy of Turkey in the 1980s" in M. Heper, ed. (1991).

102. Apart from the already discussed cases of East Asian countries, the experience of the British economy under Thacher also provides an example to this. See A. Gamble, *The Free Market Economy and the Strong State: The Politics of Thacherism* (London: MacMillan, 1988).

103. For the pre–1987 figures, see table 2.2. For the post–1987 ones, see TÜSİAD, *1991 Yılına Girerken Türk Ekonomisi* (Istanbul, 1991).

104. TÜSİAD, *1989 Yılına Girerken Türk Ekonomisi* (Istanbul, 1989) 34; and TÜSİAD, *1991 Yılına Girerken Türk Ekonomisi* (Istanbul, 1991) 41.

105. See TÜSİAD, *The Turkish Economy 1988* (Istanbul, 1988) VI; and TÜSİAD (1991) 80.

106. TÜSİAD (1991) 63.

107. The share of the public sector in total Central Bank credits was 58 percent in 1989 and 46 percent in 1990. TÜSİAD (1991) 64–65.

108. For a discussion of these organizational changes, see, Ayşe Öncü and Deniz Gökçe, "Macro-Politics of De-Regulation and Micro-Politics of Banks" in Metin Heper, ed. (1991).

109. In fact, even before the elections, the MP government authorities seemed to have lost track of the mechanism. One of the MP ministers responsible for the economy openly admitted, for example, that he had difficulties remembering the number of funds in existence (*Meydan*, 12 July 1991). Several months after the elections, the new Minister of the State responsible for the economy said that the new government was still unable to estimate the assets and liabilities of different funds (*Milliyet*, 18 December 1991).

110. Öncü and Gökçe (1991).

111. For an analysis of public deficits as the major cause of inflation in Turkey, see Tansu Çiller and Mehmet Kaytaz, *Kamu Kesimi Açıkları ve Enflasyon* (Istanbul: Istanbul Ticaret Odası, 1989).

112. Some economists have, in fact, pointed at the significance of these crowding-out effects on the decline of private investment quite early in the decade. See, for example, Demir Demirgil, "Özel Sektörün Yatırım Eğilimindeki Durgunluk," *Türk Tarihi Dergisi*, 2 (Nisan 1985).

113. Panel discussion on television, "Industrialization and Alternative Policies," 5 May 1989.

114. This question was specifically raised by an article attempting to interpret the logic behind the policy move in question. See Deniz Gökçe, "Terk," *Ekonomik Bülten*, 7–13 November 1988.

115. See Günlük, "Belirsizlikler Ülkesi," *Dünya*, 5 December 1988.

116. For different reactions to the new tax in question see, *Dünya*, 25 January 1989.

117. See, for example, Z. Öniş, "Organization of Export Oriented Industrialization: The Turkish Foreign Trade Companies in Comparative

Perspective" in Tevfik Nas and M. Odekon, *Politics and Economics of Turkish Liberalization* (New York: Associated Universities Press, 1992).

118. Although the estimation of the actual value of fictitious exports is very difficult, there were some attempts in this direction. See, for example, Dani Rodrik, "Türkiye'nin İhracat Patlamasının Ne Kadarı Hayali?," *Toplum ve Bilim*, 42 (Yaz 1988).

119. See the interview with Murat Vargı in *Dış Ticarette Durum*, May-June 1989. See also, in the same issue, Mustafa Özel, "İhracatta Model Tartışmalarına Katkı."

120. See *Milliyet*, 14 August 1989.

121. See *Cumhuriyet*, 17 August 1989.

122. See *Barometre*, 11–17 June 1990.

123. *Cumhuriyet*, 3 February 1989.

124. *Cumhuriyet*, 25 October 1989.

125. See, for example, *Cumhuriyet*, 12 April 1990; and *Barometre*, 16–22 April 1990.

126. *Cumhuriyet*, 8 February 1989; and *Miliyet*, 10 November 1989.

127. See *Cumhuriyet*, 30 December 1989, and 28 January 1990.

128. See the interview with Ali Koçman in *Sabah*, 10 September 1989.

129. See Heper (1985).

130. See, for a survey, Metin Heper, *Türk Kamu Bürokrasisinde Gelenekçilik ve Modernleşme* (İstanbul: Boğaziçi Üniversitesi Yayınları, 1977) 70–81.

131. For a discussion of the fusion of bureaucratic and political power creating the authority structure of the single-party period, see L. L. Roos and N. P. Roos, *Managers of Modernization: Organizations and Elites in Turkey: 1950–1969* (Cambridge, Mass.: Harvard University Press, 1971) chapter 2.

132. The typology of such a bureaucrat internalizing the official ideology of the single-party era can be found in a recent biographical novel, Erhan Bener, *Bir Büyük Bürokratın Romanı:Memduh Aytür* (Ankara: Bilgi Yayınevi, 1991). The biography is especially interesting in presenting the successive disillusionments of the protoganist in the multiparty period as the conflicts between the political process and bureaucratic rationality have become increasingly severe.

133. Faik Ökte (1951) presents a full picture of the confusion of well-meaning bureaucrats in the face of the unusual task that they were assigned to fulfill by the politicians.

134. See Lütfü Duran, *Türkiye Yönetiminde Karmaşa* (Istanbul: Çağdaş Yayınları, 1988) 113.

135. See *Forum*, 15 July 1954. See also Duran (1988) 113–114; and Heper (1977) 99–100.

136. See Heper (1977) 71–2 and 78–79; and Bener (1991) 178–183.

137. See the special issue on the "Two Decades of Planned Development in Turkey" of the (Middle East Technical University) *Studies in Development*, 1981. See, especially, Gencay Şaylan, "Planlama ve Bürokrasi"; Turgut Tan, "20 Yıllık Planlama Deneyimi Işığında Türkiye'de Planlamanın İdari ve Hukuki Sorunları"; and Deha Sezer, "Türkiye'de Planlamanın Hukuki Çerçevesine İlişkin Sorunlar ve Seçenekler Üstüne Bazı Gözlemler" in this issue.

138. See, for example, Duran (1988) 92.

139. See Tan (1981).

140. Saylan (1981).

141. Saylan (1981).

142. Tan (1981).

143. The problem of bureaucratic fragmentation in the institution of the foreign trade regime in the 1980s is also mentioned by Öniş (1992).

144. See "Özal'ın Prensleri (6): Prensler Prensi," *Milliyet*, 10 February 1990.

145. *Cumhuriyet*, 10 May 1990; and Osman Ulagay, "Kurmaylar Anlaşamıyor," *Cumhuriyet*, 17 May 1990

146. See, for example, "Ekonomi Yönetiminde Çokbaşlılık Depreşti," *Barometre*, 14–20 May 1990.

147. See, for example, "İş Dünyasını Terör Değil Çokbaşlı Ekonomi Korkutuyor," *Barometre*, 19–26 March 1990.

148. For example, industrialists in particular supported the firm stand of the Central Bank against the expansionist pressures steming from the fiscal policy process in spite of the difficulties associated with a restrictive monetary policy orientation. See "Sanayiciden Saracoğlu'nun Politikasına Destek," *Güneş*, 18 January 1990. This does not imply, however, that they

would not complain when they actually begin to feel the impact of the restrictive policy. Nevertheless, the initial choice to side with the bureaucrat against the politician was unambigious.

149. Eczacıbaşı (1982) 43.

150. Akkaya (1989) 122–125.

151. See, for example, Roos and Roos (1971).

152. Sabancı (1985) 202.

153. See, for example, the bar members' reaction to Özal's declarations concerning constitutional reform in *Cumhuriyet*, 24 May 1990; and Mümtaz Sosyal, "İşbitiricilik ve Hukuk," *Milliyet*, 28 October 1989.

154. See Taha Parla, *Türkiye'de Anayasalar* (Istanbul: İletişim Yayınları, 1991) 50.

155. *Cumhuriyet*, 10 May 1957.

156. *Cumhuriyet*, 3 October 1957.

157. See *Forum*, 15 April 1961.

158. In the course of my interviews, several businessmen complained, for example, that the elimination of export tax rebates at the end of 1988 was effective even in cases where there were already signed contracts.

159. Şerif Mardin, "Politikanın İnanç Muhtevası," *Forum*, 1 July 1954.

160. A very strong criticism of this measure was published in *Forum*, 1 August 1989.

161. The recent cases of some exporters who have taken court action against the government, although still quite exceptional, might, nevertheless, be pointing at some changes in this area. See, on these cases, S. İlkin, "Exporters: Favored Dependency" in M. Heper, ed. (1991).

162. Kemal Karpat, *Türk Demokrasi Tarihi* (Istanbul, 1967) 254.

## CHAPTER 4

1. A. D. Chandler, Jr., *Strategy and Structure: Chapters in the History of Industrial Enterprise* (Cambridge, Mass.: The M.I.T. Press, 1962).

2. Chandler (1962) 382–384.

3. C. H. Kirkpatrick, et al. *Industrial Structure and Policy in Less Developed Countries* (London: George Allen and Unwin, 1984) 58–62.

4. A. F. Brimmer (1955); and Shoi Ito, "Ownership and Management in Indian Zaibatsu" in Akio Okochi and Shigeaki Yasuka, eds., *Family Business in the Era of Industrial Growth* (Tokyo: University of Tokyo Press, 1984).

5. On the role of multiactivity firms in these countries, see, for example, Jürgen Brocksted, "Family Enterprise and the Rise of Large scale Enterprise in Germany (1871–1914)—Ownership and Management—"; Shoichi Asajima, "Financing of the Japanese Zaibatsu: Sumitomo as a Case Study"; and S. Yasuoka, "Capital Ownership in Family Companies: Japanese Firms Compared with Those in Other Countries." in Akio Okochi and Shigeaki Yasuoka (eds., 1984). See also Richard Jankowski (1989).

6. See Brocksted (1984), Asajima (1984), and Yasuoka (1984).

7. See Jones and Sakong (1980) and D. McNamara (1989).

8. *"Les geants sud-coreens sont contraints de se specialiser,"* Le Monde, 10 mai 1991.

9. For a general survey of the role of the family in the development of business enterprises in different Western and non-Western societies, see, Okochi and Yusuoka (eds., 1984).

10. David Landes (1949).

11. See Peter Payne, "Family Business in Britain: A Historical and Analytical Survey" in Okochi and Yasuoko, eds. (1984).

12. Maurice Levy-Leboyer, "The Large Family Firm in the French Manufacturing Industry" in Okochi and Yasuoko, (1984).

13. Alberto Martinelli and Atonio M. Chiesi, "Italy" in Bottomore and Brym, eds. *The Capitalist Class: An International Study* (New York: New York University Press, 1989).

14. A survey of these recent approaches can be found in the "Introduction" to Leslie Hannah, ed. *From Family to Professional Management* (Proceedings of the Eight International Economic History Congress, Budapest, 1982).

15. See M. Blaug, "Entrepreneurship before and after Schumpeter" in M. Blaug, *Economic History and the History of Economics* (New York: New York University Press, 1987).

16. Hannah (1982). See also Brocksted (1984).

17. It was indeed the occupation forces that disbanded the *zaibatsu* by deliberate action to break the political power of prominent entrepre-

neurial families. See, for example, T. Ishida, "The development of Interest Groups and the Pattern of Political Modernization in Japan" in R. E. Ward, ed., *Political Development in Modern Japan*, (Princeton, N.J.: Princeton University Press, 1968).

18. See Matao Miyamoto, "The Position and Role of Family Business in the Development of the Japanese Company System" in A.Okochi and S.Yasuoka, eds. (1984).

19. See Tamio Hattori, "The Relationship between Zaibatsu and Family Structure: The Korean Case" in Okochi and Yasuoka, eds. (1984).

20. Landes (1949) and E. Suleiman, *Elites in French Society* (Princeton: Princeton University Press, 1978).

21. N. Leff (1978).

22. H. Leibenstein, "Entrepreneurship and Development," *American Economic Review*, 58 (May 1968).

23. Leff (1978) 668.

24. Leff (1978) 670.

25. Leff (1978) 673.

26. Jankowski (1989) and M. Olson, *The Rise and Decline of Nations* (New Haven: Yale University Press, 1982).

27. Jankowski (1989) 985.

28. Leff (1978) 674.

29. For the activity diversification structures, as well as the statistical figures for sales and profits, of these groups see Sönmez (1990).

30. This information was gathered through a truly painstaking operation which involved identifying each one of the 405 private enterprises by using holding company reports and, basically, by asking around. The data compiled was checked in a two-hour-long second interview with the president of the board of directors of the Istanbul Chamber of Industry who has kindly accepted to help me on this subject although I had already interviewed him in relation to the present study. It was still impossible to find information on the share-holding structure of twelve enterprises. For the list of the five hundred largest companies, see the *Journal of Istanbul Chamber of Industry*, 24:282 (15 August 1989).

31. See Ayşe Öncü and Deniz Gökçe, "Macro-Politics of De-Regulation and Micro-Politics of Banks" in Metin Heper, ed. (1991). The

information given by Öncü and Gökçe on the ownership structure of Türk Ticaret Bankası was checked and corrected with reference to *Banks and Banking System*, IBAR Co., Inc. (Istanbul, 1991), 7th ed., and Ö. Akgüç, *100 Soruda Türkiye'de Bankacılık* (Istanbul: Gerçek Yayınları, 1989).

32. Data compiled on the basis of the information given by the *Journal of the Istanbul Chamber of Industry*, 25:294 (22 August 1990). I could not find information on the ownership structure of nine private Turkish firms in joint ventures with foreign enterprises.

33. See Güven Alpay, *Holding Yönetimine Gelince* (Istanbul: BETA, 1988).

34. See Güven Alpay (1988) and M. Şükrü Tekbaş, "Türkiye'de Holding Şirket Uygulaması Üzerine bir Çalışma," unpublished doctoral dissertation, (Istanbul: Istanbul Üniversitesi İşletme Fakültesi, 1972).

35. Türkiye Ticaret Odaları, Sanayi, Odaları ve Ticaret Borsaları Birliği, 7 Mart 1963 Tarihli Toplantıda Ilgili Bakanlara Takdim Olunan *Özel Sektörü Ilgilendiren Başlıca Konular Hakkında Rapor* (Ankara, 1963). See especially 11.

36. Türkiye Ticaret Odaları, Sanayi Odaları ve Ticaret Borsaları Birliği (1963), 7.

37. For the pioneering case of Koç, see, in particular, Nahum (1988), 275 and the 1964 Annual Report of the Koç group.

38. Sabancı (1985) 221.

39. Sabancı (1985) 172–176.

40. Enka and Süzer provide examples of this strategy of restricting export activities in the late 1980s. See *Cumhuriyet*, 16 December 1989.

41. Only Net, Koç, Enka, and Yaşar Holdings were in the tourism business prior to 1980. After 1980, we see that Tekfen, Akkök, Inci, Alarko, Kavala, Sabancı, Eczacıbaşı, and Anadolu Endüstri have also entered this sector.

42. This was indeed a point made by several individuals whom I interviewed.

43. See B. Yaşer, *A Comparative Analysis of Selected Financial Ratios of Private Private Manufacturing Firms in the U.S.A. and in Turkey, 1983–1984* (Istanbul: Istanbul Chamber of Industry Publications, 1988).

44. These limitations which had begun to be gradually introduced starting with the 1970s have culminated in the Banking Law amendments

of 1985. Among other restrictions that they involve, these amendments include the limitation of the credit extended to affiliated enterprises to 15 percent of total credits and the restriction of credits extended to any one single enterprise to less than 10 percent of own capital.

45. Although it obviously constitutes a major preoccupation of someone such as Vehbi Koç, given his efforts to devise ways of maximizing the managerial control of the family and, also, given the references, in his autobiography, to Bennett, "the evil manager who has almost caused the ruin of the Ford family."

46. See *Cumhuriyet*, 28 December 1988.

47. See *Cumhuriyet*, 12 September 1989.

48. See Öniş (1992) on the comparative foreign trade performance of Turkish and Korean enterprises.

## CHAPTER 5

1. R. Bianchi, *Interest Groups and Political Development in Turkey* (Princeton,N.J.: Princeton University Press, 1984); M. Heper, "The State and Interest Groups with Special Reference to Turkey" in M. Heper, ed. (1991).

2. M. Heper (1991) 4, 6.

3. P.Schmitter, "Still the Century of Corporatism?" in F. Pike and T. Stritch, eds., *The New Corporatism* (Notre Dame: Notre Dame University Press, 1974).

4. W. Grant, "Introduction" in W. Grant, ed., *The Political Economy of Corporatism* (London: MacMillan, 1985).

5. Grant (1985).

6. Grant (1985).

7. Offe (1981).

8. T. Skocpol (1985) 7.

9. Both the changes that have occurred in South Korean state big business relations in the Park era and the developments in the Indian business environment after the recent attempts to follow a more export-oriented strategy provide support to such an hypothesis. See, in particular, D. McNamara (1989), and R. Boyd (1987). A similar trend is observed in the

Indian context by A. Kohli, "Politics of Economic Liberalization in India," *World Development*, 17:3 (March 1989).

10. McNamara (1989).

11. See T. Ishida (1968).

12. R. Boyd (1987).

13. E. Suleiman's (1978) account of the relationship between the French elites in private and public executive positions, in particular, supports this observation.

14. McNamara (1989). T. Wakiyama, for example, suggests that the administrative guidance of the MITI is directly conveyed to business executives without the intermediation of associations, except in the case of competitive industries with a large number of firms. See T. Wakiyama, "The Implications and Effectiveness of MITI's Administrative Guidance" in Wilks and Wright, eds. (1987).

15. Useem (1984) 165.

16. Useem (1984) 111–113.

17. Offe (1981).

18. Grant (1985) 6–7.

19. C. Johnson (1987).

20. To give the reader some idea about the atmosphere of the late 1970s in Turkey, it would probably suffice to state that, during the first eight months of 1980, before the military intervention in September of the same year, there were more than 1600 political assassinations. Among the people killed, there were several well-known university professors, members of parliament, and local authorities from the RPP. The president of the Metal Workers' Union, an important figure in the history of the Turkish labor movement was also among the victims of these political assassinations. The years 1979 and 1980 were also characterized by an unprecedented spread of long strikes. In 1979, 269 strikes took place involving more than 40,000 workers. By May 1980, strikes had taken place in 388 work places with nearly 55,000 workers involved. For a general atmoshere of the economic and sociopolitical atmosphere of the country before the 1980 coup, see A. (Buğra) Trak and Ç. Turan, "Is Democracy A Luxury Item for Turkey?", *Labour, Capital and Society* 13:2 (November 1980).

21. For a detailed taxonomy of the Turkish Chambers and evolution of the relevant legislation in the Republican era, see A. Öncü, "Cumhuriyet Döneminde Odalar," *Cumhuriyet Dönemi Türkiye Ansiklopedisi,* 50 (1984) 1566–1576. Also, K.Sayıbaşılı, "Chambers of Commerce and Industry, Political Parties, and Governments: A Comparative Analysis of The British and the Turkish Cases," (Middle East Technical University) *Studies in Development,* 11 (Spring 1976); and Bianchi (1984).

22. Öncü (1984).

23. Öncü (1980) discusses the detailed and intricate nature of the provisions of the 1924 Law. "Even the most liberal Turkish associational regulations," writes Bianchi, "tend to be so complex, limiting, and unclear that it is virtually inevitable that association leaders will violate them sooner or later and thus be subject to official reprisal." See Bianchi (1984) 114.

24. K. Sayıbaşılı (1976).

25. Sayıbaşılı (1976).

26. See A. Öncü (1980).

27. Sayıbaşılı (1976).

28. Later, the founder of the Islamic National Order, National Salvation, and Welfare Parties.

29. See E.Özbudun, "The Post–1980 Legal Framework for Interest Group Association," and, especially, Ü. Cizre Sakallıoğlu, "Labor: The Battered Community" in M. Heper, ed. (1991).

30. For the history of Turkish labor unionism in the Republican period, see, for example, K.Sülker, *Türkiye'de İşçi Hareketleri* (Istanbul: Gerçek Yayinevi, 1968); and M. Kutal and M. Ekonomi, *Türk Endüstri İlişkileri Sisteminin Yasal Çerçevesi ve Başlıca Sorunları* (Istanbul, 1976).

31. In the 1980s, the Confederation leaders were especially hostile toward any demands for even minor revisions of the labor legislation prepared during the military government before 1983. See, for example, *Cumhuriyet,* 2 March 1985. In this period, the Confederation has also shown a strong reaction against the critical interference of the ILO for an improvement of the Turkish labor legislation. *Cumhuriyet,* 26 November 1984.

32. N. Eczacıbaşı (1982) 148–158.

33. Vehbi Koç (Koç group), Nejat Eczacıbaşı (Eczacıbaşı), Sakıp Sabancı (Sabancı), Selçuk Yaşar (Yaşar), Raşit Özsaruhan (Özsaruhan), Ahmet Sapmaz (Güney Sanayi), Feyyaz Berker (Tekfen), Özakat (Özakat), Ibrahim Bodur (Bodur), Hikmet Erenyol (Joint Stock Co. Electro-Metalurgy), Osman Boyner (Altınyıldız), and Muzaffer Gazioğlu (Joint Stock Co. Cement Industries).

34. For such attempts which remain quite unconvincing, see, for example, Arat (1991); Bianchi (1984) 274; and K. Boratav, "Contradictions of 'Structural Adjustment': Capital and the State in Post–1980 Turkey," paper presented at the conference on Socio-Economic Transformation, State and Political Regimes, Cairo, 24–25 May 1991.

35. Eczacıbaşı (1982) 169–170.

36. See Bianchi (1984) 265.

37. See Cumhuriyet, 10 April 1971.

38. See Hürriyet, 21 January 1988.

39. The expert legal opinion that the prosecutor's office consulted to settle the matter served to dismiss the case on the grounds that there was nothing against the prevailing law of associations in Boyner's public speeches. The Report of Experts to the Prosecutor's Office, 2 August 1990.

40. Cumhuriyet, 28 February 1992.

41. See, for example, the founding members Feyyaz Berker and Ali Koçman's reaction to a public criticism of the government by Boyner, Milliyet, 15 August 1989.

42. Ş.Gülfidan, "Big Business and the State in Turkey: The Case of TÜSİAD," unpublished doctoral dissertation (Istanbul: Boğaziçi University, 1990).

43. Eczacıbaşı (1982), for example, comments on this suspicious attitude of the involuntary associations against TÜSİAD in the formative years of the association. In the course of my private interviews with them, several TÜSİAD members—as well as the president of the board of directors of the Istanbul Chamber of Industry, a sympathetic outsider to the Association—have made references to feelings of rivalry and fear that certain representatives of involuntary associations entertain vis-à-vis TÜSİAD, without, according to my interviewees, much rational reason behind them.

44. See Cumhuriyet, 1 May 1986.

45. Güneş, 20 January 1988. Also quoted by Y.Esmer, "Manufacturing Industries: Giants with Hesitant Voices" in Heper and Metin, eds. (1991).

46. See *Barometre,* 4 December 1989.

47. *Cumhuriyet,* 31 January 1992.

48. *Cumhuriyet,* 2 April 1988.

49. See *Milliyet,* 1 December 1989.

50. *Cumhuriyet,* 6 September 1989.

51. *Cumhuriyet,* 14 March 1990.

52. Founded in the 1980s by Demirel as a continuation of the JP, closed by the military.

53. *Cumhuriyet,* 30 March 1990.

54. *Cumhuriyet,* 14 December 1989

55. *Barometre,* 21–28 May 1990.

56. *Cumhuriyet,* 14 May 1990.

57. *Cumhuriyet,* 9 January 1990.

58. See, for example, *Cumhuriyet* 9 September 1989.

59. The Istanbul Chamber of Industry, for example, has forty such professional committees in which small, medium, and big enterprises in a given sector are jointly represented.

60. These professional associations became active mainly in the 1980s. Since they are—along with all the other associations of many different characters ranging from those founded for the beautification of a particular neighbourhood to societies for the protection of animals—placed under the control of the Ministry of Interior, it is extremely difficult to have exact information about the number, membership structures, and activities of these associations. On the basis of the press coverage of their activities, as well as the frequent references to the significance of their role by my interviewees, I could suggest that a few associations—such as the Associations of Chemical Industrialists, Textile Producers, Garment Industrialists, and Leather Producers—dominate the scene as far as the social and economic significance of associational activity is concerned. Very little is heard about other professional associations active in other sectors.

61. *Hürriyet,* 29 June 1990.

62. See *Ekonomik Bülten,* 2–8 April 1990.

63. See the interview with Feyyaz Berker, the president of DEİK, in *Dış Ticarette Durum,* November/December 1988.

CHAPTER 6

1. See, for example, Barry W.Ickes, "Obstacles to Economic Reform of Socialism: An Institutional Choice Approach"; and Jan Winiecki, "Obstacles to Economic Reform of Socialism: A Property Rights Approach," both articles in *The Annals of the American Academy of Political and Social Science,* special issue on privatizing and marketizing socialism, January 1990.

# BIBLIOGRAPHY

Ahmad, Feroz, *Turkish Experiment in Democracy* (London: C. Hurst and Co., 1977).

――――. "Vanguard of a Nascent Bourgeoisie: The Social and Economic Policy of the Young Turks 1908–1918" in Osman Okyar and H. Inalcık, eds., *Social and Economic History of Turkey* (Ankara: Meteksan Ltd., 1980).

Akgüç, Öztin, *100 Soruda Türkiye'de Bankacılık* (Istanbul: Gerçek Yayınları, 1989).

Akkaya, Fevzi, *Ömrümüzün Kilometre Taşları: ST-FA'nın Hikayesi* (Istanbul: Fevzi Akkaya Temel Eğitim Vakfı, 1989).

Alpay, Güven, *Holding Yönetimine Gelince* (Istanbul: BETA, 1988).

Alpender, Güvenç G., "Big Business and Big Business Leaders in Turkey," unpublished doctoral dissertation, Department of Management (East Lansing, Michigan; Michigan State University, 1966).

Amsden, Alice, "The State and Taiwan's Economic Development" in Peter B. Evans, D. Rueschemeyer, and T. Skocpol, eds., *Bringing the State Back In* (Cambridge: 1985).

――――. "Third World Industrialization: Global Fordism or A New Model," *New Left Review,* 182 (July/August 1990).

Appleby, Joan, *Economic Thought and Ideology in Seventeenth-Century England* (Princeton, N.J.: Princeton University Press, 1979).

Arat, Yeşim, "Politics and Big Business: Janus-Faced Link to the State" in Metin Heper, ed., *Strong State and Economic Interest Groups: The*

*Post–1980 Turkish Experience* (Berlin and New York: De Gruyter, 1991).

Arzık, Nimet, *Ak Altının Ağası: Hacı Ömer Sabancı'nın Hayatı* (Istanbul: Faik Yolaç Ofset Basım, 1985).

Asajima, Shoichi, "Financing of the Japanese Zaibatsu: Sumitomo as a Case Study" in Akio Okochi and S. Yasuoka, eds., *Family Business in the Era of Industrial Growth* (Tokyo: University of Tokyo, 1984).

Aşıkoğlu, Rıza, *Türkiye'de Yatırım Teşvik Tedbirleri*, 278 (Eskişehir: Anadolu Üniversitesi Yayınları, 1988).

Atay, Falih Rıfkı, *Moskova-Roma* (Istanbul, 1932).

Attali, Jacques, *Au propre et au figure* (Paris: Fayard, 1988).

Avcıoğlu, Doğan, *Türkiye'nin Düzeni*, 2 vols. (Istanbul: Cem Yayınevi, 1973).

Balassa, Bela, "The Lessons of East Asian Development," *Economic Development and Cultural Change*, 16:4 (April 1988).

Başar, Ahmet Hamdi, *İktisadi Devletcilik*, 6 vols. (Istanbul: Privately printed, 1931–1943).

———. "Sanayici Efendilerimiz Biraz Susar mısınız?," *Kooperatif*, 1:5 (1932).

Bates, Donald La Vere, "The Origins and Career Path Development of the Modern Turkish Business Elite," unpublished doctoral dissertation, Department of Business Administration, University of Arkansas, 1973.

Bener, Erhan, *Bir Büyük Bürokratın Romanı: Memduh Aytür* (Ankara: Bilgi Yayınevi, 1991).

Berksoy, Taner, A. S. Doğruel, and F. Doğruel, *Türkiye'de Yabancı Sermaye* (Istanbul: Türkiye Sosyal Ekonomik Siyasal Araştırmalar Vakfı, 1989).

Bianchi, Robert, *Interest Groups and Political Development in Turkey* (Princeton, N.J.: Princeton University Press, 1984).

Bilen, Alber, *Türk Sanayiinde Kırk Zorlu Yıl* (Istanbul: Final Ofset Matbaası, 1988).

Blaug, Mark, "Entrepreneurship before and after Schumpeter" in Mark Blaug, ed., *Economic History and the History of Economics* (New York: New York University Press, 1987).

Boratav, Korkut, *Türkiye'de Devletcilik* (Istanbul: Gerçek Yayınevi, 1974).

————. "Contradictions of 'Structural Adjustment': Capital and State in Post–1980 Turkey" paper presented at the conference on Socio-Economic Transformation, State and Political Regimes in Cairo, 24–25 May 1991.

Bottomore, Tom, and R. J. Brym, *The Capitalist Class: An International Study* (New York: New York University Press, 1989).

Boyd, R., "Government-Industry Relations in Japan: Access, Communication, and Competitive Collaboration" in Stephen Wilks and M. Wright, eds., *Comparative Government-Industry Relations* (Oxford: Clarendon Press, 1987).

Brimmer, Andrew F., "The Setting of Entrepreneurship in India," *Quartely Journal of Economics*, 69:4 (November 1955).

Brocksted, Jürgen, "Family Enterprise and the Rise of Large Scale Enterprise in Germany" in Akio Okochi and S. Yasuoka, eds., *Family Business in the Era of Industrial Growth* (Tokyo: University of Tokyo, 1984).

Brym, Robert J., "Canada" in Tom Bottomore and R. J. Brym, eds., *The Capitalist Class: An International Study* (New York: New York University Press, 1989).

Buğra, Ayşe, "The Late Coming Tycoons of Turkey," *Journal of Economics and Administrative Studies*, 1:1 (Winter 1987).

(Buğra) Trak, Ayşe, "Liberalizm-Devletcilik Tartışması: 1923–1939," *Cumhuriyet Dönemi Türkiye Ansiklopedisi*, 4, pp. 1085–1089.

————. "Development Literature and Writers from Underdeveloped Countries: The Case of Turkey," *Current Anthropology*, 6:1 (February 1985).

(Buğra) Trak, Ayşe and Ç. Turan, "Is Democracy A Luxury Item for Turkey?," *Labour, Capital and Society*, 13:2 (November 1980).

Cardoso, Fernando H., "The Industrial Elite" in M. Lipset and A. Solari, *Elites in Latin America* (New York: Oxford University Press, 1967).

Carroll, G. R., J. Delacroix and J. Goodstein, "The Political Environments of Organizations: An Ecological View" in B. M. Staw and L. L. Cummings, eds., *The Evolution and Adaptation of Organizations* (Greenwich, Conn.: JAI Press, 1990).

Chandler, Alfred D., Jr., *Strategy and Structure: Chapters in the History of Industrial Enterprise* (Cambridge, Mass: The M.I.T. Press, 1962).

Coates, David, "Britain" in Tom Bottomore and R. J. Brym, eds., *The Capitalist Class: An International Study* (New York: New York University Press, 1989).

Crouzet, F., *The First Industrialists: The Problem of Origins* (Cambridge: Cambridge University Press, 1988).

Cummings, Bruce, "The Origins and Development of the Northeast Asian Political Economy: Industrial Sectors, Product Cycles and Political Consequences," *Industrial Organization*, 38:1 (Winter 1984).

————. "The Abortive Apertura: South Korea in the Light of Latin American Experience, *New Left Review*, 173 (February 1989).

Çiller, Tansu, and M. Kaytaz, *Kamu Kesimi Açıkları ve Enflasyon* (Istanbul: Istanbul Ticaret Odası, 1989).

Demirgil, Demir, "Özel Sektörün Yatırım Eğilimindeki Durgunluk," *Türk Tarihi Dergisi*, 2 (Nisan 1985).

Derin, Haldun, *Türkiye'de Devletcilik* (Istanbul: Çituri Biraderler, 1940).

Deyo, Frederic C., ed., *The Political Economy of New Asian Industrialism* (Ithaca, N.Y.: Cornell University Press, 1987).

Drucker, Peter F., *The New Realities* (London: Heineman, 1989).

Dumont, Louis, *From Mandeville to Marx* (Chicago: University of Chicago Press, 1977).

Duran, Lütfü, *Türkiye Yönetiminde Karmaşa* (Istanbul: Çağdaş Yayınları, 1988).

Eczacıbaşı, Nejat, *Kuşaktan Kuşağa* (Istanbul: Nejat Eczacıbaşı Vakfı Yayını, 1982).

Effimianidis, Yorgaki, *Cihan İktisad Buhranı Önünde Türkiye* (Istanbul: Kağıtcılık ve Matbaacılık A.Ş., 1935).

Esmer, Yılmaz, "Manufacturing Industries: Giants with Hesitant Voices" in Metin Heper, ed., *Strong State and Economic Interest Groups: The Post–1980 Turkish Experience* (Berlin and New York: De Gruyter, 1991).

Evans, Peter, "Class, State, and Dependence in East Asia: Lessons for Latin Americanists" in Frederic C. Deyo, ed., *The Political Economy of New Asian Industrialism* (Ithaca, N.Y.: Cornell University Press, 1987).

Evans, Peter B., D. Rueschemeyer, and T. Skocpol, eds., *Bringing the State Back In* (Cambridge: Cambridge University Press, 1985).

Fleck, James D., "The Business Council on National Issues and Canadian International Competitiveness" in V. V. Murray, ed., *Theories of Business-Government Relations* (Toronto: Trans-Canada Press, 1985).

Gamble, Andrew, *The Free Market Economy and the Strong State: The Politics of Thacherism* (London: MacMillan, 1988).

Gereffi, Gary, "Big Business and the State" in Gary, Gereffi and D. L. Wyman, eds., *Manufacturing Miracles: Paths of Industrialization in Latin America and East Asia* (Princeton, N.J.: Princeton University Press, 1990).

Gerschenkron, A., *Economic Development in Historical Perspective* (Cambridge, Mass.: Harvard University Press, 1962).

Gökçe, Deniz, "Terk," *Ekonomik Bülten*, 7–13 November 1988.

Göymen, Korel, "The Stages of Etatist Development in Turkey," *Studies in Development*, 10 (Middle East Technical University: 1979).

Grant, Wyn, "Introduction" in Wyn Grant, ed., *The Political Economy of Corporatism* (London: MacMillan, 1985).

————. "Why Employer Organization Matters: A Comparative Analysis of Business Association Activity in Britain and West Germany," Politics Working Papers, 42 (Coventry: University of Warwick, June 1986).

Gülfidan, Şebnem, "Big Business and the State in Turkey: The Case of TÜSİAD," unpublished doctoral dissertation (Istanbul:, Boğaziçi University, 1990).

Hamilton, Gary G., and Nicole W. Biggart, "Market, Culture, and Authority: A Comparative Analysis of Management and Organization in the Far East," *American Journal of Sociology*, 94 (1988).

Hannah, Leslie, "Introduction" in Leslie Hannah, ed., *From Family to Professional Management: Structure and Performance of Business Enterprise*, Proceedings of the Eighth International Economic History Congress, Budapest, 1982.

Hattori, Tamio, "The Relationship between Zaibatsu and Family Structure: The Korean Case" in Akio Okochi and S. Yasuoka, eds., *Family Business in the Era of Industrial Growth* (Tokyo: Uinversity of Tokyo, 1984).

Heper, Metin, *Türk Kamu Bürokrasisinde Gelenekçilik ve Modernleşme* (Istanbul: Boğaziçi Üniversitesi Yayınları, 1977).

————. *The State Tradition in Turkey* (London: The Eothen Press, 1985).

Heper, Metin, "The State and Interest Groups with Special Reference to Turkey" in Metin Heper, ed., *Strong State and Economic Interest Groups: The Post–1980 Turkish Experience* (Berlin and New York: De Gruyter, 1991).

Hofstede, Geert, "The Cultural Relativity of Organizational Practices and Theories," *Journal of International Business Studies*, 14:2 (Fall 1983).

Iacocca, Lee, *Iacocca: An Autobiography* (New York: Bantam Books, 1985).

Ickes, Barry W., "Obstacles to Economic Reform of Socialism: An Institutional Choice Appoach," *The Annals of the American Academy of Political and Social Science*, special issue on privatizing and marketizing socialism (January 1990).

İlkin, Selim, "Exporters: Favored Dependency" in Metin Heper, ed., *Strong State and Economic Interest Groups: The Post–1980 Turkish Experience* (Berlin and New York: De Gruyter, 1991).

İlkin, Selim, and İ. Tekeli, *Savaş Sonrası Ortamında 1947 Türkiye İktisadi Kalkınma Planı* (Ankara: Orta Doğu Teknik Üniversitesi, 1974).

———. *1929 Dünya Buhranında Türkiye'nin İktisadi Politika Arayışları* (Ankara: Orta Doğu Teknik Üniversitesi, 1977).

———. *Uygulamaya Geçerken Türkiye'de Devletçiliğin Oluşumu* (Ankara: Orta Doğu Teknik Üniversitesi Yayınları, 1982).

İlmen, Süreyya, *Türkiye'de Tayyarecilik ve Balonculuk Tarihi* (Istanbul: Hilmi Kitabevi, 1947).

———. *Hatıralarım*, Book 2: *Teşebbüslerim ve Reisliklerim* (Istanbul: Hilmi Kitabevi, 1949).

———. *Zavallı Serbest Fırka* (Istanbul: Muallim Fuat Gücüyener Kitabevi, 1951).

İnan, Afet, *Izmir İktisat Kongresi: 17 Şubat–4 Mart 1923* (Ankara: Türk Tarih Kurumu, 1989).

İnönü, İsmet, "Fırkamızın Devletcilik Vasfı," *Kadro*, 221 (1934).

Ishida, Takeshi, "The Development of Interest Groups and the Pattern of Political Modernization in Japan" in R. E. Ward, ed., *Political Development in Modern Asia* (Princeton, N.J.: Princeton University Press, 1968).

Ito, Shoi, "Ownership and Management in Indian Zaibatsu" in Akio Okochi and S. Yasuoka, eds., *Family Business in the Era of Industrial Growth* (Tokyo: University of Tokyo, 1984).

Jankowski, Richard, "Preference Aggregation in Firms and Cellular Encompassing Organizations," *American Journal of Political Science*, 33:4 (November 1989).

Jenkins, Rhys, "The Political Economy of Industrialization: A Comparison of Latin American and East Asian Newly Industrializing Countries," *Development and Change*, 22, (1991).

Johnson, Chalmers, "Political Institutions and Economic Performance: The Government-Business Relationship in Japan, South Korea and Taiwan" in Frederic Deyo, ed., *The Political Economy of New Asian Industrialism* (Ithaca, N.Y.: Cornell University Press, 1987).

Jones, Lee P., and I. Sakong, *Government, Business and Entrepreneurship in Economic Development: The Korean Case* (Cambridge, Mass.: Harvard University, Council on East Asian Studies, 1980).

Kafadar, Cemal, "A Death in Venice, 1575: Anatolian Muslim Merchants Trading in the Serenissima," *Journal of Turkish Studies*, 10, special issue of essays presented to Halil İnalcık on his seventieth birthday (1986).

Karakoyunlu, Erdoğan, *Türkiye'de Yatırım ve İhracat Teşvikleri* (Istanbul: Yased, 1987).

Karakoyunlu, Yılmaz, *Salkım Hanımın Taneleri* (Istanbul: Semavi Yayınları, 1990).

Karpat, Kemal, *Türk Demokrasi Tarihi* (Istanbul, 1967).

Katzenstein, Peter, "Introduction and Conclusion: Domestic and International Structures and Strategies of Foreign Economic Policy," *International Organization*, 31:4 (Autumn 1977).

Kerwin, Robert W., "Private Enterprise in Turkish Economic Development," *Middle East Journal*, 5:1 (Winter 1951).

Keyder, Çağlar, *State and Class in Turkey: A Study in Capitalist Development* (London: Verso, 1987).

———. "The Agrarian Sector and the Genesis of The Turkish Bourgeoisie," paper presented at the conference on Socio-Economic Tranformation, State and Political Regimes: Egypt and Turkey, in Cairo. 24–25 May 1991.

Keynes, John M., *Essays in Persuation* (New York: W. W. Norton and Co., 1963).

Kirkpatrick, Colin H., N. Lee, and F. I. Nixon, *Industrial Structure and Policy in Less Developed Countries* (London: George Allen and Unwin, 1984).

Kochanek, Stanley A., "The Federation of Indian Chambers of Commerce and Industry and Politics," *Asian Survey*, xl:9 (September 1971).

Koç, Vehbi, *Hayat Hikayem* (Istanbul: Apa Ofset Basımevi, 1979).

Kohli, A., "Politics of Economic Liberalization in India," *World Development*, 17:3 (March 1989).

Koray, Enver, ed., *Selahattin Adil Paşa'nın Anıları* (Istanbul: Zafer Matbaası, 1982).

Kuruç, Bilsay, *İktisat Politikasının Resmi Belgeleri: Söylev, Demeç ve Yazılar* (Ankara: Siyasal Bilgiler Fakültesi Maliye Enstitüsü, 1964).

———. *Mustafa Kemal Döneminde Ekonomi* (Ankara: Bilgi Yayınevi, 1987).

Kutal, Metin, and M. Ekonomi, *Türk Endüstri İlişkileri Sisteminin Yasal Çerçevesi ve Başlıca Sorunları* (Istanbul: 1976).

Kutay, Cemal, *Cumhuriyet Devrinde Suistimaller* (Istanbul: Ercan Matbaası, 1958).

Lall, S., "Industrial Success in the Developing World" in V. N. Balasubramanyan and S. Lall, eds., *Current Issues in Development Economics* (London: MacMillan, 1991).

Landes, David, "French Entrepreneurship and Economic Development in the Nineteenth Century," *Journal of Economic History*, 9 (May 1949).

Leff, Nathaniel, "Industrial Organization and Entrepreneurship in Developing Countries: The Economic Groups," *Economic Development and Cultural Change*, 28:4 (July 1978).

Leibenstein, Harvey, "Entrepreneurship and Development," *American Economic Review*, 58 (May 1968).

Levy-Leboyer, Maurice, "The Large Family Firm in the French Manufacturing Industry" in Akio Okochi and S. Yasuoka, eds., *Family Business in the Era of Industrial Growth* (Tokyo: University of Tokyo, 1984).

Lewis, W. Arthur, "Reflections on Development" in Gustav Ranis and T. P. Schultz, eds., *The State of Development Economics: Progress and Perspective* (Oxford: Basil Blackwell, 1990).

Leys, Colin, "Thacherism and British Manufacturing: A Question of Hegemony," *New Left Review*, 151 (May/June 1985).

Lindblom, Charles, *Politics and Markets: The World's Political-Economic Systems* (New York: Basic Books, 1977).

Maine, H.S., *The Ancient Law* (Gloucester, Mass.: Peter Smith, 1970).

Mardin, Şerif, "Politikanın İnanç Muhtevası," *Forum*, 1 July 1954.

————. "Power, Civil Society, and Culture in the Ottoman Empire," *Comparative Studies in Society and History*, 11 (June 1969).

Mardin, Şerif, "The Transformation of an Economic Code" in Aydın Ulusan and E. Özbudun, eds., *The Political Economy of Income Distribution in Turkey* (New York: Holmes and Meier Publishers, Inc., 1980).

Martinelli, Alberto, and A. M. Chiesi, "Italy" in Tom Bottomore and R. J. Brym, eds., *The Capitalist Class: An International Study* (New York: New York University Press, 1989).

Mason, Edward S. Mahn Ke Kim, D. H. Perkins, Kwang Suk Kim, and D. C. Cole, *The Economic and Social Modernization of the Republic of Korea* (Cambridge, Mass.: Harvard University Press, 1980).

McEachen, David, *The Expanding State: Class and Economy in Europe Since 1945* (New York: Harvester Wheatsheaf, 1990).

McNamara, David, "Origins of Concentration in Korean Private Enterprise," paper presented at the Conference of the International Sociological Association Research Committee on Economy and Society in Milan, 1989.

McNamee, Stephen J., "Du Pont-State Relations," *Social Problems*, 3:1 (February 1987).

Miliband, Ralph, *The State in Capitalist Society* (London: Quartet Books, 1973).

Miyamoto, Matao, "The Position and the Role of Family Business in the Development of the Japanese Company System" in Akio Okochi and S. Yasuoka, eds., *Family Business in the Era of Industrial Growth* (Tokyo: University of Tokyo, 1984).

Nader, Ralph, and W. Taylor, *The Big Boys: Power and Position in American Business* (New York: Pantheon Books, 1986).

Nafziger, Wayne E., *Entrepreneurship, Equity and Development* (London: Jai Press, Inc., 1986).

Nahum, Bernar, *Koç'ta 44 Yılım* (Istanbul: Milliyet Yayınları, 1988).

Nezihi, Hakkı, *50 Yıllık Oda Hayatı: 1882–1932* (Istanbul: Sanayii Nefise Matbaası, 1932).

Offe, Claus, "The Attribution of Public Status to Interest Groups" in S. Berger, A. O. Hirschman, and C. Meier, eds., *Organizing Interests in Western Europe: Pluralism, Corporatism, and the Transformation of Politics* (Cambridge: Cambridge University Press, 1981).

Okochi, Akio, and Yasuoko, S., eds., *Family Business in the Era of Industrial Growth* (Tokyo: University of Tokyo, 1984).

Okyar, Osman, "İktisadi Sistemimiz Üzerine Düşünceler," *Forum*, 1 January 1960.

Olson, Mancur, *The Rise and Decline of Nations* (New Haven: Yale University Press, 1982).

Ökçün, Gündüz, *Osmanlı Sanayii: 1913, 1915 Yılları Sanayi İstatistiki* (Ankara: Ankara Siyasal Bilgiler Fakültesi Yayınları, 1971).

————. "1909–1930 Yılları Arasında Anonim Şirket Olarak Kurulan Bankalar" in Osman Okyar, ed., *Türkiye İktisat Tarihi Semineri* (Ankara: Hacettepe Üniversitesi Yayınları, 1975).

Ökte, Faik, *Varlık Vergisi Faciası* (Istanbul: Nebioğlu Yayınevi, 1950).

Öncü, Ayşe, "Chambers of Industry in Turkey: An Inquiry into State-Industry Relations as A Distributive Domain" in Aydın Ulusan and E. Özbudun, eds., *The Political Economy of Income Distribution in Turkey* (New York: Holmes and Meier Publishers, Inc., 1980).

————. "Cumhuriyet Döneminde Odalar," *Cumhuriyet Dönemi Türkiye Ansiklopedisi*, 50 (1984).

Öncü, Ayşe, and D. Gökçe, "Macro-Politics of De-Regulation and Micro-Politics of Banks" in Metin Heper, ed., *Strong State and Economic Interest Groups: The Post–1980 Turkish Experience* (Berlin and New York: De Gruyter, 1991).

Öniş, Ziya, "Anatomy of Unorthodox Liberalism; The Political Economy of Turkey in the 1980s" in Metin Heper, ed., *Strong State and Economic Interest Groups: The Post–1980 Turkish Experience* (Berlin and New York: De Gruyter, 1991).

————. "Organization of Export Oriented Industrialization: The Turkish Foreign Trade Companies in Comparative Perspective" in Tevfik Nas and M. Odekon, eds., *Politics and Economics of Turkish Liberation* (New York: Associated Universities Press, 1992).

Özbudun, Ergun, "The Post–1980 Framework for Interest Group Association" in Metin Heper, ed., *Strong State and Economic Interest Groups: The Post–1980 Turkish Experience* (Berlin and New York: De Gruyter, 1991).

Özel, Mustafa, "İhracatta Model Tartışmalarına Katkı," *Dış Ticarette Durum*, May–June 1989.

Parla, Taha, *Türkiye'de Anayasalar* (Istanbul: İletişim Yayınları, 1991).

Payaslıoğlu, Arif, *Türkiye'de Özel Sanayi Alanında Müteşebbisler ve Teşebbüsler* (Ankara: Siyasal Bilgiler Fakültesi Maliye Enstitüsü, 1961).

———. "Türkiye'de Siyasi Partilerin Ekonomik Görüşleri" in *Türkiye Ekonomisinin Elli Yılı Semineri* (Bursa: İktisadi ve Ticari İlimler Akademisi, 1973).

Payne, Peter, "Family Business in Britain: A Historical and Analytical Survey" in Akio Okochi and S. Yasuoka, eds., *Family Business in the Era of Industrial Growth* (Tokyo: University of Tokyo, 1984).

Peker, Recep, *İnkılap Dersleri Notları* (Ankara: Ülkü'nün Kitapları, 1936).

Polanyi, Karl, *The Great Transformation* (Boston: Beacon Press, 1957a).

———. "The Economy as an Instituted Process" in Karl Polanyi, C. M. Arensberg, and H. W. Pearson, eds., *Trade and Market in the Early Empires* (Chicago: Gateway, 1957b).

Poulantzas, Nicos, *Les Classes sociales dans le capitalisme d'aujourd'hui* (Paris: Editions du Seuil, 1974).

Ranis, Gustav, and J. C. H. Fei, "Development Economics: What Next?" in Gustav Ranis and T. P. Schultz, eds., *The State of Development Economics: Progress and Perspectives* (Oxford: Basil Blackwell, 1990).

Rodrik, Dani, "Türkiye'nin İhracat Patlamasının Ne Kadarı Hayali?," *Toplum ve Bilim*, 42 (Yaz 1988).

Roos, Leslie L., Jr., and N. P. Roos, *Managers of Modernization: Organizations and Elites in Turkey: 1950–1969* (Cambridge, Mass.: Harvard University Press, 1971).

Sabancı, Sakıp, *İşte Hayatım* (Istanbul: Aksoy Matbaacılık, 1985).

Sakallıoğlu, Ümit, "Labor: The Battered Community" in Metin Heper, ed., *Strong State and Economic Interest Groups: The Post–1980 Turkish Experience* (Berlin and New York: De Gruyter, 1991).

Sayıbaşılı, Kemalettin, "Chambers of Commerce and Industry, Political Parties, and Governments: A Comparative Analysis of the British and the Turkish Cases," (Middle East Technical University) *Studies in Development*, 11 (Spring 1976).

Şaylan, Gencay, "Planlama ve Bürokrasi," (Middle East Technical University) *Studies in Development*, special issue on the two decades of planned development in Turkey (1981).

Schmitter, Philippe, "Still the Century of Corporatism?" in Fredrick Pike and T. Stritch, eds., *The New Corporatism* (Notre Dame: Notre Dame University Press, 1974).

Schumpeter, Joseph, *Capitalism, Socialism and Democracy* (New York: Harper Torchbooks, 1963).

Sezer, Deha, "Türkiye'de Planlamanın Hukuki Çerçevesine İlişkin Sorunlar ve Seçenekler Üstüne Bazı Gözlemler," (Middle East Technical University) *Studies in Development,* special issue on the two decades of planned development in Turkey (1981).

Shimuzi, M., *Introductory Notes for the Study of Pressure Groups in Egypt* (Cairo: Middle East Studies Series, 1988).

Silier, Oya, *Türkiye'de Tarımsal Yapının Gelişimi (1923–1938)* (Istanbul: Boğaziçi Üniversitesi, İdari Bilimler Fakültesi, 1981).

Silin, Robert H., *Leadership and Values* (Cambridge, Mass: Harvard East Asian Monographs, 62, 1976).

Sönmez, Mustafa, *Kırk Haramiler: Türkiye'de Holdingler* (Ankara: Arkadaş Yayınevi, 1990).

Soral, Erdoğan, *Özel Kesimde Türk Müteşebbisleri* (Ankara: Ankara İktisadi ve Ticari İlimler Akademisi Yayınları, 1974).

Soysal, Mümtaz, "İşbitiricilik ve Hukuk," *Milliyet,* 28 October 1989.

Stalings, Barbara, "The Role of Foreign Capital in Economic Development" in Gary Gereffi and D. L. Wyman, eds., *Manufacturing Miracles: Paths of Industrialization in Latin American and East Asia* (Princeton, N.J.: Princeton University Press, 1990).

Stewart, Frances, *Technology and Underdevelopment* (Boulder, Colo.: Westview Press, 1977).

Suleiman, Ezra, *Elites in French Society* (Princeton, N.J.: Princeton University Press, 1978).

Sülker, Kemal, *Türkiye'de İşçi Hareketleri* (Istanbul: Gerçek Yayınevi, 1986).

Tan, Turgut, "20 Yıllık Planlama Deneyimi Işığında Türkiye'de Planlamanın İdari ve Hukuki Sorunları," (Middle East Technical University) *Studies in Development,* special issue on the two decades of planned development in Turkey (1981).

Tanju, Sadun, *Hacı Ömer* (Istanbul: Apa Ofset, 1983).

Tekbaş, Şükrü M., "Türkiye'de Holding Şirket Uygulaması Üzerine Bir Çalışma," unpublished doctoral dissertation (Istanbul: İstanbul Üniversitesi İşletme Falkültesi, 1972).

Tengirşenk, Yusuf Kemal, Türk İnkılabı Dersleri: Ekonomik Değişmeler (Istanbul: Resimli Ay, 1935).

Tigar, Michael E., and M. R. Levy, Law and the Rise of Capitalism (New York: Monthly Review Press, 1977).

Toprak, Zafer, Türkiye'de Milli İktisat (1908–1918) (Ankara: Yurt Yayınları, 1982).

Tökin, İsmail Hüsrev, Türkiye'de Köy İktisadiyatı (Ankara: Kadro Mecmuası, 1934).

Tör, Vedat Nedim, "Bizde Hususi Teşebbüsün Zaferi," Kadro, 131 (1933).

Ulagay, Osman, "Kurmaylar Anlaşamıyor," Cumhuriyet, 17 May 1990.

Ulusan, Aydın, and E. Özbudun, The Political Economy of Income Distribution in Turkey (New York: Holmes and Meier Publishers, Inc., 1980).

Useem, Michael, The Inner Circle: Large Corporations and the Rise of Business Political Activity in the U.S. and U.K. (Oxford: Oxford University Press, 1984).

Ülgener, Sabri, "Value Patterns of Traditional Societies" in Conference Board on Economic and Social Issues, Social Aspects of Development (Istanbul, 1964).

Üstünel, Besim, "Devalüasyon ya da . . . ," Cumhuriyet, 19 September 1968.

Vogel, David, "Why Businessmen Distrust Their State?," British Journal of Political Science, 8 (January 1978).

Wade, Robert, "Industrial Policy in East Asia: Does It Lead or Follow the Market?" in Gary Gereffi and D. L. Wyman, eds., Manufacturing Miracles: Paths of Industrialization in Latin America and East Asia (Princeton, N.J.: Princeton University, 1990).

Wakiyama, T., "The Implications and Effectiveness of MITI's Administrative Guidance" in Stephen Wilks and M. Wright, eds., Comparative Government-Industry Relations (Oxford: Clarendon Press, 1987).

Whitley, Richard D., "East Asian Enterprise Structures and the Comparative Analysis of Forms of Business Organization," Organization Studies, 11:1 (1990).

———. "The Social Construction of Business Systems in East Asia," *Organization Studies*, 12:1 (1991).

Wilks, Stephen, and M. Wright, eds., *Comparative Government-Industry Relations* (Oxford: Clarendon Press, 1987).

Williamson, Oliver E., *Markets and Hierarchies* (New York: Free Press, 1975).

———. "The Economics of Organization," *American Journal of Sociology*, 87 (1981).

Winiecki, Jan, "Obstacles to Economic Reform of Socialism: A Property Rights Approach," *The Annals of the American Academy of Political and Social Science*, special issue on privatizing and marketizing socialism, (January 1990).

Yasuoka, Shigeaki, "Capital Ownership in Family Companies: Japanese Firms Compared with Those in Other Countries" in Akio Okochi and S. Yasuoka, eds., *Family Business in the Era of Industrial Growth* (Tokyo: University of Tokyo, 1984).

Yaşer, Betty S., R. Marchesini, and N. Weed, *A Comparative Analysis of Selected Financial Ratios of Private Manufacturing Firms in the U.S.A. and in Turkey, 1983–1984* (Istanbul: Istanbul Chamber Of Industry Publications, 1988).

## OFFICIAL DOCUMENTS AND REPORTS

Istanbul Ticaret Odası, *Türk Sanayiinde Teşvik Tedbirleri Semineri*, Istanbul, 25 December 1978.
———. *Türkiye'de Küçük ve Orta Ölçekli İşletmeler: Yapısal ve Finansal Sorunlar*, Çözümler, Istanbul, 1991.
Türkiye Ticaret Odaları, Sanayi Odaları ve Ticaret Borsaları Birliği, *Kalkınma Planı Hakkında Özel Sektörün Görüş ve Dilekleri*, Ankara, 1962a.
———. (16 Nisan 1962 tarihli toplantıda ilgili bakanlara takdim olunan) *Özel Sektörü İlgilendiren Başlıca Konular Hakkında Rapor*, Ankara, 1962b.
———. (10 Mart 1964 tarihli toplantıda ilgili bakanlara takdim olunan) *Özel Sektörü İlgilendiren Başlıca Konular Hakkında Rapor*, Ankara, 1964.
———. (7 Mart 1963 tarihli toplantıda ilgili bakanlara takdim olunan) *Özel Sektörü İlgilendiren Başlıca Konular Hakkında Rapor*, Ankara, 1963.
———. *Türkiye'de Özel Sektör ve Kalkınma*, Ankara, 1966.
TÜSİAD, *The Turkish Economy 1988*, Istanbul, 1988.

———. *1989 Yılına Girerken Türk Ekonomisi*, Istanbul 1989.
———. *Kim Kimdir? '88/'89, Istanbul, 1990*.
———. *TÜSİAD Members' Company Profiles 1989*, Istanbul, 1990.
———. *1991 Yılına Girerken Türk Ekonomisi*, Istanbul, 1991.

## ANNUAL COMPANY REPORTS:

Koç, 1964 and 1988
Akkök, 1988
Altınyıldız, 1988
Borusan, 1988
Sabancı, 1988
Tamek, 1988
Tekfen, 1988
Yaşar, 1988
*Banks and Banking System*, Istanbul: IBAR Co. Inc., 1991, 7th ed.

## PERIODICALS

Akşam
Barometre
Cumhuriyet
Dış Ticarette Durum
Dünya
Ekonomik Bülten
Forum
Güneş
Hürriyet
Journal of the Istanbul Chamber of Industry
Meydan
Milliyet
Sabah

INDEX

Akın group, 57, 61–62, 191, 205–06
Akkaya, Fevzi, 68–69, 92–93, 116,
    162
Akkök group, 56–57, 190, 203, 207,
    212, 249
Alarko group, 57, 123, 205–06
Altınyıldız group, 57, 61–62, 183,
    190, 202, 248
Amsden, Alice, 7
Anadolu Endüstri group, 56–57,
    154, 182, 190–91, 196–97
army. *See* military
Army Mutual Aid Society (OYAK),
    81, 206
Atatürk, Mustafa Kemal, 43, 108,
    111–2, 114

banks. *See* financial system
Başar, Ahmet Hamdi, 109
Bates, D. La Vere, 59
Bayar, Celal, 83, 86, 102, 104–06,
    108, 111–12
Baydur, Refik, 253, 255
Bianci, Robert, 225–28
Biggart, Nicole, 25–26
Bilen, Alber, 68–69, 89, 90–91

Borusan group, 57, 190–91, 198
Boyner, Cem, 250–51
bureaucracy, 17, 23–24, 28, 70, 93,
    97, 156–164. *See also* mecha-
    nisms of intermediation (in
    government-business relations)
business associations, 8–9, 30–33,
    225, 231, 233–35; in Turkey, 30–
    32, 237–38, 243–45, 247–48,
    257–63; and groups, 30, 169,
    223–24, 248; sectorial, 258–59;
    voluntary, 32, 229, 237–38, 240,
    245. *See also* interest representa-
    tion; Chambers; DEIK; IKV;
    TISK; TUSIAD
business councils, 135, 259–60
Bylaw against Overproduction
    (Sürprodüksüyon Kararnamesi),
    105

capitulary regime, 37, 39
Cardoso, Fernando H., 16
Central Commission for the Or-
    ganization of Credit Allocations,
    122

323

chaebol, 27, 29–30, 175–76, 222, 231

Chambers, 117, 129–30, 132–34, 140, 237, 239–45, 257–59; of commerce, 116–17, 239; of industry, 239; of commerce and industry, 85, 239; Ankara Chamber of Commerce and Industry, 130, 242; Eskişehir Chamber of Industry, 254; Istanbul Chamber of Commerce, 39, 61, 65, 129–30, 181–82, 240, 242, 254, 260; Istanbul Chamber of Industry, 182, 240, 253–55, 259–60; Izmir Chamber of Commerce, 127. See also business associations; interest representation

Chandler, Alfred, 25, 171–75, 177, 187

coalition models of state-society relations, 14

Committee for Union and Progress (CUP), 35, 38–42, 50–52, 70, 75, 98, 240. See also Young Turks

Conference Board on Economic and Social Issues, 88–89, 138–39, 246–47

corporatism, 14, 225–26, 228, 231; neo-, 8–9, 14, 32, 225–26, 229, 236, 257, 262–62; societal, 227; state, 227

Çukurova group, 56–57, 59, 182–83, 191, 199, 206

DEIK (Foreign Economic Relations Organization), 260

Demirel, Süleyman, 138

Democrat Party (DP), 56, 76, 78, 83, 91, 97, 118–21, 123–29, 136, 143, 158, 166, 238, 241–42

Dinçkök, Ömer, 212, 249–51, 253

DISK (Revolutionary Confederation of Labor Unions), 245

Doğuş group, 123, 183, 199, 206

Dumont, Louis, 3

East Asia: state and class, 6–8, 18–24, 32, 93, 223, 230–32, 236, 262; big business enterprises, 27–30, 173–76, 178–79, 199, 222

Ecevit, Bülent, 140–42, 244

Economic Measures Bill, 126, 129, 166

Eczacıbaşı: group, 56–57, 86, 88; Bülent, 250; Nejat, 86–89, 133, 138–9, 162, 246–8

endogenesis, 87

Enka group, 57, 123, 154–55, 191, 205

Ercan: group, 57, 154–155, 191; Tevfik, 155

etatism, 56, 98, 101–20, 124, 142, 146

Export Credit Bank (Eximbank), 161

extrabudgetary funds (off-budget funds), 145, 153

financial system, 18–19, 222–23; commercial banks, 40–42, 85, 174, 183, 199, 202–06

Five Year Plans (FYP), 128, 131, 134, 137–38, 159; before 1960, 104, 109, 112, 118–19; First, 134, 136, 159, 237; Second, 137; Fourth, 160

foreign direct investment and investors, 21, 28, 65–69, 75–77, 84, 90–92, 153, 183, 199, 204–05; in East Asia, 21, 28, 67; in Latin America, 21, 28, 67

foreign trade companies, 88, 123, 149–50, 160–61, 182–83, 189, 191
foreign trade regime, 39, 81, 99–102, 105–07, 110–03, 116–17, 122, 124–25, 127, 131, 136–37, 142, 149–53, 189–90, 264
France: state and business in, 231–32

Gezgin, Nurullah, 253
Grant, William, 227
Great Depression, 10, 12, 21–22, 100–101, 106
groups (multiactivity enterprises), 24–25, 27–28, 30, 171, 173–76, 179–80, 222, 265, See also holding companies; managing agency system; chaebol; keiretsu; zaibatsu

Hacıoğlu, Memduh, 253
Hamilton, Garry G., 25–26
Heper, Metin, 225–28
Hofstede, Geert, 27
holding companies, 24, 175, 177; and groups in Turkey, 27, 29–30, 50, 56–57, 59, 61–62, 169, 171, 178, 180–86, 190–98, 200–04, 220–02; and banks, 183, 199, 201, 204–6; and business associations, 169, 223–24, 248; and the state, 123, 136, 155, 169, 180, 187–90, 199, 201, 217–8, 221–23; and foreign enterprises, 183, 204–06; and foreign trade companies, 88, 182–3, 189; as family firms, 28, 79, 136, 169, 189–81, 185–86, 207–19

IKV (Economic Development Foundation), 260
İlmen, Süreyya (Süreyya Pasha), 70–76, 88
Industry and Mining Bank, 103
Industrial Development Bank of Turkey, 83–84, 87, 122, 136
Industrial Investment and Credit Bank, 136
İnönü, İsmet, 108–09, 133, 136
interest representation, 179–80, 223–24, 227–32, 234–36; in Turkey, 226–27, 238, 242–45, 244–45, 256–57, 259, 261; as a matter of political design, 8, 13–14, 229–30. See also busines associations; Chambers; labor unions
International Monetary Fund (IMF), 141–42, 146, 266
International Bank for Reconstruction and Development (IBRD). See World Bank
İş Bankası, 43, 183, 191
Izmir National Economic Congress of 1923, 98–99

Jankowski, Richard, 179–80
Johnson, Chalmers, 236
joint stock companies, 40, 42, 175, 177
Justice Party (JP), 138–42, 243–44, 249

Kadro movement, 109, 118
keiretsu, 176, 179, 199. See also zaibatsu
Kerwin, Robert, 63
Keynes, John M., 3; Keynesian revolution, 14
Kocatopçu, Şahap, 208–10

Koç: group: 56–57, 79–82, 84–85, 88, 182, 185–86, 191, 196, 199, 206–11, 214, 248; Vehbi, 76–82, 85, 133–34, 136, 209, 211, 249
Kutlutaş group, 56–57

labor, 235–36, 255; unions, 135, 141, 235, 238, 244–46, 248–49, 255, 261–62
Landes, David, 176, 178
landowners and landownership, 20–21, 41, 59, 60, 83, 111, 117–18, 140, 165
land reform, 21, 60, 111, 117–18, 140, 165; in East Asia, 20–21
late capitalism, 15–16, 249
late industrialization, 16–17, 171–72, 175, 230; late-industrializing countries, 15–17, 24, 61, 65, 67, 109, 171–73, 176–77, 230, 232, 265–67; late coming, 15
Latin America: state and class in, 18–21, 24; big business enterprises, 28, 173
Lausanne Treaty, 21, 99–101
Law for the Encouragement of Industry, 39–40, 75, 98–99, 102, 104, 106, 109, 121, 136
Law for the Prevention and Punishment of Smuggling, 110
Law for the Protection of Turkish Currency, 101–02, 167
Law for the Regulation of Profits, 125
Leff, Nathaniel, 179–80
legal system, 17, 23–24, 28, 51, 97, 148, 156–57, 164–68, 218, 228. See also mechanisms of intermediation (in government-business relations)

Leibenstein, Harvey, 179
liberal: model, 11, 232; orthodoxy, 5; value system, 5
liberalism, 107–08, 111; neo-, 10–11; in Turkey, 98, 120–21, 123–24, 143–44
Lindblom, Charles, 15–16

managing agency system, 173–74, 176
Marshall Plan, 78, 118
marxian approach, 1–2, 4, 6, 11, 13; functionalism, 2; instrumentalism, 2
Mass Housing and Public Participation Fund, 145, 153
mechanisms of intermediation (in government-business relations), 17, 23–24, 28, 97, 156, 159, 167, 228. See also bureaucracy; legal system
Menderes, Adnan, 123, 125, 128–29
military: career and businessmen, 70–76; and business, 41, 72, 74–76, 80–81, 85, 87, 207; intervention, 78, 85, 130–33, 139, 142, 158, 166, 242–44
minorities, 20, 36–37, 39, 42, 51, 53, 60, 67, 73, 77, 82–83, 86, 92, 114–16, 187; Greek, 60, 82, 87, 92; Armenian, 40, 60, 71–72, 75–76, 82, 86, 92; Jewish, 77–78, 80–82, 86, 89–91, 116
mixed economy, 50, 134, 140, 249
multinational companies. See foreign direct investment and investors
Motherland Party (MP), 97, 142–43, 145–46, 151, 153–54, 161,

164–66, 221, 238, 244, 249, 250–51, 154–55, 259, 264

Nahum, Bernar, 78, 80–82
National Defense Law, 112, 117, 125–26, 127, 129, 166
National Development Party, 119
National Factory Builders' Association, 52
National Salvation Party, 141, 244
National Union of Industrialists, 103–05
nationalism, 3, 92, 98
non-Muslims. See minorities

OECD (Organization for Economic Cooperation and Development), 125, 127–28, 135
Claus, Offe, 13–14, 229, 235
Özakat group, 57, 181, 206, 248
Özal, Turgut, 84, 86, 146, 152, 154, 161, 164, 249–50
Özsaruhan group, 57, 181, 248

Peker, Recep, 109, 111–12, 119
pluralism, 14, 225–28
Polanyi, Karl, 12–15
policy network, 24, 29, 96–97, 143, 165, 228, 232
populism, 141
professional management, 28–29, 79, 173, 177–78, 185–86, 213–16, 218; managers, 43, 169, 172, 176, 204, 207–08, 213–18, 220. See also holding companies as family firms
property: private and individual, 3–4, 13, 115; regime, 40, 98, 111; rights, 4, 107, 111–12, 117, 165–66

rent-seeking activity, 19, 22, 29, 110, 114, 121, 124, 143, 150–1, 188, 222, 261, 264
Republican People's Party (RPP), 78, 106, 108, 111, 113, 119–21, 123, 128, 142, 157, 242, 244

Sabancı: group, 56–7, 82–84, 86, 88, 95, 153, 182, 186, 190–93, 199, 206, 219, 248; family, 84–6, 115; Hacı Ömer, 76–77, 82–85; Sakıp, 83, 85, 95–96, 115, 163, 186, 188
Santral Holding, 57, 207, 211–12
Schimitter, Philippe, 227
Schumpeter, Joseph, 3; Schumpeterian, 171, 179, 219
Scocpol, Theda, 230
Selahaddin Adil Pasha (Adil Pasha), 74–76, 78
small business, 59, 61, 86, 105, 131, 148, 235, 243, 246, 253–54, 257, 261
social democracy, 140, 244, 255
socialism, 88, 108, 111, 139–40, 142, 246–47
Soral, Erdoğan, 58
state: autonomy, 18–21, 103, 222, 265; capacity, 18–19, 24; -centered approaches, 14
State Economic Enterprises (public enterprises), 38, 43, 50, 99, 103–05, 108–09, 117, 119, 123, 127, 144
State Industrial Office, 103–04
State Investment Bank, 136
State Organization for Agricultural Equipment, 163
State Planning Organization (SPO),

84, 86, 138, 152, 158–60, 164,
243, 250. *See also* Five Year Plans
Sümerbank, 104
Special Commission for Com-
merce (Heyet-i Mahsusa-i
Ticariyye), 42
Special Commission to Prevent
Speculative Activity (Men-i
İhtikar Heyeti), 42
STFA group, 57, 92, 191
stock market, 153, 205, 207; Istan-
bul Stock Exchange, 144
Suleiman, Ezra, 178
Şeref, Mustafa, 102–05

Tamek group, 57, 190, 204
Tanzimat (Reform Period), 37
Tekfen group, 57, 123, 190–91,
200–01, 205–06
TİSK (Turkish Confederation of
Employers' Unions), 246, 248,
253–55, 260
transaction costs, 25
True Path Party, 255
TÜSİAD (Turkish Industrialists'
and Businessmen's Association),
55, 65–66, 132, 139–42, 147,
247–58, 260
Türk-İş (Confederation of Turkish
Labor Unions), 245

U.K. and U.S.A.: state and class in,
14, 32, 233–34
Union of Chambers of Commerce
and Industry and Commodities
Exchanges (Union of Chambers),
85, 126, 135, 137, 149, 181, 185,
239, 242–44, 253–54, 260. *See
also* Chambers
Union of Exporters and Importers,
117
Useem, Michael, 233–34

Vakko group, 57, 182

Wealth Levy (varlık vergisi), 51, 83,
89, 114–6, 157
Whitley, Richard, 26–27
Williamson, Oliver, 25
World Bank, 84, 92, 125

Yaşar group, 56–57, 154, 182, 190–
91, 194–95, 206, 248
Young Turks, 35–36, 38. *See also*
Committee for Union and Progress (CUP)

zaibatsu, 176, 178. *See also* keiretsu
zero-sum entrepreneurship, 29,
151, 264